Paul Pettit

Science for the 70's

Science for the 70's

BOOK ONE

A. J. Mee

Patricia Boyd
Head of Biology Department
Broughton Secondary School, Edinburgh

David Ritchie
Deputy Headmaster and Principal Physics Teacher
Balwearie School, Kirkcaldy

Heinemann Educational Books
London and Edinburgh

Heinemann Educational Books Ltd

London Edinburgh Melbourne Auckland Toronto
Hong Kong Singapore Kuala Lumpur
Ibadan Nairobi Johannesburg
Lusaka New Delhi

ISBN 0 435 57574 0
© A. J. Mee, P. Boyd, and D. Ritchie 1971

First published 1971
Reprinted 1971 (twice), 1972
Second Edition in full colour 1973
Reprinted 1975

Published by Heinemann Educational Books Ltd
48 Charles Street, London W1X 8AH

Printed in Great Britain by
Jarrold and Sons Ltd, Norwich

A Note to the Teacher

Science for the Seventies, a series of two pupils' books with Teachers' Guides, comprises a complete experimental Integrated Science Course for the first two or three years of secondary education. It follows the order of the Scottish Integrated Science syllabus laid down in *Curriculum Paper Number 7 : Science in General Education* (H.M.S.O.).

It can be used in conjunction with the Scottish Secondary Science Working Party's **Science Worksheets** (Heinemann Educational Books) or independently.

The *Teachers' Guide* for each book functions both with **Science for the Seventies** and the **Science Worksheets**. Teachers are recommended to consult the *Guides* in order to make full use of the pupils' books.

A.J.M.
P.B.
D.R.

1971

A Note for Pupils only

THIS BOOK has been written for your enjoyment. You may think this is a strange thing to say about a school text-book; an adventure story, yes – but not a school book! But, you see, we do not believe that any subject, least of all science, should be dry and distasteful. Let us assure you that this is not just another old-fashioned kind of school book, giving you only the facts about the subject which you must learn – or else!

We do not believe in telling you everything. Being intelligent young people there is much that you can work out, and so quite often we have left you to do the thinking, and we are sure you will enjoy doing that. Science cannot really be learnt from a book anyway, but only by carrying out experiments for yourselves. This book is full of them, and we hope you will be able to do most, if not all, of these experiments either in your school laboratory or at home.

In order that you may be sure that you really have learnt something we have put a summary at the end of each unit showing the points you should know about and remember.

A. J. Mee
Patricia Boyd
David Ritchie

1971

Contents

Acknowledgements

Acknowledgements for permission to publish Photographs are due as follows:

A–Z Collection, 6.11 (bottom), 6.20 (top left, bottom centre)

Aldus Books, 8.20

Australian News and Information, 5.8

Heather Angel, 2.6, 6.6, 6.11 (top), 6.14, 6.18 (bottom), 6.19 (top right, bottom right), 6.20 (top left, top centre, bottom left), 8.14 (top left)

Ardea Photos, 6.19, (top left, bottom left, bottom centre), 8.14 (top right, bottom right)

Berger Paints Ltd., 5.21

British Oxygen Co., 8.26, 8.27

Maurice Broomfield, 5.11

Gene Cox, 6.3

Mary Evans, 4.27

Anne Fischer, 2.3 (centre – ponies)

M. Holford, 1.16 (centre, right), 3.25

Imperial Chemical Industries, 5.21

Institute of Geological Science, 5.18 (left)

P. Lloyd, 4.21, 7.8, 7.12

Meteorological Office, 4.2

Ministry of Defence, 5.9

Ken Moreman, 6.18

N.A.S.A., 3.11, 4.16

Natural History Photographic Agency, 2.2 (top), 2.3 (bottom right), 6.7, 8.14 (centre left, centre, bottom left)

P and A Photos, 1.10, 3.16, 4.35, 5.16, 5.18 (top and bottom right), 7.13, 7.22, 7.25, 7.27

Picturepoint Ltd., 1.3, 1.5, 1.6, 1.14, 1.16 (top and bottom right), 2.3 (top left, centre – blue tit, bottom left), 3.2, 3.3 (left), 3.4, 3.6, 4.6, 4.17, 4.28, 5.10, 5.14, 5.32, 7.1, 8.10, 8.12, 8.22, 8.30

U.K.A.E.A., 1.1, 3.3 (right), 7.6

Unit One
Introducing Science

1.1 THE SCIENTIST'S WORK

What does a scientist do? To answer this question would require many, many books. Look at the books in your own school library which deal with science, and see if you can write down twenty things that scientists are interested in. You will find that they range from finding out about metals so as to discover the best one with which to build an aeroplane, a bridge, or a rocket – to making new medicines which will cure people suffering from diseases; from making the best washing powder – to making the best rocket fuel; from making very powerful beams of light which can trigger off explosions miles away – to discovering the best chemical to kill off pests which rob us of our food.

Fig. 1.2

Fig. 1.1 A scientist working with radiosotopes for medical, industrial, and scientific use

These are just a few of the ways in which the scientist helps us all; you will find many more for yourselves. There are other things that a scientist does which do not seem to have any very direct use. If you look around the laboratory in which you are now you should find plenty of problems to which you would like to find the answer. You should see, for instance, that some boys and girls have dark hair, and some have fair, and possibly a few have red; some of you have blue eyes, some grey, some brown. Some are fat and some thin, some are tall and some short.

How can we account for the fact that we are not all the same? This is the sort of question to which the scientist tries to find an answer. How can we explain that when we throw something into the air it always comes down again, but that if a rocket is launched with sufficient power it doesn't seem to come down again, but keeps going round the earth? How is it that if we connect a lamp to a battery it lights? Where does the salt in the sea come from? How is it that a dog can hear sounds that we cannot hear? Where did you come from? To these, and many, many other interesting questions scientists have found the answers.

Very often in looking at problems like these, which do not seem to be of much direct help to us in everyday life, the scientist finds out things which turn out to be very useful indeed! For instance, Michael Faraday was looking at the interesting things that happen when a coil of wire is slipped over the end of a magnet; he found that an electric current was generated in the coil, and as a result of this discovery a machine called a dynamo was constructed. We now use this machine to generate all our electricity. Just think what a different place the world would be without electricity – no cars, no aeroplanes, no radio, no

TV! Similarly, by looking at some moulds, Sir Alexander Fleming discovered penicillin, the forerunner of all modern antibiotics – medicines which have conquered many diseases, and may possibly have saved your own life. It is worth reading about this in a book which you can borrow from the library.

To put it all in a nutshell, the scientist tries to find out the truth about the world in which he lives. He is a curious person – not of course soft in the head – but curious about things, wanting to know why they do this or that, and trying to find out the way in which the universe behaves. To do this he must be a detective – a super-detective in fact, because these secrets are very well hidden – greater than Sherlock Holmes or Inspector Barlow, or any of the others you have read about or seen on TV. Now this is just what you are going to be in your work in the science laboratory in school. You are going to find out lots of things for yourselves – and that is really what makes science so interesting.

Although a detective who investigates crime may want to keep his discoveries to himself for a while, there comes a time when he has to tell someone, possibly the police or the judge, what he has found out and how he did it. In science, too, we cannot make much progress without telling other scientists about our work; you can imagine that we would never get anywhere if we all had to start from the beginning and discover everything afresh for ourselves. We must therefore be able to record what we do and what we see in such a way that others will understand exactly what we have been doing and what we have observed. It is possible that at the beginning of this course your teacher will not ask you to write down what you have done, but he will expect you to be able to write down what you have seen. You may possibly be provided with a worksheet on which the instructions for carrying out an experiment are given to you, and you will be asked to fill in what you observe. Let's see how good you are at this.

1.2 HOW GOOD ARE YOU AT LOOKING?

Before starting on the first experiment you must know the meaning of two words. A chemical, like salt, or sugar, or sand is called a **substance**. Some substances when put into water dissolve, forming **solutions**.

Experiment 1.1

You will be provided with some substances dissolved in water. Here is a list of possible ones but your teacher may provide others.

1. lead nitrate
2. potassium iodide
3. sodium chloride
4. copper sulphate
5. sodium carbonate
6. silver nitrate
7. potassium chromate
8. ammonia solution
9. acetic acid

These solutions are in labelled bottles. **Note very carefully what the label says.** Pour a little of any one of them into a test-tube. (A depth of about 3 cm is enough.) **Remember to put the stopper back in the bottle immediately after you have taken what you want.** Then add about the same quantity of any other solution in the list. Note carefully what happens. You may have some surprises, so be prepared. If you use four pairs of solutions it will be enough. If other members of the class use different pairs you could look at their results too. You could look to see if there are any changes of colour, if the mixture turns cloudy, if it fizzes or if it gets hot. It saves writing if you put your results down in a table, like this.

Solutions mixed	Observation
3 and 7	White, cloudy liquid
7 and 8	
4 and 9	
2 and 4	

Compare your results with those of other pupils. Are they the same?

Your teacher will discuss the results of these experiments with you, and you can see how good you were at looking and recording your observations.

1.3 CAN WE TRUST OUR SENSES?

All detectives start on their work of discovery by looking for clues. How do we do this? First of all we must realize that all our information comes to us through our senses; we look at things, we feel them, we smell and taste them (not very often in the laboratory because so many of the things we deal with are poisonous), and we listen. Perhaps we should find out how reliable our senses are.

Fig. 1.3 The men in this picture earn their living by their sense of smell — they are called perfume snifters and work for a famous French perfume manufacturer

Some people say 'Seeing is believing'. Are they right?

Experiment 1.2
Can we believe our eyes?

Look at the pictures in Fig. 1.4. What do you think?

Experiment 1.3
Can we trust our sense of touch?

Get three beakers. Into one put some fairly hot water (not hot enough to burn you), in another put some tepid water, and in the third some cold water.

Put a finger of your left hand into the hot water, and one of your right hand in the cold water. Then take them out and put them both into the tepid water. How does the tepid water feel to your left hand and to your right hand?

Can you trust your sense of touch?

(a) Something wrong?

(b) A vase, or . . . . . . ?

(c) Is the hat taller than the width of the brim?

(d) Which way up?

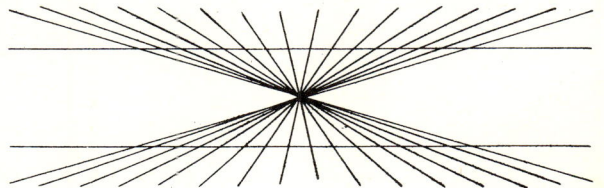

(e) Are the lines parallel?

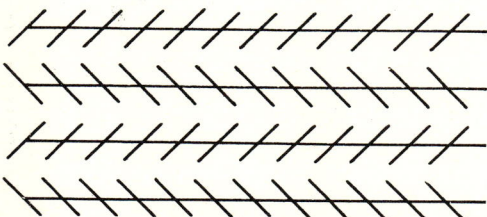

(f) Are the lines parallel?

(g) Are these lines the same length?

(h) Who is tallest?

Fig. 1.4 Can we believe our eyes?

Experiment 1.4
Can we trust our ears?

We shall use an apparatus called a signal generator connected to a loudspeaker.

The signal generator can produce sounds of different pitch from low notes to very high notes. By turning the knob we can make the note higher and higher. Turn it until the note is so high that you cannot hear it any more. Then try the same thing with some of your neighbours. You will probably find that they will say that they cannot hear anything while you can, or vice versa. Is the sound still there or not? Who is right? It is no use arguing about it. You are both right. But can you trust your ears to decide whether there is a sound there or not?

Experiment 1.5
Can we trust our sense of taste?

Here is an extra experiment you can do at home if you wish. Eat a piece of orange; eat a sweet; then eat another piece of the same orange.

Does the orange taste as sweet as it would have done if you had not eaten the sweet first? Can you trust your sense of taste?

Experiment 1.6
Can you judge distances accurately?

You can take part in this experiment with all the other members of the class. Have a look at a metre stick first to see how long a metre is, and then estimate the length of the bench in metres. Put the estimates up on the blackboard. Do they all agree? How could we find out how near any of you are to the correct length?

Obviously you will require some measuring instrument to do this. You could use the metre stick you saw before.

Your ruler is marked off in centimetres, and most rulers are about 30 cm long. Would measuring the length of the bench with a ruler be likely to give you a very accurate result? If not, why? Would the metre stick be any better?

Experiment 1.7
Can you judge times accurately?

See how accurately you can estimate a minute. Get your partner to time you with his watch, if it has a seconds hand. If not, the teacher will provide you with a stop watch or a stop clock.

1.4 HELPING OUR SENSES

This may seem to be a very discouraging start. If we cannot rely on our senses how can we be sure of the results of any of our experiments? Yet it is most important in science to be able to observe and measure things accurately. If we are to do this we have to use instruments which will help us. As a rule these let us see things which otherwise we would have to judge by touch, or by hearing; and, although it is possible to fool our eyes, as you have seen in Experiment 1.2, sight is the most sensitive of the senses, and is the one with which we can judge most accurately. We must remember, though, that no instrument can give a perfectly accurate result. This is where science differs from mathematics. Provided you do your sums correctly, arithmetic will always give you an accurate answer. In science we depend upon instruments which themselves may be at fault; and not only that, the result will depend on how carefully we use the instrument.

To try this out, all members of the class should measure the length of this page with a ruler. Write down your result in your note book, then collect all the results for the class and put them on the blackboard. Are they all the same? Should they have been all the same? If they are not, why aren't they?

We are going to use some of the instruments which you will see in the laboratory. You will be using these over and over again in your science course and you will gradually become better and better at using them.

1.5 HOW HOT?

Not so long ago we decided that we could not use our sense of touch to find out how warm a thing was because the result depended on what we had been touching just before; and of course we could not use our fingers to find out how hot a boiling liquid was, or a piece of red hot iron. Is there any way in which we could *see* how hot a thing was instead of relying on our sense of touch? Fortunately there is. We use an instrument which translates hotness into something we can see. This instrument is called a **thermometer** (Fig. 1.5).

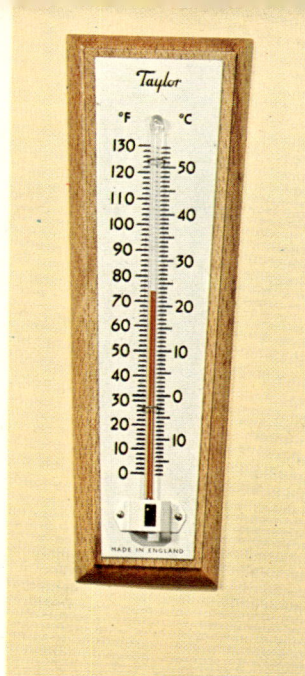

Fig. 1.5 A thermometer

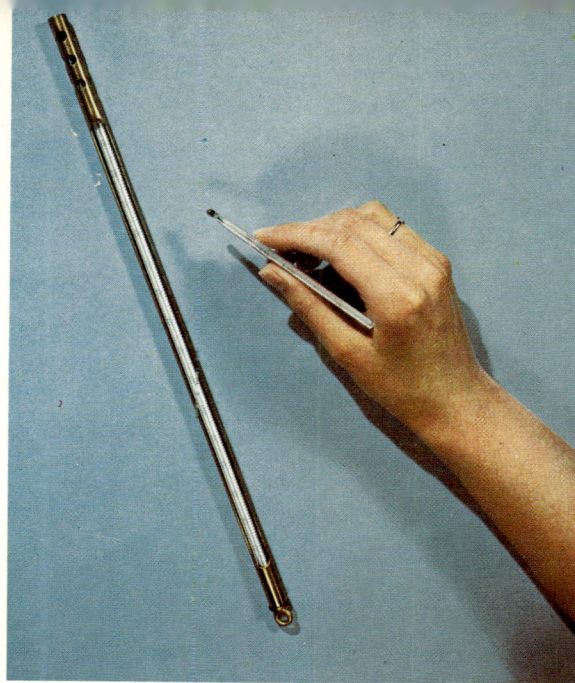

Fig. 1.6 Thermometers vary in size. The small thermometer in the picture is a clinical thermometer and is used to find the temperature of the body. The large thermometer, which is also filled with mercury, is used in a laboratory

You have probably seen one before, because there is often one hanging in the classroom to show us how hot the room is. Possibly you may have used one to find out how hot you are when you are not feeling well.

How hot a body is is called its **temperature**. You have probably met this term before. When you have had 'flu you may have heard the doctor say that you have a temperature. This means that you are hotter than you would usually be if you were well.

If we are to measure anything we have to use a scale. Your ruler has a scale marked on it so that you can measure lengths with it. You have probably learnt how to measure with a ruler in the primary school and in fact, you measured the length of this page not so long ago. If, however, you are not sure about this you should practise measuring the lengths of some things before you go any further. One of the things we must be able to do is to read a scale.

1.6 THERMOMETERS

Look at a thermometer. You will see the scale engraved on the glass. To make a scale we have to decide first where it is to begin – we call that point 0. Then we have to decide on another fixed point. In the case of a ruler we would have to decide how long a metre is going to be; this was fixed a long time ago as the distance between two marks on a piece of metal. (Try to find out how the length of a metre was fixed originally; it is very interesting.) Having marked just how long a metre is on our strip of wood we can then divide this up into as many equal parts as we like. It has been decided to divide it first into a thousand parts; each one of these is a millimetre. Ten of these small divisions is called a centimetre (one hundredth of a metre). We could go on dividing up the millimetre if we wanted to, but the marks would then be so close together that we would not be able to see them properly.

It has been decided to call the temperature of melting ice zero; so if we put an unmarked thermometer into melting ice we can put the mark 0 against where the liquid comes to.

The other fixed point is the temperature of boiling water, and this is called 100. The distance between 0 and 100 is divided into a hundred equal parts. Each part is called a **degree**. This method of subdividing the interval was proposed by a Swedish scientist called Celsius, after whom the scale has been named. This scale is called

Fig. 1.7 Part of a thermometer

the **Celsius scale**. We put a letter C after the reading that we measure on the scale to show that it is a Celsius scale we are using. Thus 50 °C is read as 'fifty degrees Celsius'.

To make sure that you can read the thermometer scale properly two drawings of part of a thermometer are given in the margin.

What temperatures do they indicate? The answer is given at the foot of the next column*.

Experiment 1.8
Using a thermometer

Now we are ready to use a thermometer. Note these points about it. What is it made of? What is there inside it? Look for the 0 °C and the 100 °C marks, and see how the scale is divided. It is not always easy to see where the liquid stands and you may need some practice, but when you are quite sure that you can read the scale and are accustomed to finding the top of the column of liquid you can use the thermometer to find out how hot or how cold things are.

Find the temperature of the cold water from the tap.

Is the air in the room hotter or colder than tap water? (Be careful not to hold the thermometer by the bulb when you do this.)

What is the temperature of your hand? Is the temperature of everyone's hand the same?

What is the temperature of the water from the hot tap? Write down these temperatures in your note book or on your worksheet.

What would you do to find out if your thermometer was accurate?

1.7 MELTING

Many solid substances melt when they are warmed.

Experiment 1.9
Do all solids melt at the same temperature?

To find out, take a test-tube with a little naphthalene in it and clamp it in a stand, as shown in Fig. 1.8. Put a thermometer in the tube so that its bulb is in the naphthalene. Then heat the tube gently. This is best done by

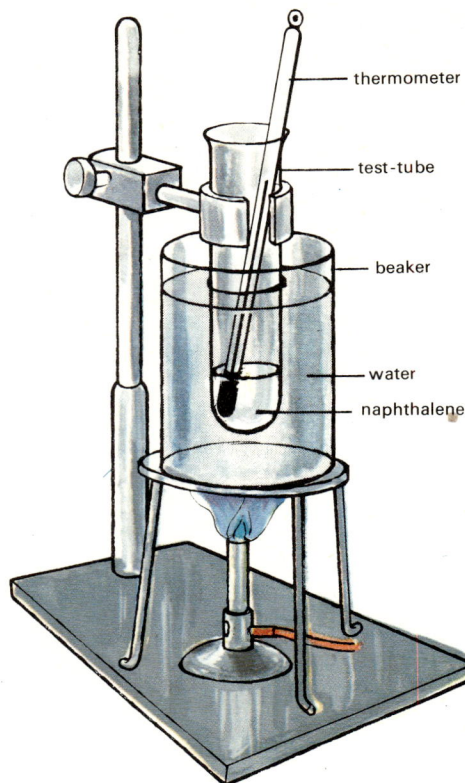

Fig. 1.8

placing it in a beaker of water and heating the water. Read the temperature when the naphthalene melts.

Repeat the experiment with salol, and with paraffin wax.

The temperature at which a substance melts is called its melting point.

Put down your results in a table like this:

Substance	Melting point
Naphthalene	
Salol	
Wax	

(It is not necessary for you to find the melting points of all three substances. You might do two of them.)

You already know the melting point of ice, and so you can put that in the table too.

What is the answer to the problem you set out to solve?

*Readings: *top*, 78 °C; *bottom*, 32 °C.

1.8 WEIGHING

Another job we often have to do in science is to find out how much things weigh. For this purpose we use a balance. One kind of balance is like a pair of scales, but we shall use a special sort of balance which is very easy to read. There is a picture of one in Fig. 1.9. All you have to do

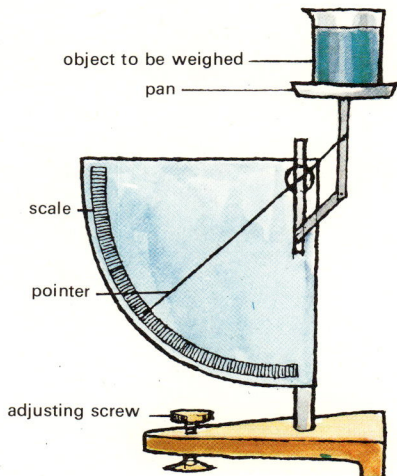

Fig. 1.10 This van is being weighed. Find out how

Fig. 1.9

is to put what you want to weigh on the pan at the top and note the reading on the scale opposite the pointer.

(It is possible that you may have a different kind of balance in your laboratory. If so, your teacher will show you how to use it.)

Of course, if you want to find the weight of something accurately you must first see that the pointer reads o when there is nothing on the scale. You can do this by altering the adjusting screw at the base. You must also read the scale very carefully, and so before you weigh anything look at the scale and see exactly how the numbers go.

We measure the weight of things in grammes, and the scale of your balance is graduated in grammes. The word 'gramme' is often abbreviated to g. Thus 10 g means 10 grammes.

Here is a simple experiment to start with.

Experiment 1.10
Does a ten-penny piece weigh twice as much as a five-penny piece?

Weigh both and put down your results in your note book or on the worksheet.

Which is heavier, wood or metal? This is really a silly question to ask. Why? Perhaps you will see the answer from the following experiment.

Experiment 1.11

Weigh a cube of wood and then a cube of metal the same size as the wood. Which is the heavier?

Experiment 1.11(a)

How would you find the weight of a sheet of paper? Try to find out for yourself.

Something to do at home

Would you like to make for yourself a simple weighing machine? You can do this at home. First of all get a strong rubber band. From wood or Meccano, make a stand like the one shown in the diagram on the next page, and hang the rubber band from the nail (or arm) at the top. Make a cardboard pan (or use a tin lid in which you have bored three holes at the side) and tie threads through the holes so that you can attach it to the rubber band. This is done by bending a paper clip to make a pointer and slipping the rubber band through it. The pan is then tied on to the paper clip. Put a piece of cardboard behind the rubber band so that the pointer just moves over it. This is going to be our scale. Make a pencil mark on the cardboard at the place where the

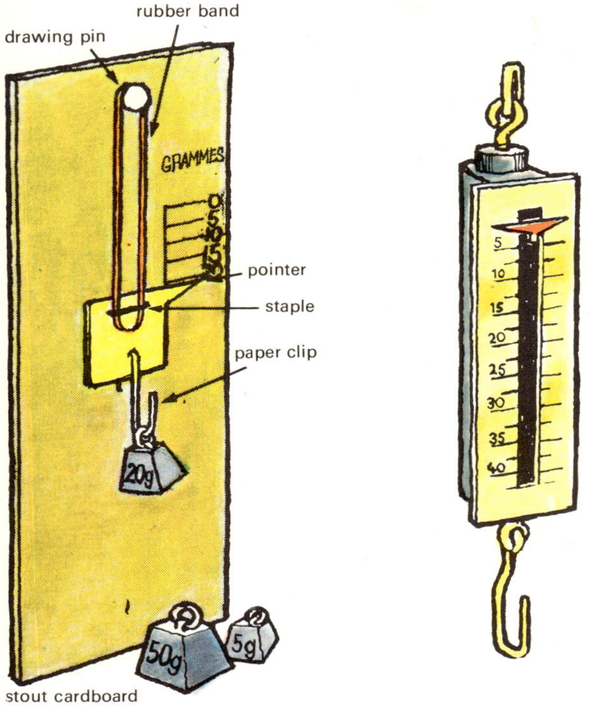
rubber band
drawing pin
GRAMMES
0
5
10
15
pointer
staple
paper clip
20g
50g
5g
stout cardboard
5
10
15
20
25
30
35
40

Fig. 1.11 *(left)* A rubber-band balance and *(right)* a spring balance

pointer comes. As there is nothing in the pan this will be our zero, so put 0 against it. Now put a 10 g weight on the pan. This will make the rubber band stretch and so the pointer moves down. Make a mark where it comes to. Take the 10 g weight off and put on a 20 g weight. This should stretch the band more. Make a mark where the pointer stands now. (How much more do you think the 20 g weight will stretch the band? Check your guess and see if you are right.) Now we can fill in the other numbers and make a complete scale between 0 and 20 g. You can now use your balance to weigh anything up to 20 g. Would it be possible to weigh more than 20 g? If so how could you do this?

If you have a very slack rubber band you may find that 10 g and 20 g are too much for it; or, if it is a very strong band it may not stretch very much with these weights, and you will have to choose more suitable bands. If you do not have weights at home you could use the ten-penny piece that you weighed at school instead; then your scale would be in ten-penny weights instead of in grammes, but you could easily change from ten-penny weights to grammes because you know how much a ten-penny piece weighs in grammes.

The rubber-band balance works in just the same way as a spring balance, and if you have a spring (or can make one from a coil of wire), you can use it instead of a rubber band. Of course, the stronger the spring the more 'pull' you will have to use to stretch it, and the greater the weights it can weigh. When we put a scale on to an instrument we say that we **calibrate** it.

You can also make at home a balance that will weigh a hair. Get a milk straw and flatten it at one end. This makes a little platform on which you will be able to put tiny weights. Stick a bristle or a very fine wire on the end to make a pointer. Stick a needle through the straw at about the point A as shown in Fig. 1.12.

Now we want to balance the straw with the needle as a pivot so we make a stand like the one shown in the diagram. To balance the straw we stick little bits of plasticine or wax near end A until it just balances. Then we fix a strip of cardboard in a clip or on to a wooden block and stand it behind the wire on the end of the straw. We are going to make this into our scale. Now comes the tricky part. How are we going to make the scale? The balance is so delicate that, if we were to put a weight like a 5 g weight on the flattened end of the straw, the pointer would move down a very long way; so we need some very small weights. To do this we get a big sheet of squared paper and weigh it. (You remember how you did this in Experiment 1.11 (a).) Suppose it weighs 1 g. Count up the number of squares on the paper. Suppose there are 1000. Each square therefore weighs a thousandth of a gramme. Now if we want a weight of 0.01 g (or 1/100 g) we can cut off the required number of squares. How many will it be? (Of course, it is unlikely that the arithmetic will be as easy as this, because your sheet of paper will not weigh exactly 1 g, but if you are reasonably good at calculating you should not find it too difficult to find out how much one square weighs.) If you put your 0.01 g weight on the flattened end of the straw (of course you can fold the paper to do this) the pointer will move down. Mark where it comes to and put 0.01 against the mark. Now put an extra 0.01 g weight on and mark the place again. Go on doing this until you have a good scale.

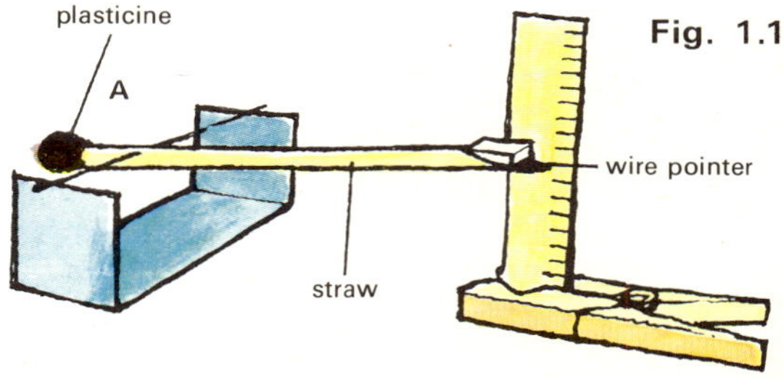
plasticine
A
wire pointer
straw

Fig. 1.12

You can use your balance to weigh very tiny objects – a hair, a nail clipping, or perhaps a dead fly!

1.9 HOW MUCH SPACE?

Another fact we often want to know about a body (this is what a scientist calls a 'thing' – a book, a pencil, a weight, a rubber band, a coin – all these are 'bodies') is the space it takes up. This is called its **volume**. Volume is measured in cubic centimetres (usually abbreviated to cm³). You may find that the measuring instruments at school are calibrated in millilitres (ml) which are almost exactly the same as cubic centimetres. We shall use the cubic centimetre throughout this book.

To find the volumes of liquids such as water or milk at home you would use a graduated jug. Have a look at the one in the larder. It may be graduated in four ways – in pints, in fluid ounces, in tablespoons, or in fractions of a litre. In science we never use pints, fluid ounces, or tablespoons.

We use a similar kind of 'jug' in the science laboratory, but it has a different shape. We call it a measuring cylinder. We use a graduated beaker if we do not require to be very accurate. The scale is marked on the side of the vessel, and you will see that at the top it says c.cm. (which means cubic centimetres) or ml. Look at the scale carefully and see that you understand which way it goes. Show your neighbour where 55 cm³ comes and let him check this. Now ask him to show you where 35 cm³ comes.

What are the advantages and disadvantages of a measuring cylinder compared with a graduated jug?

Experiment 1.12
Using a measuring cylinder; finding the weight of 50 cm³ of water

---

First weigh a beaker which is large enough to contain 50 cm³ of water and put it on one side for use later.

Fill up your measuring cylinder with water to a little above the 50 cm³ mark. When you read the level of the water in the cylinder you must **stand the cylinder on the bench** and you must bend down to look at it so that **your eye is on a level with the surface of the water**. Why must you do this?

Fig. 1.13 The right and wrong way to measure the volume of a liquid

When you look at the surface of the water in the cylinder, you will find that it is not flat, but curls up at the edges forming a curved surface. When measuring the volumes of liquids we always read the **bottom** of this curve. The curved surface is called a **meniscus**. It is a help to view the meniscus from below — it looks like a mirror — and raise the eye until the reflection disappears.

Fig. 1.14 Examples of (*left*) a water meniscus and (*right*) a mercury meniscus

We have in our cylinder a little more than 50 cm³ of water. Pour a little away down the sink until the level is exactly at the 50 cm³ mark. (If you pour too much away you will have to fill it again and repeat the job, so be careful.) Pour the 50 cm³ of water into the weighed beaker and weigh it again. Calculate the weight of the water from these results. Write up your results in a table like this.

Weight of beaker + 50 cm³ of water =   g
Weight of beaker =   g
Weight of 50 cm³ of water =   g

Try to answer the following questions:

1. Does the beaker have to be dry at first?
2. Would the result be as accurate if you weighed the beaker + water first, then poured the water away, and weighed the beaker by itself?

We shall collect the result that each group gets and find the average. Why do we do this? Why are not all the results the same?

Are you surprised at the result? It is not as odd as it seems, because when scientists fixed their units of weight they decided to take the weight of 1 cm³ of water as 1 gramme.

Experiment 1.13
How to find the volume of a stone

As you are fast becoming a scientist, we are not going to tell you how to do this experiment. Try to work out a way of doing it for yourself.

Make a table of your readings as you did in the last experiment.

Now here is a harder experiment.

Experiment 1.14
How to find the volume of a cork

No hints for this one. Write in your note book, or on the back of the worksheet, a brief account of the way in which you did this experiment, so that anyone else, not knowing how to do it, would be able to follow your instructions.

Experiment 1.15
Does 1 cm³ of all liquids weigh the same?

Start this experiment by finding if it is easy to measure out exactly 1 cm³ of a liquid with a measuring cylinder. If you come to the conclusion that it is not, how would you set about finding the weight of 1 cm³ of a liquid?

Different groups in the class should try different liquids, for example paraffin, methylated spirit, turpentine, and glycerol (the proper name for glycerine). Make up a table showing the results for the class. You know how much 50 cm³ of water weigh, so you can include this in the table as well.

1.10 TIMING

We now want to find out how we can time things accurately. You have already discovered how good (or how bad) you are at guessing times, and you have checked yourself with a stop watch or a stop clock. Here are some more experiments for you to do.

Experiment 1.16
What is your pulse rate?

You do not really need a stop watch for this. A watch with a seconds hand will do. Locate your pulse in your wrist, and make sure you can count it easily. Do a 'count down', starting at 10, 9, 8 . . . 4, 3, 2, 1, 0. Note the time on the seconds hand when you reach 0, then count forward for one minute, and note the number of beats in that time. Repeat this two or three times. Your teacher will collect the results for the class, and put them on the board. Is everybody's pulse rate the same? Do you think it should be?

Now run round the playground, or up and down the stairs. Does this make any difference to your pulse rate?

Experiment 1.17
How fast does your heart beat?

If you have a stethoscope in the laboratory you can count your heart beats and time them in the same way as you found your pulse rate. If you do not have this instrument you can easily make a model one, and Fig. 1.15 will show you how this can be done.

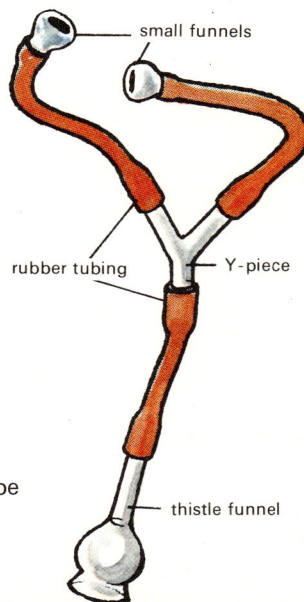

Fig. 1.15 A home-made stethoscope

Another way of doing this experiment is to amplify the sound of your heart beat. Everyone can hear it then, and the whole class can time it for you. A small microphone is held against your chest. It is connected to an amplifier and a loud-speaker, and you should hear 'lub-dub, lub-dub, lub-dub . . .' coming from the loud-speaker as your heart beats.

Try the effect on your heart beat of running round the playground. You probably know what to expect. When you come back, time your heart beat for a number of minutes, noting the number in each minute as the rate returns to normal.

Fig. 1.16 Some interesting devices for measuring time. Can you see how they work?

Is there a good runner in the class? Find out whether taking exercise has as much effect on his heart beat rate as it has on yours. It is sometimes said that good athletes have a slower heart beat rate than ordinary mortals. Is that true of the good runners in your class?

Here is an experiment you can do for homework. Set up a pendulum and find its time of swing. A pendulum is easily made by tying a weight to a piece of thread with a loop on the end. Put the loop over a nail or a hook in the wall so that the weight can swing freely, i.e. so that it does not scrape against the wall. Find the time it takes to swing back to its original position (that is a 'swing-swang'). You can best do this by doing a 'count down' as you did when you measured your pulse rate, and then counting the time taken to do, say, 20 swing-swangs. You will be able to do this with a watch with a seconds hand or with a stop watch. Try the effect of using different lengths of thread, and different weights on the end. The weight on the end of the thread is called the 'bob'.

It is very interesting to find out how people have measured time through the ages, using hour-glasses, water clocks, and so on. Some interesting timing devices are shown in the opposite figure. Look them up in an encyclopaedia in your school library and find out how they work.

Fig. 1.17 Robert Bunsen — find out all you can about him and his work

1.11 A COMPLEX PROBLEM

Now you are going to do an experiment which combines several of the operations you have learnt to carry out.

When you boiled water, and when you found melting points earlier in this unit, you used a bunsen burner to heat things. Your teacher probably told you how to adjust the burner, and you found that by altering the collar at the foot of the tube you could make a yellow flame or a blue flame. By mixing more air with the gas that you burn you change the colour from yellow to blue.

The problem is to find out whether the blue flame is hotter than the yellow one. You should be able to design an experiment for this purpose. Ask yourself these questions.

1. Could I find out by putting an ordinary thermometer in the flame?
2. If not, could I find out by heating something and seeing which flame heated it up more quickly?
3. If I decide to do it this way, would I take different amounts of the thing I heat, or must they be the same?
4. If I had no thermometer, what substance would I choose to heat?

When you have thought about this, look at the instructions given below and see if you were right.

Experiment 1.18
Is the yellow flame of the burner hotter than the blue flame?

Measure out 50 cm³ of tap water into an aluminium beaker. Time how long it takes to boil the water using the yellow flame. Pour the water away and cool the beaker.

Measure out another 50 cm³ of water into the beaker. Without touching the gas tap change the flame to blue, and find how long it takes to boil the water this time.

Which flame heats the 50 cm³ of water more quickly?

Now think back to the answers to your questions. Did you say that you must heat the same amounts of substance? Why must they be the same?

Why was it necessary not to touch the gas tap when you changed from one flame to the other?

Were you right in your answer to question 4? We use water because it is a common liquid and we can tell when the temperature has risen to a certain point without using a thermometer. The boiling point of the water is the same no matter how the water is heated. We could, of course, have used any other liquid, but water is used because it is very, very, cheap and because many other common liquids burn when they are heated (for example, paraffin, turpentine or methylated spirit).

Did you notice anything else about the flames? Clue – look at the bottom of the beaker.

Which is the more economical flame to use?

If you have time you can try this experiment another way, using a thermometer. Think out how to do it.

1.12 SEPARATING OR UN-MIXING

Now we are going to turn to something quite different. We found in Experiment 1.1 that sometimes (but not always) when two solutions of chemicals are mixed some of the liquid forms into a solid. The problem is how to separate the solid from the liquid.

Experiment 1.19
How can we separate a solid from a liquid?

Liquid A is a solution of copper sulphate and liquid B is a solution of sodium carbonate. Take about 5 cm depth of liquid A in a test-tube and add about the same quantity of liquid B. What happens?

We want to separate the solid formed. Will it do just to let the solid settle? You can wait quite a long time and nothing seems to settle out.

How does your mother separate the tea leaves from the tea when a visitor comes to tea with you? Could we use the same method here? You will probably come to the conclusion that (1) the holes in the strainer would be too big and (2) the metal may be attacked by the chemicals you are using. Many chemicals attack metals; they may dissolve them altogether. How could we overcome these difficulties?

Obviously we need a strainer with very small holes, and one not made of metal. What about muslin — the sort of material your mother uses when she is making jelly and wants to separate the fruit skins and pips from the liquid? Would this do? Try it to see. Were you successful? Probably not; the holes were again too big, and the solid came through. Let us try something else. Ordinary uncoated paper (such as newspaper or blotting paper) has a lot of very small holes — called pores — in it. Writing paper is coated with a chemical to fill up the holes so that it does not soak up the ink too quickly when you are writing on it.

Perhaps then we could use blotting paper as a strainer. In fact this is just what we do, but we use a special kind of blotting paper called **filter paper**.

We have next to find some sort of support for the paper. As you will discover if you try it, it is not very satisfactory to put the paper on top of a beaker and pour the liquid on to it. It usually spills all over the edges.

We therefore use a funnel and fit the paper into it. This is done by folding the paper into quarters, and then opening it out with three thicknesses on one side and one on the other. You will find that this fits neatly into a funnel. Fold the paper, then, and fit it into a funnel and stand the funnel in a test-tube or over a beaker. Pour the liquid you want to separate into the paper and observe what happens. This should solve your problem.

For this experiment you must use a beaker and a funnel made of glass or plastic — not metal.

We call this process **filtering**. The liquid which comes through the filter paper is called the **filtrate**.

filter paper

filter funnel

filter paper in quarters

filter paper shaped into cone

Fig. 1.18

1.13 SWINDLED – OR NOT?

Experiment 1.20

You are now going to do a little detective work. You have bought a simple indigestion remedy from a chemist's shop. It is, in fact, a mixture of powdered chalk and water. It says on the bottle that 100 g of the mixture contains at least 10 g of chalk. How would you find out if the chemist was swindling you?

You should be able to work out how to do this, but if you are in doubt here are some clues.

You will have to separate the chalk from the water.

You will have to know what weight of mixture you start with and find out the weight of chalk in it.

First shake the bottle (Why?). Weigh a beaker and add the mixture until the total weight has increased by 100 g. Filter off the chalk and collect the water in another weighed beaker. Weigh the beaker plus water.

You started off with 100 g of mixture. Suppose the water that comes through weighs 95 g. How much must the chalk weigh? Are you being swindled? Suppose the water weighs 85 g, are you being swindled this time?

This experiment is not very accurate. Why not? What would you have to do to find out exactly how much chalk there was in 100 g of mixture? Is it necessary to start with 100 g of the mixture? What would you do if you have not as much as this? The answer to this depends on how good you are at arithmetic.

1.14 AN ODD METAL

Here is an interesting experiment. You are going to observe what happens when calcium is added to water.

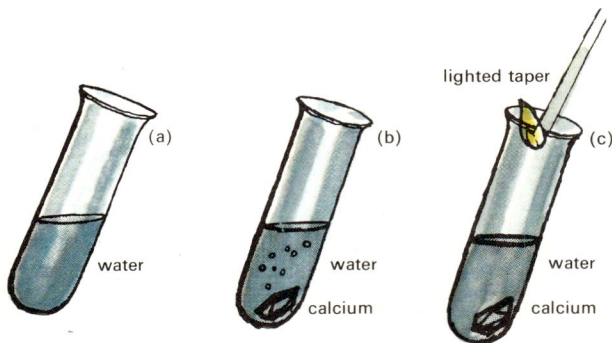

Experiment 1.21
An experiment with calcium

Calcium is a metal, although you might not think so. The calcium in the bottle does not look like a metal at all, but if you take a small piece and scrape off the rust with a knife you will see that it is shiny underneath.

Take about 3 cm depth of water in a test-tube and add a small piece of calcium, as in Fig. 1.19. What happens? Hold a lighted taper at the mouth of the tube. What happens? What does the liquid remaining in the tube look like? Filter this liquid and, using a milk straw, breathe out through the filtrate. What happens?

When a liquid fizzes, little bubbles of gas are rising through it. In the experiment you have just carried out the gas is hydrogen. You have not come across this gas before.

1.15 A JAMBOREE

You have now had quite a good introduction to the tools that the scientist uses. Now you are going to carry out more experiments which will show you some of the things that scientists do. Your teacher will probably have these experiments set up round the laboratory, and will give you a worksheet or instruction cards telling you what you have to do and what you have to look for. You should do all the experiments, but, as it

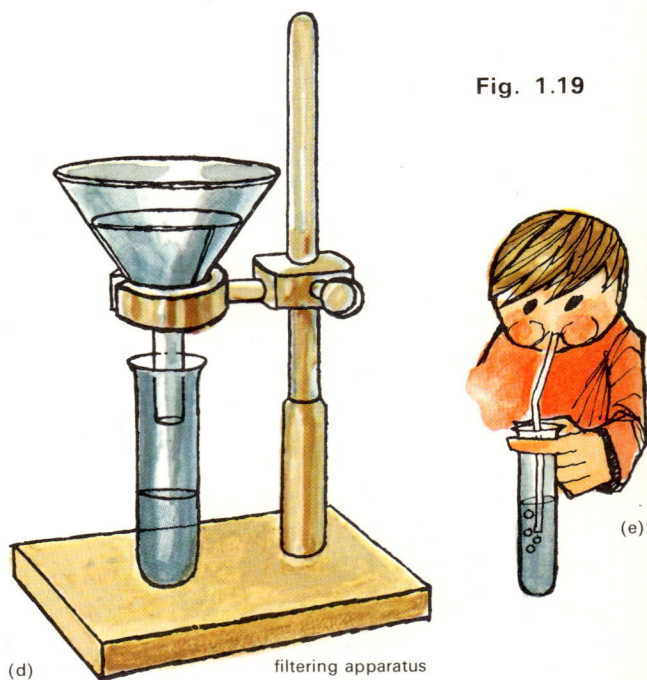

Fig. 1.19

(a) water
(b) water, calcium
(c) lighted taper, water, calcium
(d) filtering apparatus
(e)

does not matter what order you do them in, you will pass from one experiment to another when the teacher tells you to do so. Some possible experiments are set down here.

Experiment 1.22

Fig. 1.20

Sing into the microphone and watch the pattern on the oscilloscope screen. Sing a low note for as long as you can. Then sing a high note. Draw the pattern you see.

Which note gives the closer waves?

Experiment 1.23

Fig. 1.21

You will find a number of different substances on the bench, along with a magnet. Bring the magnet up to each substance in turn. Write down the names of those which are attracted.

To which subset do these belong?

Experiment 1.24

Find the volume of air which you can let out of your lungs in one breath, using the apparatus provided. Record your own and your colleagues'

Fig. 1.22

results. What conclusion can you draw about the volume of a pupil's breath?

Experiment 1.25

Fig. 1.23

Push the rubber hemispheres together, and then try to separate them.

What has happened?

Experiment 1.26

Find out as much as you can about the metal rings provided.

Fig. 1.24

Experiment 1.27

Fig. 1.25

Rub the rod with the material provided, and then hold it *near* but not touching the water jet. What happens?

Experiment 1.28

Fig. 1.26

Blow hard into the bottle through the tube. What happens? What happens when you stop blowing and pinch the rubber tubing? Why does this happen?

Experiment 1.29

To a little of the white powder A in a dry test-tube, add about 3 cm depth of water.
    What happens?
    Hold a lighted taper to the mouth of the tube. What happens?
    Compare this result with the one you get when you hold a lighted taper to the mouth of an empty test-tube.

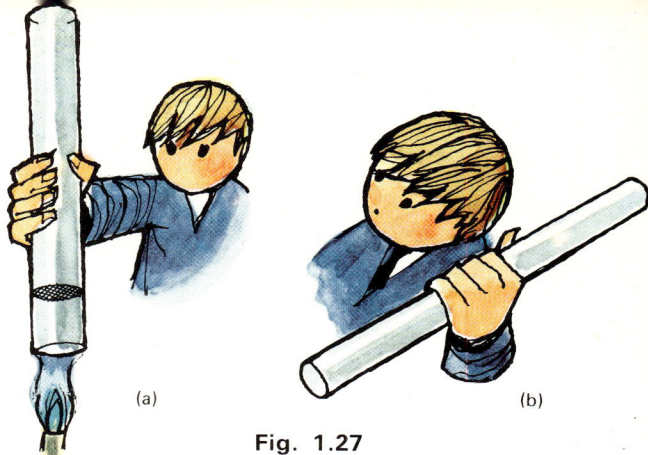

(a)   (b)

Fig. 1.27

Experiment 1.30

Light the Bunsen burner and lower the long metal tube over it. Then take it away from the flame. What happens?

Experiment 1.31

Fig. 1.28

Put your hands on the flask which is attached to a tube with its end passing under water. What happens? What happens when you take your hands away?

Experiment 1.32

Add a few drops of liquid A to about 20 cm³ of liquid B in a beaker. What happens? Now add to the mixture about 20 cm³ of liquid C. What happens?

Experiment 1.33

For this experiment a filter paper has been coated with a yellow substance. What happens when you write on it with the glass pen?

Experiment 1.34

Fig. 1.29

You will find a number of sealed boxes on the bench. Without opening the boxes, find out as much as you can about the contents of each one.

1.16 THE BLACK BOX

The last experiment really shows the scientist-detective at work. Very often the scientist cannot see what is inside a thing, and he has to try to find out by using his experience of things he can see, feel, or hear, and so on. Thus you might come to the conclusion that there is a rubber in your black box. You think this is so because you have seen a rubber; you know what it does when you drop it on the bench – it does not make the sort of noise that a penny makes, or a pencil. So the knowledge about rubbers that you have picked up during the years helps you to decide. There are some facts about the materials in the box, however, that you can never be sure of without opening the box to see for yourself. For instance you will not be able to guess what colour the rubber is, or what its exact size is, whether it has been used or not or if it has anyone's name on it. You might be able to guess what shape it had, but if someone had cut it into the shape of an animal, shall we say, you would probably not be able to guess that.

If there were a coin in the box you would not be sure whether it was a French, British, Irish or American one.

So the scientist can never be quite sure about the things he cannot see, although he can make some very good guesses. In Unit 4 you will come across a very good example of this when you yourselves will make some guesses about what substances are made up of although you cannot see inside them.

1.17 LIVING THINGS

So far we have been looking mainly at things which are not living – magnets, rulers, watches, cathode ray oscilloscopes, pieces of calcium, and so on. There is one great advantage when we are examining things such as these – they always do the same thing when we do the same thing to them, or, as the scientist would put it, they always respond in the same way to the same conditions.

A piece of calcium, for instance, always fizzes when you put it into water, and the gas which comes off is always hydrogen. When the class did an experiment like this all the pupils found the same result. Perhaps they did not all write down exactly the same words when they described what they saw, but the fact is that the same thing happened in everybody's test-tube. You have done a few experiments in which living things took part. For example you found your pulse rate and the rate of your heart beat. Was this the same for everybody?

When we look at living things we find that they do not all behave in the same way when you do the same things to them. If you stroke one cat it might purr; if you stroke another it might scratch you. All crystals of sugar and salt look the same, but you are all boys and girls and you do *not* look the same. Even if you were all dressed alike and were of the same size and shape, your teacher could still tell who was Smith and who was Jones because you at least have different faces. Sometimes, of course, twins look so much alike that it is difficult to tell one from the other, but there is usually some little difference between them –

Fig. 1.30 You cannot tell them apart!

perhaps one has a mole on his cheek and the other has not, or one's ears stick out and the other's do not. The study of living things – a branch of science called biology – is therefore sometimes more difficult than chemistry and physics which deal with non-living matter. However, although we cannot always say how a particular individual animal or plant will behave, we can, by looking at the behaviour of a lot of animals or plants of the same type, say what *most* of them will do.

1.18 HOW ODD ARE YOU?

Experiment 1.35

We are going to study the differences between the boys and girls who are in your year at school to see what conclusions we can arrive at. In order to gather all the information you will need, it is best to work in groups. Fill up a table like the one below. In entering colour of eyes you should choose one of the following four types – blue, grey, brown, and 'any other colour', and for colour of hair one of the following – dark, fair, red.

Look at the table you have filled up and you will soon realize how much you differ from each other. Collect the results for all the First Year pupils. Your teacher will show you another and quicker way of doing this. Find out who is the shortest. Say his height is 148 cm. Count up now how many are 149 cm, 150 cm, 151 cm, and so on until you get to the tallest. Then draw a column graph – called a histogram – like the one in Fig. 1.31.

Note the shape of the diagram you get. Do the same thing for length of hand span and pulse rate. If you have a statistics board you can use it in the same way, and it will give you the same sort of diagram as your graph.

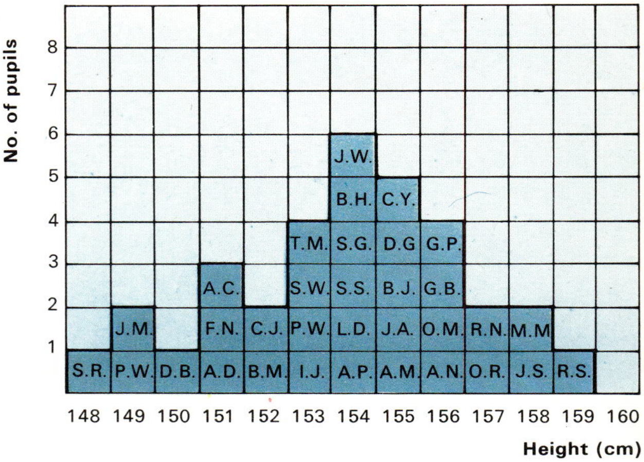

Fig. 1.31

Answer the following questions.

Is the shape of the diagram the same for height, hand span, and pulse rate?

You should find that there are comparatively few short pupils and comparatively few tall pupils in the class. Most seem to have nearly the same height.

What is the most usual height for pupils in the First Year?

What is the most usual hand span?
What is the most usual pulse rate?
What is the commonest eye colour?
What is the least common eye colour?
What is the commonest colour of hair?

Name	Height (cm)	Colour of eyes	Colour of hair	Can roll tongue?	Length of hand span (mm)	Pulse rate (beats/min)	Left or right handed
J. Smith	158	Blue	Dark	No	170	80	Right

What is the most unusual colour of hair?

What is the percentage of left-handed people in your Year or Form?

Can you say from this what coloured eyes and what coloured hair your future husband or wife is *most likely* to have? Is he or she *most likely* to be right or left handed? Of course, no one can be *certain*, but you can get some idea of what the odds are.

1.19 PLANTS TOO!

Of course, animals are not the only living creatures which show variation between themselves. Plants do too. All the flowers on a plant are not all the same size, some plants grow taller than others of the same kind and so on. You can convince yourself of this by looking at leaves, all of which come from the same tree.

Experiment 1.36

Collect some leaves from a tree near the school or in your garden. Trace the outline of one. Then see if you can find at least two ways in which the other leaves you have collected differ from the one you have drawn.

1.20 SORTING THINGS OUT

If you were asked to sort out the boys and girls in your class into groups you could do this by making use of the information you have already gathered about their hair colour, their eye colour, and so on.

Make a list of all the boys with blue eyes, those with brown eyes, those with grey eyes, and those with eyes of some other colour; do the same for the girls. Then make a list of all the boys with fair hair, those with dark hair, and those with red hair, and do the same for the girls. You will find these lists useful when you come to Unit 2, so you should keep them by you.

Scientists often have to sort things out like this. When we set out to classify substances, one of the most obvious things to do is to sort them out into solids, liquids, and gases. From the following list of substances pick out those which are solids, those which are liquids, and those which are gases.

glass	methylated	oil
tin	spirit	washing powder
water	ice	silk
oxygen	air	hydrogen
paraffin	salt	brick
milk	petrol	copper
	lemonade	

Another way of sorting things out is to put them into groups of metals and non-metals. Pick out from the following list those substances which are metals and those which are non-metals.

wood	marble	nylon
copper	calcium	water
paper	bronze	brass
iron	rubber	silver
cotton	hair	aluminium

WHAT YOU HAVE LEARNT IN THIS UNIT

1.   You have discovered some of the things that everyone who is going to study science must be able to do. First of all you must be able to look carefully and describe what you have seen and what you have done. You have learnt that the senses by themselves are often unreliable if we use them for measuring things, and so we have to devise instruments to help them. The list below shows you the things you have learnt to do and the instruments you have used. It also gives the units in which you measure things.

Job	*Instrument*	*Unit*
measuring lengths	ruler	m
measuring volumes	measuring cylinder	cm^3
measuring weights	balance	g
measuring times	watch or clock	min and s
measuring temperatures	thermometer	°C

2.   You have also learnt how to separate a solid from a liquid by filtration.

Of course these are not by any means all the operations you will have to do in the science laboratory, but they are a good start. You will come across more and more of them as you go on.

3.   You have learnt that although non-living matter always responds in the same way when you do something to it, living things do not. Nor are living things of the same type exactly alike. No two boys are the same, nor are two frogs.

Scientists often have to sort things out into groups (classify them) in order to cut down the work they have to do.

Unit Two
Looking at Living Things

2.1 HOW MANY ARE THERE?

Look at the picture below (Fig. 2.1)

In your notebook write down the names of the animals in the picture

   (a) that have 4 legs,
   (b) that have wings,
   (c) that are covered with feathers.

Write down the names of plants that (a) have flowers and (b) have no flowers.

From this picture we can see that animals and plants vary in shape. Only a few animals and plants are shown here. How many kinds of animals are there?

There are about 950 000 kinds of groups of animals in the world – nearly a million! The animals in each group are similar to each other in appearance, but they differ from those in the remaining groups. There must therefore be about 950 000 different shapes of animals.

Could you draw the shape of an animal, say an elephant or a blackbird, in one minute? Try this to see if you can. If you allowed only one minute for each drawing you could draw 360 in 6 hours, which is the time you spend in school each day. If you spent 6 hours every day of the year doing nothing else but drawing an animal each minute, it would take you over 7 years to complete 950 000 pictures. If you started doing

Fig. 2.1

this today, how old would you be when you finished the task?

Make a list in your note book of as many different animals and plants as you can find, say during the week-end. You will find them by looking under stones, piles of leaves, or in the soil. The animals you find might include snails, spiders, earthworms, earwigs, caterpillars, centipedes, and woodlice (slaters). Make rough drawings of those you find. You could bring some of them to school.

If you live near a pond, a stream, or the sea, see what you can find there.

Experiment 2.1
Looking at plants and animals

Look at the drawings of the plants and animals you and the other members of your class have found, or brought to school. Your teacher has provided some too. Look at the shapes of the **organisms**. This is the name given to living things. They are all different. In what ways do they differ from each other? Make lists of the organisms in two groups, plants and animals.

2.2 HOW DIFFERENT ARE THEY?

You have looked closely at the animals and noted the differences in their shapes, but do these animals have any similarities? As both the mouse and the hamster are covered with hair and have four legs, we can say they are similar. Is the mouse similar in any way to the goldfish? By looking at them there appear to be no similarities. The mouse is covered with hair, but the fish is covered with scales. The mouse has four legs and the fish

appears to have none. However the mouse and the fish have one feature in common. Do you know what it is? If you opened each animal you would find a backbone inside.

Look again at your list of animals and write down the names of those that have a backbone. We call animals with backbones **vertebrates**. Your teacher may have to help you because you cannot see inside the animals, and obviously we cannot open them up just to see if they have a backbone or not.

The remaining animals in your list do not have backbones. We call them **invertebrates**. Write down the names of the invertebrates.

2.3 SORTING THINGS OUT

The need for sorting things out, or classifying them, was mentioned at the end of the last chapter. You can now do this for living things. You have already divided living things into two groups, plants and animals. Then you divided the animals into two groups, vertebrates and invertebrates.

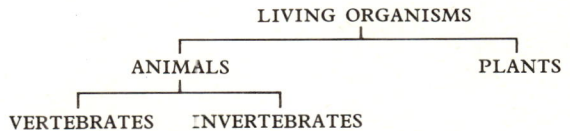

```
                    LIVING ORGANISMS
              ┌──────────┴──────────┐
           ANIMALS                 PLANTS
       ┌──────┴──────┐
  VERTEBRATES   INVERTEBRATES
```

Can you divide vertebrates into several small groups?

Fig. 2.2 (*left*) Mouse and (*right*) goldfish

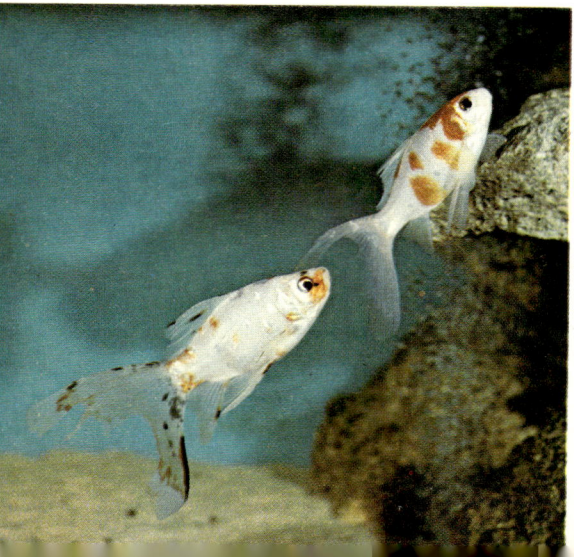

You will probably have some vertebrates in your laboratory, and you may have some at home as pets. Look at them and make up a table like the one at the top of the opposite page and fill in the spaces.

All the animals in the table share one common feature. What is this feature? However, you can see that these animals vary. Some are covered with hair, some with scales, and some with feathers. Vertebrates that have hair are called **mammals**, those that have feathers are called **birds**. Vertebrates that are covered with scales and live in water are called **fish**; those that live on land are called **reptiles**. Look at the table and try to find one other difference between fish and reptiles. Vertebrates that are covered with damp skin and can live both in water and on land are called **amphibians**.

Look again at the vertebrates in your laboratory. Write down the names of the mammals and the amphibians.

We have now divided the vertebrates into 5 smaller groups.

VERTEBRATES

FISH   AMPHIBIANS   REPTILES   BIRDS   MAMMALS

Vertebrates represent only a small proportion of all living animals. There are about 54 000 kinds of them, so there must be about 896 000 kinds of invertebrates. (How do we get this figure?) Obviously the invertebrates can also be divided up into groups, each containing animals with similar features. If you started to classify the invertebrates and the plants, it would take you many months. As you have many more interesting things to do and to look at we must leave classification for now.

Fig. 2.3 Sort these vertebrates into the correct groups – see Experiment 2.2

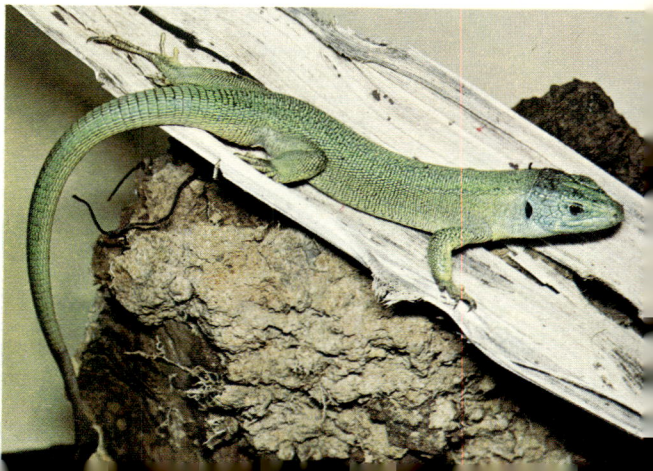

Animals with backbones											
		1	2	3	4	5	6	7	8	9	10
		goldfish	pigeon	man	frog	mouse	budgerigar	lizard	herring		
Skin structure	hair present										
	feathers present										
	scales present										
	none of above present										
Appendages	wings										
	legs										
	fins										

Something to do at home

Can you divide other things into groups? Perhaps at home you have a collection of stamps or post-cards. Look at your collection, and using one or more than one feature, divide your collection into groups. You could start a note book and put a different group on each page. When you have completed your note book, bring it into school and show it to your friends.

2.4 COLLECTING PLANTS

You can also make a class note book. When you are outside school look for plants growing on waste ground, on embankments or in the country. If there are many flowers of one kind you could pick **one** and bring it into school. If you can, try to bring the whole plant. As it is important to say where you found your plant, before you go collecting prepare a number of cards as follows.

Name		
Class		
Date	Name of plant	Where found

Do not be worried if you do not know the name of the plants you find, because you will soon be learning how to name organisms you may never have seen before.

When you bring your plants into school you can press them, so that they can be kept for a long time. Press your plants by placing them between sheets of blotting paper or newspaper. Cover this with more sheets of newspaper, and then place some heavy books on top. The paper will absorb water from the plants, and so you should change it every few days. When the plants are completely dry, stick them on to a sheet of paper or cardboard. Beside the specimen write all the details you noted when collecting them.

Arrange all the pressed plants around the laboratory and then divide them into groups. Remember that all the plants in one group must have similar features. What features will you choose? When you have classified your plants arrange them in a folder.

2.5 MAKING A ZOO

At the beginning of this unit you were asked to collect different animals and bring them into school. You examined them and put them into groups. However, you can study the behaviour and habits of some of the animals if you can keep them alive in your laboratory. You will have to free some of the animals, e.g. spiders and centipedes, by taking them back to where you found them. These animals are difficult to feed and would probably die if you kept them in school. On the other hand some animals can be kept quite easily in school, and these include earthworms, woodlice, and caterpillars.

Investigation of living organisms

In order to keep any organism alive in school, you must provide it with the conditions under which it lives normally. If you were taken from your natural surroundings, i.e. your home, and sent to live on the moon or the bottom of the sea, what would you require to take with you? You would need food similar to that which you usually eat, a supply of the air you breathe, and building material of some kind to build a protective covering. In other words, you would need all the conditions which you are used to. In the same way you must provide for the animals in your laboratory conditions similar to those in which you found them.

You found the earthworms in soil and so you must keep them in soil. You found the caterpillars on leaves and so you must supply them with leaves. What other conditions must you provide? What kind of food will you give them?

You can find this out for yourself. If you have managed to find several caterpillars, some groups can study them; if not, you can all study earthworms.

2.6 LOOKING AT EARTHWORMS AND CATERPILLARS

Experiment 2.3
Finding out what earthworms eat

Put about 10 earthworms in a box of soil. On the surface of the soil place about 20 leaves,

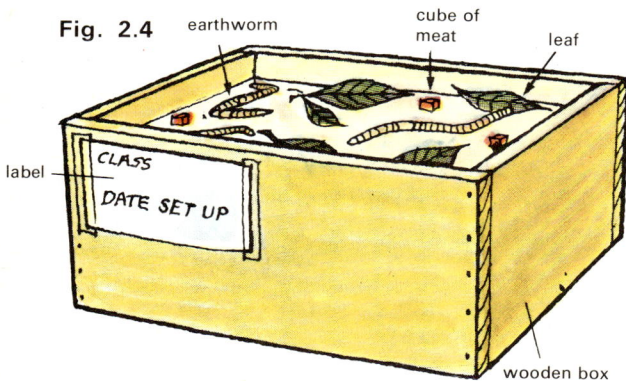

Fig. 2.4   earthworm   cube of meat   leaf   label   CLASS   DATE SET UP   wooden box

several stones, and a few pieces of raw meat. Write down the number of leaves, stones, and pieces of meat placed on the surface, making a table like the one below. Cover the box with

Number of worms			
Date set up			
Date	Number of leaves on surface of soil	Number of stones on surface of soil	Number of pieces of meat on surface of soil

polythene, that has been pricked to allow air to enter. Label the box with the name of your class and the date. Leave the box in a cool place for one week. Remove the polythene, and then look carefully to see what has happened. Enter your results in the table.

What has happened to the leaves? Have the worms eaten any raw meat? From the results of this experiment do you think worms eat grubs in the soil? What *do* they eat?

Experiment 2.4
Do earthworms prefer some foods to others?

No help this time. Work out a way of finding this out for yourself.

Do you prefer some foods to others? Write down a list of the foods you like most and the foods you like least.

What is the most popular food amongst the numbers of your class? Do the girls like the same food as the boys?

Experiment 2.5
What do caterpillars like to eat?

Some of you may have caterpillars to look at. Can you find out what they like to eat? Before

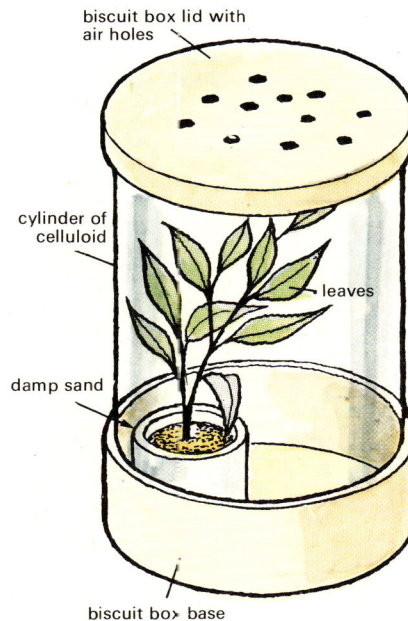

Fig. 2.5 Various types of insect cage

you can do this you must prepare something in which the caterpillar can live. You can do this quite easily if you use jam jars.

Make an insect cage, and then see if you can find out what your caterpillar eats. You will have to provide it with different kinds of leaves. Make a table of your results.

You have found out where your organisms like to live and what they eat. You should now be able to keep them alive in your laboratory and so find out more about them.

Experiment 2.6
Looking at the structure of an earthworm

Put an earthworm on a sheet of paper. What shape of body does it have?

Turn the worm over. Which surface is the darker? Look at the worm carefully. Which end do you think is the head? Give a reason for your answer. Look for the swollen part on the worm. This is called the **saddle**. Is the saddle near the head end or the rear?

Draw the shape of your earthworm and label the head, the saddle, and the rear. You are now going to look more closely at your earthworm. In order to see small structures, they will have to be made larger or magnified. To do this we use a lens.

Experiment 2.7
How to use a lens

Hold the lens about 5 cm from one eye. Holding the earthworm in your other hand, bring it up to the lens. The earthworm will gradually become clear. When you can see it clearly it is said to be **in focus**.

Can you see the rings on the worm? These rings are called **segments**. Are there any segments on the saddle? Draw the segments on your diagram of the earthworm.

Turn the worm over and using your lens look closely at the segments. What do you see? Gently stroke the underside of the worm. What do you feel?

On the underside of the worm are many bristles or hair-like structures.

Experiment 2.8
The structure of the caterpillar

Look at the caterpillar. In what way is the caterpillar similar to the earthworm? Do they differ? Make a list of similarities and differences. You can have a competition. See which group can collect the longest list of similarities and of differences.

Fig. 2.6 Caterpillars on privet leaves

Experiment 2.9
How does the earthworm move?

Put the worm on a sheet of paper and watch it closely. What happens to the shape of the worm when it moves?

Put your head near the paper and listen carefully. In order to hear anything you must be very quiet. What do you hear? What do you

think is making the noise? How do you think you could magnify the sound? If you have the equipment you could try it out.

In your note book write a brief account of how the worm moves so that anyone who had never studied earthworms could understand your description.

Experiment 2.10
Movement in the caterpillar

Put the caterpillar on a piece of paper and watch it closely.

Write down *two* ways in which the movement of the caterpillar differs from that of the worm.

If you had a race between a worm and a caterpillar, which do you think would win? Give a reason for your answer. If you have time you could try this to see if you are correct.

In Experiment 2.3 you found out that worms pull leaves below the surface of the soil. Unfortunately you could not see what happened to the leaves. If you put the worms into a narrow box with glass sides you will be able to observe what happens under the soil.

Fig. 2.7 A common garden worm

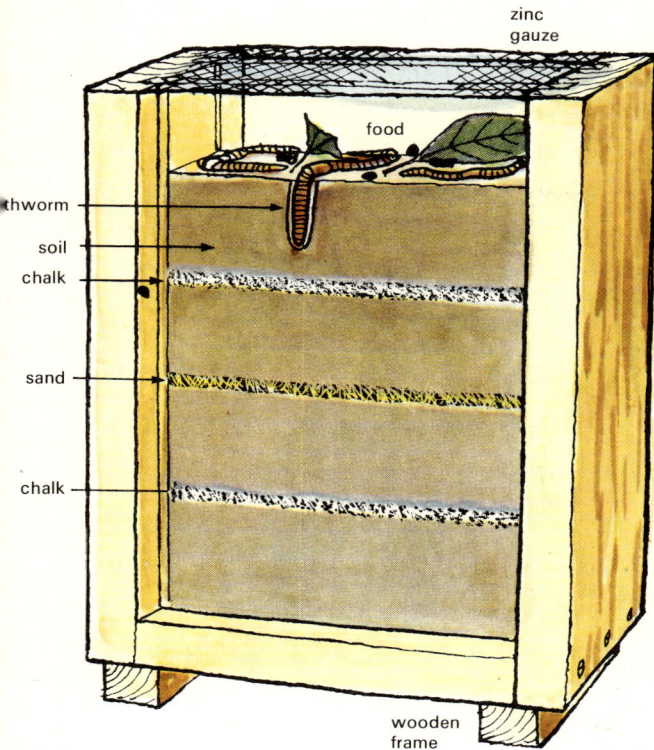

Fig. 2.8 A wormery

Labels on figure: zinc gauze, food, earthworm, soil, chalk, sand, chalk, wooden frame

Cut two pieces of cardboard and fit them over the glass sides.

Leave the wormery for about a week. Read the following questions, and then remove the pieces of cardboard.

Some questions to answer

1. What happened to the worms when you removed the cardboard?
2. What has happened to the leaves lying on top of the soil? Pull some leaves from a burrow. Do they show signs of having been eaten?
3. For what purpose does the worm plug its burrow?
4. What shape are the burrows?
5. How are the burrows formed?
6. What is happening to the layers as a result of the worms burrowing?
7. Why were the glass sides covered with cardboard?
8. Do worms prefer daylight or dark surroundings? Find this out for yourself.

Experiment 2.11
Setting up a wormery

Using a spoon, put a layer of damp garden soil (about 5 cm deep) in the bottom of the wormery (see Fig. 2.8).

Level this off with a ruler. Sprinkle in a very thin layer of sand or chalk. Level off, add more soil, then chalk. Repeat this, ending with a layer of soil, until you are 5 cm from the top of the wormery.

Put five worms on the surface of the soil. Watch them burrow. How do they move through the soil? Place some food on top of the soil and cover the wormery with zinc gauze.

Label the wormery as follows.

Class . . . .

Date set up . . . .

Number of worms . . . .

Experiment 2.12
Do earthworms prefer daylight or dark surroundings?

To find this out you will need long glass tubes, black paper, and a bench lamp or torch. Do caterpillars react in the same way?

2.7 IMPORTANCE OF EARTHWORMS

By keeping earthworms in school you have been able to observe their behaviour. You have seen that they pull leaves under the ground. When they burrow, they pass soil through their bodies and so make it finer.

Earthworms are very useful to the gardener. They pull into the ground leaves which decay and make the soil richer. Their burrows allow air and water to reach the roots of plants. They mix the soil and so bring fresh soil up to the surface.

If you had a choice of putting 10 000 earthworms into your garden or 10 000 caterpillars, which would you choose? Give a reason for your answer.

2.8 KEEPING YOUR CATERPILLAR

When you have finished studying the behaviour of your caterpillar, keep it in the laboratory for a few weeks. Place its cage in a cool spot and feed it with its favourite food. Look at it once a week and you may see a strange thing happening.

For the letter writers

You have a friend in another town who knows nothing about earthworms, but he would like to keep some in school. Write a letter to him, giving him the instructions he will need to keep his earthworms successfully in the laboratory.

For the night owls

If you go into your garden after dark on a warm damp night, you will probably see worms lying on the lawn. Shine a torch over some worms. What happens? If you are very quick try to catch a worm. Can you pull it from its burrow? Give a reason for your answer.

2.9 IDENTIFYING PLANTS AND ANIMALS

You have compared two animals, the earthworm and the caterpillar, and have found that they vary in appearance and behaviour. As the worm and the caterpillar belong to different groups of animals, you would expect them to be different. By noting the differences between types of animal or plant we can identify them. To do this we have to draw up a **key**, which really consists of pairs of clues. By looking at our animal or plant and seeing which clues apply to it, we are able to say what it is.

Here is an example of a key, and how to use it.

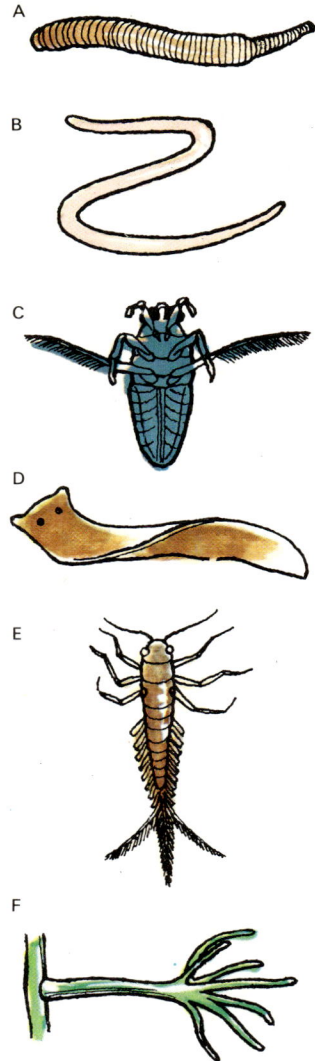

Fig. 2.9

Fig. 2.9 shows six animals which are found in pond water. Here is the key.

1.	Body divided into segments ..	(2)
	Body not divided into segments ..	(4)
2.	Animals with jointed limbs ..	(3)
	No limbs .. .. LEECH	
3.	Third pair of limbs fringed WATER BOATMAN	
	Third pair of limbs not fringed MAYFLY LARVA	
4.	Tentacles at end of body ..	HYDRA
	No tentacles..	(5)
5.	Body round and thread-like NEMATODE WORM	
	Body flat .. .. .. FLATWORM	

Name	Height (cm)	Colour of eyes	Colour of hair	Length hand span (mm)	Pulse rate (beats/min)	Left or right handed
J. Smith	158	Blue	Dark	170	80	RIGHT
S. Robertson	148	Brown	Dark	175	87	RIGHT
I. Jackson	153	Blue	Fair	170	93	RIGHT
P. Wilson	149	Blue	Dark	165	79	LEFT
A. Duncan	151	Blue	Fair	170	89	LEFT
D. Brown	150	Grey	Dark	170	96	RIGHT

Look at animal A, and then at clue 1. You will see that the clue is made up of two parts. Is the body of A divided into segments or not? You can see that it *is* divided. Opposite 'Body divided into segments' you will see the number (2). This means you must go on and look at clue 2.

Look at animal A again. Does it have limbs? It has no limbs. Opposite 'No limbs' you will see the name LEECH. This means that animal A is a leech; so you have found out this one very quickly.

Now let's look at animal B. Applying clue 1 we have to look to see if the animal is divided into segments or not. It is not. Opposite 'Body not divided into segments' you will see the number (4). This means that you have to go to clue 4. Clues 2 and 3 refer only to animals with segmented bodies. Does the animal have tentacles or not? It has no tentacles, and so we have to go on to clue 5. Is the body round or flat? As it is round and thread-like, animal B is a NEMATODE WORM.

Using the key, name the remaining animals C, D, E, and F. Remember you must always begin at clue 1 and ask yourself whether the animal has a segmented body or not. Write down the name of each animal. Your teacher will tell you if you are correct.

2.10 MAKING A KEY

You are now going to try to make up a key for yourselves. In Unit 1 you noted that there was variation between the different members of the class, and you made a table showing the different heights, eye colour, hair colour, and so on for all the boys and girls in your class. We can use this information to make a key from which you will be able to identify all the boys and girls in the class by looking at them, even if you did not know their names to start with.

Above is a table similar to the one you filled up before.

Can you divide these six boys into two groups so that all in one group share a common feature, but none in the second group have it? You could use eye colour. How many boys have blue eyes? There are four with blue eyes, and two with eyes that are a different colour. Our first division will therefore be this

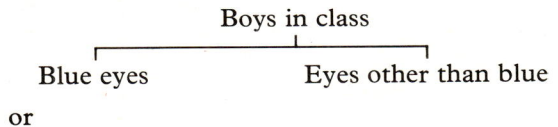

Boys in class

Blue eyes   Eyes other than blue

or

1. Blue eyes .. ..
   Eyes other than blue

Look at the boys with blue eyes. What feature can you use to divide them into two groups? What about hair colour? Two of them have fair hair and two have dark.

We can add to the key as follows.

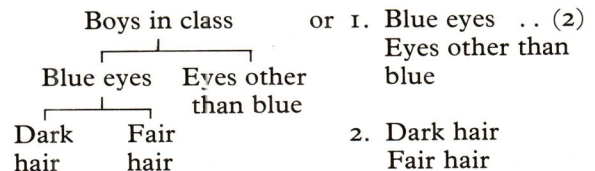

Boys in class   or 1. Blue eyes .. (2)
                              Eyes other than
Blue eyes   Eyes other   blue
            than blue
Dark   Fair
hair   hair   2. Dark hair
                                 Fair hair

Look for the names of boys with blue eyes and dark hair. They are J. Smith and P. Wilson. What features can we use to separate these two? What about height? Smith is 158 cm. Wilson is 149 cm.

We can add some further information to our key.

```
                    Boys in class
              ┌───────────┴───────────┐
          Blue eyes          Eyes other than
                                   blue
          ┌───┴───┐
        Dark      Fair
        hair      hair
      ┌───┴───┐
   Height   Height
   158 cm   149 cm
      │        │
    SMITH    WILSON
```

or

1. Blue eyes   ..   ..   ..   (2)
   Eyes other than blue

2. Dark hair   ..   ..   ..   (3)
   Fair hair

3. Height 158 cm   ..   ..   SMITH
   Height 149 cm   ..   ..   WILSON

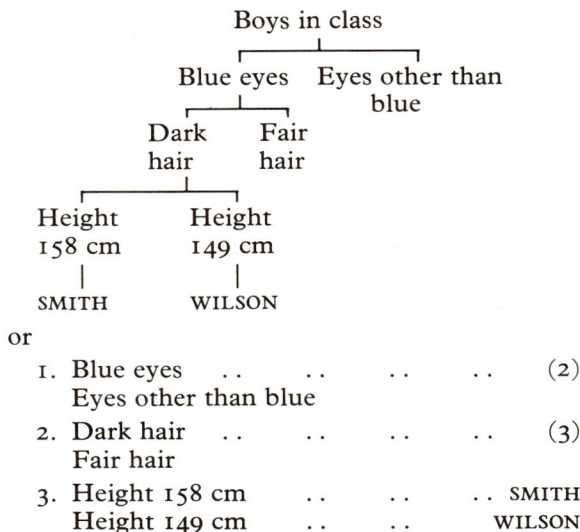

Note that (3) has been written opposite 'Dark hair'. What does this mean? Now look for the names of the boys with blue eyes and fair hair. Who are they? Jackson is right-handed. Duncan is left-handed. Our key will now look like this.

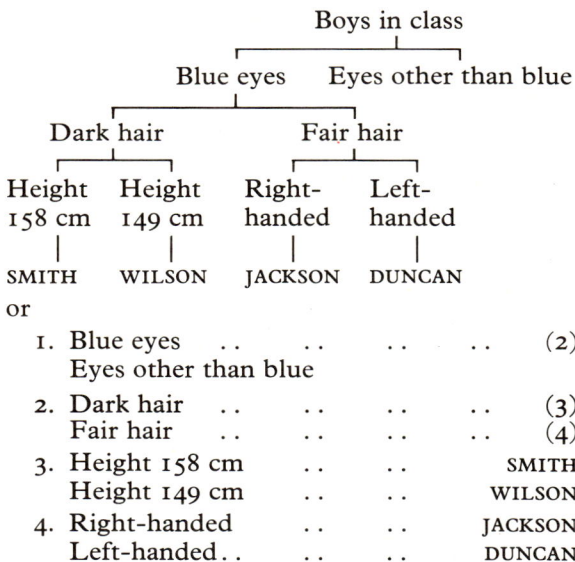

```
                         Boys in class
                 ┌─────────────┴─────────────┐
            Blue eyes              Eyes other than blue
        ┌────────┴────────┐
     Dark hair          Fair hair
   ┌────┴────┐       ┌──────┴──────┐
 Height  Height    Right-        Left-
 158 cm  149 cm    handed        handed
   │        │         │             │
 SMITH   WILSON    JACKSON       DUNCAN
```

or

1. Blue eyes   ..   ..   ..   (2)
   Eyes other than blue

2. Dark hair   ..   ..   ..   (3)
   Fair hair   ..   ..   ..   (4)

3. Height 158 cm   ..   ..   SMITH
   Height 149 cm   ..   ..   WILSON

4. Right-handed   ..   ..   JACKSON
   Left-handed ..   ..   ..   DUNCAN

You will notice that the number (2) has been written opposite 'Blue eyes'. What does this mean? Why was it not written opposite 'Eyes other than blue'?

We have been dealing with boys with blue eyes. Now let us go back and look at the boys with eyes that are not blue, Robertson and Brown. You will see that they have a different pulse rate. We can now complete our key as follows.

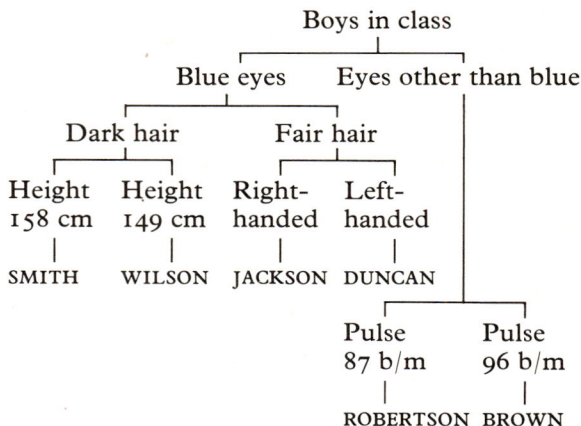

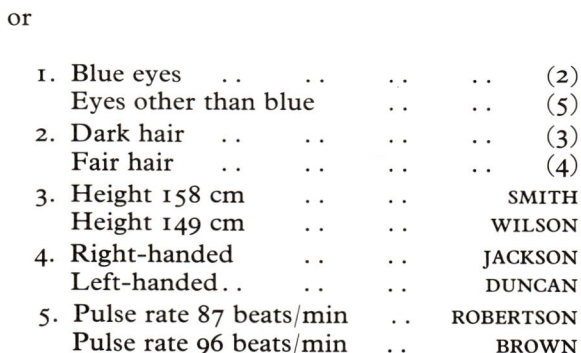

```
                            Boys in class
                   ┌─────────────┴─────────────┐
              Blue eyes              Eyes other than blue
          ┌────────┴────────┐                   │
     Dark hair            Fair hair             │
   ┌──────┴──────┐    ┌──────┴──────┐           │
 Height   Height   Right-      Left-            │
 158 cm   149 cm   handed      handed           │
   │        │         │           │             │
 SMITH   WILSON   JACKSON     DUNCAN        ┌───┴───┐
                                          Pulse   Pulse
                                          87 b/m  96 b/m
                                            │        │
                                       ROBERTSON  BROWN
```

or

1. Blue eyes   ..   ..   ..   (2)
   Eyes other than blue   ..   ..   (5)

2. Dark hair   ..   ..   ..   (3)
   Fair hair   ..   ..   ..   (4)

3. Height 158 cm   ..   ..   SMITH
   Height 149 cm   ..   ..   WILSON

4. Right-handed   ..   ..   JACKSON
   Left-handed..   ..   ..   DUNCAN

5. Pulse rate 87 beats/min   ..   ROBERTSON
   Pulse rate 96 beats/min   ..   BROWN

Make a key to identify the members of your own group. You can test your key by inviting a teacher who does not know your class to work out the names of one or two members of your group.

WHAT YOU HAVE LEARNT IN THIS UNIT

1. There are very many different kinds of animal in the world. You looked at a very few and found that they had different shapes, different numbers of legs, different coverings for their bodies, and so on.

2. Animals can be sorted into two groups – those which have backbones (called **vertebrates**), and those which do not (**invertebrates**).

3. Vertebrates can be sorted out into five groups.

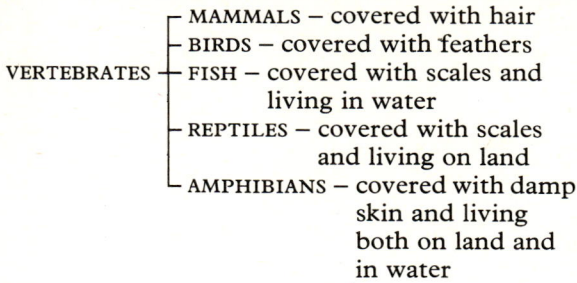

VERTEBRATES
- MAMMALS – covered with hair
- BIRDS – covered with feathers
- FISH – covered with scales and living in water
- REPTILES – covered with scales and living on land
- AMPHIBIANS – covered with damp skin and living both on land and in water

4. There are many more invertebrates than there are vertebrates, and to sort these out would take a very long time.

5. There are very many different kinds of plant, too.

6. You made a special study of the earthworm, and found out how to make a wormery.

7. The earthworm you studied had a body made up of **segments**, and looked like the diagram below, which gives the names of the various parts you noticed.

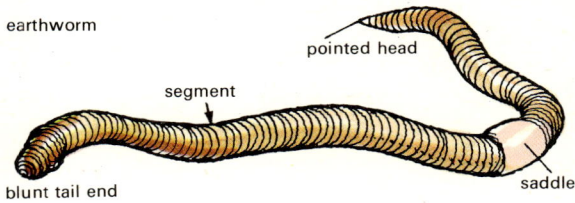

Fig. 2.10

8. Earthworms pull down leaves into the soil, but they do not touch meat.

9. The diagram below shows the main parts of a caterpillar.

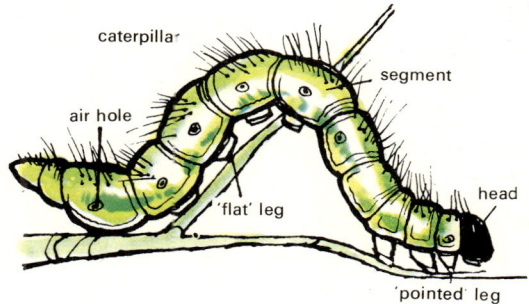

Fig. 2.11

10. You found that caterpillars would only eat certain kinds of leaves. Unlike earthworms they did not burrow into the ground.

11. Earthworms and caterpillars move in different ways. The earthworm squeezes up the segments in one part of its body and stretches others, very much like a concertina. It uses the bristles on its under surface to get a grip, particularly when burrowing. The caterpillar moves by using its legs and making a sort of hump.

12. Earthworms are very useful to the gardener and the farmer, because they (a) pull leaves into the soil, where they decay and make the ground richer; (b) let air into the soil through their burrows; and (c) mix up the soil, bringing fresh soil to the surface.

13. You have also learnt how to sort things out (classify them) and how to identify animals or plants by means of a key.

Unit Three
Energy

3.1 ENERGY, FOOD, AND MOVEMENT

Most young boys and girls love to dash about in the playground, or to play games like football and hockey, or to go swimming. In good weather the only time they want to come indoors is when they feel hungry, and want to eat.

Is there any connection between eating and playing? When you are running about we say you are energetic. You must have energy to move about. Do boys and girls who live in parts of the world where food is scarce have as much energy as you do? Perhaps you have seen pictures of them which give you the idea that they do not. Can you think of any of your favourite breakfast foods or sweets which are advertised as giving you lots of energy?

Our bodies are very wonderful; they are able to change foods into energy for us. While you are moving about, playing games, swimming and so on, the chemicals in the food you have eaten provide the energy you need to be able to do these things.

Of course energy is required to enable not only *us* to move; it is necessary for the movement of cars, planes, and everything else.

3.2 FORMS OF ENERGY

There are many other forms in which energy exists. Look at the chart in Fig. 3.1 and you will see that so far we have mentioned three:

chemical energy, which is available from food (and, as you will see, from other chemicals too); **movement energy**, which is usually called **kinetic energy** (find out from a dictionary what the word 'kinetic' means; is it connected with the cinema?) and **stored up energy**, which is usually called **potential energy.**

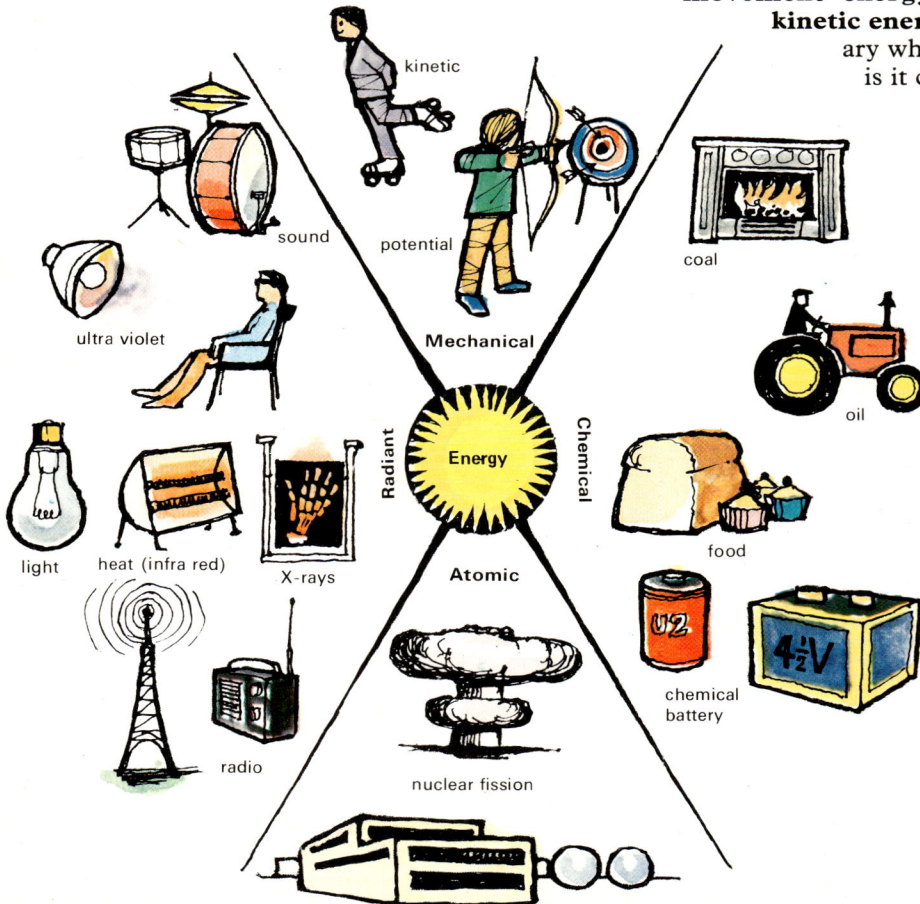

Fig. 3.1 Forms of energy

You may come across the word 'potential' in your English lessons. Perhaps someone has said of you that you are a 'potential' captain of the football team or a 'potential' scientist meaning that you have stored up within you the capacity of being a football captain or a scientist. Anything which has potential energy is able to do something with it when it is released. A very simple example is the potential energy stored up in a wound-up spring. You had to put this energy into the spring when you wound it up, and you get it back when the spring drives a toy motor-car or perhaps the hands of your wrist-watch.

3.3 FUELS

When you have been playing a game very energetically you will have found that your food has made another kind of energy for you as well as movement energy. This is **heat**, which perhaps you are more accustomed to think of as coming from the burning of fuels. Fuels, like every other substance, are, of course, chemicals. Which chemicals that you know of are used as fuels?

We could say that food too is a fuel. When a fuel is burned, the heat energy produced is often used to drive engines of one kind or another; in other words, the heat energy is converted into mechanical energy. In just the same way our food, which contains chemical energy, is burnt (you will find out later how the body does this, but of course no flame or smoke is produced!) and gives us movement energy. One of the world's greatest problems in the years ahead will be to find enough food for feeding people, and enough fuel for burning either to make heat or to make machines move. During the last hundred years scientists and engineers have discovered many ways of burning or exploding fuel to provide machines with the energy to do jobs for us which otherwise we would find very hard or perhaps impossible to do.

Here is something for you to find out. Do you know how the Pyramids in Egypt were built? How would they have been built today? What machines would we use that the ancient Egyptians did not have? You would perhaps get some idea

Fig. 3.2 The production of various fuels. Find out which they are

by looking up how the giant statues at Abu Simnel were moved some years ago.

Make a list of the kinds of engines you have heard about.

Make a list of the machines you have at home which help you to save your own energy when doing jobs.

3.4 ATOMIC ENERGY

Scientists have found out how to use the energy stored up in the very heavy metal uranium. This energy is called **atomic** energy. What are the present forms of transport which are able to use the atomic energy from uranium? Britain at present leads the world in using atomic energy in power stations to make electricity. What kinds of energy can we obtain by using this electricity?

3.5 WAVES

Energy can travel from one place to another as waves. Do you remember the experiment in which you whistled into a microphone and saw a wave form produced on the cathode ray oscilloscope? The whistle, which was of course a sound, was energy in one particular form, and this energy travels in waves. Later on in the course you will find out much more about these sound waves, how they can travel and so on.

The energy sent out by radio stations and picked up by your transistor set travels in waves also. If you look on the tuning panel of your radio set you may see the letters LW, MW, and SW. What do these letters stand for?

When anyone is unfortunate enough to break a bone in his body, some very short waves called X-rays are shot through the person on to a photographic film, and a picture of the shadow of the bones is made. The energy of these waves is, in fact, rather dangerous, and we have to be careful not to expose the body too often to them.

Try to find these forms of energy in Fig. 3.1.

3.6 WHERE DOES ENERGY COME FROM?

If you ask where did all the energy come from in the universe to start with, the answer to that would be 'No-one really knows'. But we do know where all the energy which we use on the earth comes from.

You may already know of the various changes which have taken place on the earth since it was formed. Later on in school it may be possible for you to find out what has happened in the past to the ground where you are now, how it came to be different from the kind of landscape there is in other parts of the country. At some time over the past hundreds of millions of years, the spot where you are now was notably under the sea, then a sandy desert, perhaps part of a lava field from a volcano, maybe a swamp, and possibly even covered by a thick sheet of ice. During all

Fig. 3.3 (*left*) An open-cast uranium mine in New Mexico. The grey area bears the ore, (*top*) uranium fuel elements, and (*bottom*) Dounreay nuclear reactor in Scotland

this time something was pouring out energy into our planet from about 90 million miles away. What do you think this source of energy was?

Scientists calculate that the Sun will continue to supply us with energy for a thousand million years or so into the future. The energy from the Sun travels to us in waves, and it takes about eight minutes twenty seconds to reach us.

Can you name three of the forms in which energy from the Sun reaches us?

One of the effects of heat and light energy was that, about two hundred and fifty million years ago, dense tropical forests were able to grow at some places on the Earth, including the area round about the South Pole. Do you know what is left of these forests now and how we make use of their remains?

At other times the heat and light allowed tiny plants to grow here, on which animals fed. Nowadays we find the remains of these organisms turned into oil or natural gas. When we burn any of these fuels which in the distant past were in the form of some kind of plant, it is just as if the heat we get from them today is the heat and light energy they obtained from the Sun and locked up within themselves when they were growing.

Find out from books in the school library about the tremendous energies set free in such things as earthquakes, hurricanes, and the tides. Where does this energy come from?

3.7 ENERGY CHANGES

All around us we have energy in different forms, but often energy changes from one form to another. We have seen already that the chemical energy stored in food can be changed into kinetic energy; so can the chemical energy stored in petrol or coal.

Here are some more examples to think about. When you wound up your watch you hoped it would keep on going all day. What form of energy was put in, what happened to it, and what form of energy was given out?

Obviously you used kinetic energy in winding up the watch. This was stored as potential energy in the spring, and released again as kinetic energy as the spring unwound. Of course we can take this chain of energy changes back further if we wish.

Where did the kinetic energy come from which was used in winding up the watch? It was present as chemical energy in our food. And this chemical energy came from heat and light from the Sun. So the complete chain is:

Heat $\longrightarrow$ Chemical $\rightarrow$ Kinetic $\longrightarrow$ Potential $\longrightarrow$
energy   energy   energy   energy
(from Sun) (food)   (winding) (in spring)

Kinetic
energy
(moving wheels and hands)

Here is another example to think about. A car is driven to the top of a hill. Then the engine is turned off, and the car is allowed to free wheel down the other side of the hill. Where did the energy come from to drive the car to the top of the hill? What kind of energy did the car have at the top of the hill? What was it changed into as the car coasted down the hill?

You may own a catapult, and no doubt you will have seen on films huge catapults launching aircraft from the decks of aircraft carriers. Both these kinds of catapult work by storing up energy and then suddenly releasing it as kinetic energy. Can you find out what it is that stores the energy in each case?

Fig. 3.4 Two methods by which energy is changed: work out how this happens

3.8 SOME EXPERIMENTS ON ENERGY CHANGES

Here are a number of simple experiments for you to try for yourself. In each experiment you are asked to say in what form the energy is supplied and in what form it comes out. Write up your results in a table like this.

Experiment	Energy exchange
1	
2	

(If you use worksheets the table will have been drawn out ready for you.)

The energy chain on page 35 will remind you of all the different forms in which energy can exist.

Experiment 3.1

Rub your finger backwards and forwards on the bench. In what form is the energy· you are supplying? How do your fingers feel when you have done this for some time? What kind of energy have you been able to make?

Do you think there would be any difference if you tried rubbing your finger on a different kind of surface, say a rougher one?

We call the effect of rubbing one surface on another **friction**. Generally, as you have found, the energy used up in making rough surfaces slide over each other is converted into heat and sometimes into sound too. Where on your bicycle would this effect be very important when you want to stop? Where on your bicycle would you *not* want much friction and what do you do to try to prevent it?

You must be careful not to make the mistake of thinking that friction is in itself a form of energy. It is not. To start anything moving you have to push it, or as we say 'apply a force' to it. Friction is a force which opposes and often stops motion.

Experiment 3.2

You will be provided with a tube about 1 m long with a piece of wire gauze about 10 cm up inside the tube. Heat the wire gauze with a flame for about twenty seconds, and then slide the Bunsen away. What happens?

In what form was the energy that you gave the gauze? What kind of energy did the tube give you in return?

Experiment 3.3

A circuit is set up in which a torch bulb is connected to a battery and a switch. What happens when you close the switch? Where has the energy come from to light the bulb?

Do you think the bulb would still be glowing if you left the switch closed and came back next week to see?

Dry batteries contain certain chemicals which have energy which can be changed into an electric current, but these chemicals can soon be used up if there is not much of them, and the bulb would become dim and finally go out.

Can you imagine how different our lives would be if we did not have electric light bulbs to light up our homes, streets, shops and so on. Later you will hear of the man who invented electric light bulbs.

Experiment 3.4

Here is a very simple experiment. Heat the corner of a piece of wire gauze in a blue Bunsen flame. What happens to the colour of the gauze?

If you were able to heat the gauze with a much hotter flame, you might find that instead of glowing red it would glow yellow or even white. We say that we can heat things 'red hot' or 'white hot'. It is obvious that the hot gauze is not just giving off heat; it is giving off light as well.

What energy conversion has taken place here?

This method of getting light – making things hot so that they glow – is used in electric light bulbs. If you live somewhere where you use oil for lighting, you will know that you use the burning oil to heat a 'mantle' which gives off light.

Fig. 3.5 A gas mantle and wire filament glow when hot and are said to be 'incandescent'

(a) Gas mantle   (b) Electric lamp

Experiment 3.5

A match head is wrapped up tightly in a piece of aluminium foil, such as you use in cooking, or in a milk bottle top. The match is resting on a crucible lid on a pipe-clay triangle on a tripod stand. Make sure you do not stand too close. When you heat the crucible lid what happens?

Sometimes there is a little explosion and the piece of foil jumps off the lid. This would mean that there were at least two kinds of energy produced by the heating. What are they?

Perhaps this reminds you of fireworks. These contain chemicals. When they are heated their energy is converted into other forms. What are they? Do you know which nation invented gunpowder? If you don't, look it up. The chemicals in a match head are not, however, the same as in gunpowder, and they do not explode in quite the same way.

Fig. 3.6 Striking a match – a controlled explosion

Name some important forms of transport in which the motion energy is produced from a very rapid series of explosions. Which substances contain the chemical energy which is supplied to these?

Experiment 3.6

Here is another very simple experiment. This time you are to shake a tin with nails inside it. What kind of energy do you supply? What kind of energy is made?

When you were a baby you probably liked to produce sound this way. With what?

Some musicians use instruments like your tin of nails. They are used a lot in South American music-making. What is their correct name?

Experiment 3.7

Fig. 3.7

Make a paper spiral, stick it through with a pin, and hold it about 10 cm above a Bunsen flame. Be careful that the flame does not set the paper alight, and that the spiral moves easily on the pin. You can also do this experiment with a thin piece of aluminium foil cut into sectors and bent into blades, and then mounted on a pin as a bearing; or you can use a toy windmill. The paper spiral revolves. What is the air doing to make it revolve?

What energy changes take place here?

What do you notice about the smoke from a fire when there is no wind? Is this the same sort of thing that has happened in your experiment?

Experiment 3.8

Push the friction-drive toy car along the bench or on the floor. Most of you will have had toys like this when you were younger. Before this kind of toy became so popular most toy cars were of the clockwork kind, in which a spring was wound up to store the energy which was later used to make the toy go. How does the friction-drive toy work? Perhaps you have had one which has broken and you have taken it to pieces. Is there a spring in it? If not, can you spot something which can store energy? You will see that there is a big disc or wheel, like a large coin, called a **fly-wheel**. When you push the toy this wheel starts spinning. Because it is a heavy wheel for this size of car, the fly-wheel once set spinning tends to keep on doing so, and it stores energy. Real motor-car engines have fly-wheels to keep the engine parts moving smoothly in between the separate explosions in the cylinders.

Write down the energy changes that occur in this experiment.

Experiment 3.9

In this experiment you are going to use a dangerous chemical called sodium hydroxide or caustic soda. The word **caustic** means burning, and so you should not touch this substance. It should be handled only with the forceps provided.

First pour some water to a depth of about 3 cm into a test-tube. Put one hand round the tube. How does it feel compared with the temperature of the room? Now carefully lift up one pellet of the caustic soda and drop it into the water in the test-tube. Again put your hand round the test-tube. Keep it there as long as it is comfortable. Does it feel as if the water is at the same temperature as it was to begin with? What is happening to the pellet of caustic soda? Is it as big as it was? If we say that the caustic soda has chemical energy, into what kind of energy has this changed as the pellet dissolved?

Experiment 3.10

In this experiment you are going to heat some orange crystals of ammonium dichromate. Look at this substance carefully before you start, and notice that it is made up of tiny particles of similar shape, just as sugar or salt is. See that your test-tube is quite dry, and then put into it about 0.5 cm depth of the orange crystals. Holding the tube in a test-tube holder, heat it gently with a small flame. See that the tube is not pointing at any one, and do not look directly into it yourself. What happens to the substance?

You can try this experiment in another way. Make a small heap of the ammonium dichromate on a metal plate. Heat a thick piece of copper wire red hot and then put it into the heap of crystals. You will see that you get a kind of miniature volcano. Once it is started it goes on by itself. Why should this be?

What energy changes have taken place here?

Experiment 3.11

Our next experiment works best with an accumulator. This stores up energy in chemical form which can readily be changed into electrical energy when we want it. An accumulator is used to provide the electrical energy in cars.

Connect the accumulator to the coil of wire and a switch. Switch on the current for a few seconds only. What happens to the little

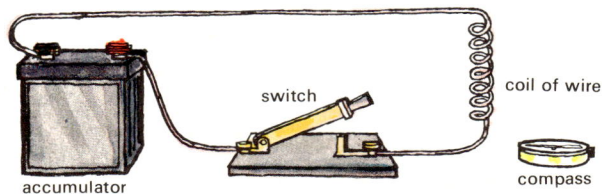

Fig. 3.8 When you open and close the switch, what happens to the compass needle?

compass needle which is near the end of the coil? What happens to it when you switch the current off? You will come across this experiment again later in the course. It will tell us something of how electric bells, telephone receivers, and so on, work.

What energy conversions have taken place here?

Experiment 3.12

In this experiment we have two wires of different metals. One is copper, the other is an alloy called constantan, and is the sort of metal of which the element in an electric fire is made. The two wires are twisted together at one end. The other ends are connected to a sensitive meter whose needle will move when an electric current is passed through the meter. Heat the wires where they are twisted together. Does the needle move?

What energy changes have taken place?

This kind of arrangement is often used as a thermometer. What advantage would it have over an ordinary kind of thermometer? What are its disadvantages?

In remote areas in Russia large numbers of these junctions of wire are heated with stoves to

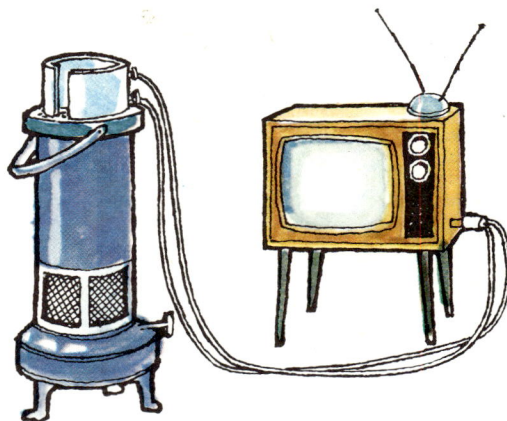

Fig. 3.9 What happens to the TV if the stove goes out?

produce sufficient electricity to run radios and even TV sets, as it is too expensive to provide the miles upon miles of electric cables that would be necessary to supply electricity from a power station.

Do you think this is a very efficient way of converting heat into electrical energy?

Experiment 3.13

Fix a paper windmill to the axle of a toy electric motor. Then connect the motor to a battery and set it going. What energy conversion has taken place here?

Write out a list of all the gadgets that you know of which have electric motors in them, and which therefore change electrical energy into kinetic energy.

Experiment 3.14

Rubbing the rod has charged it with elec- a small pith ball which is suspended by a nylon thread. What happens to the ball?

Rubbing the rod has charged it with electricity. What kind of energy did you use in charging the rod? What kind of energy did the pith ball have? Do you think you got as much energy out of this rod as you put into it?

You will understand much better what has happened in this experiment when you have reached Unit 7.

Experiment 3.15

Pull down the ball hanging on the end of a rubber band hung from a stand, and then let go. What does the ball do? What kind of energy does the stretched rubber have? What kind of energy does the ball have when released? This experiment is rather like the catapult mentioned on page 35.

Experiment 3.16

Here we have an electric bell connected through a switch to a battery. When you switch on the electric current there should be two kinds of energy you can spot easily. Can you see the coil of wire in the bell which acts like the one in Experiment 3.11?

Fig. 3.10

Experiment 3.17

This experiment requires to be done very carefully. When you are heating magnesium do not look directly at the metal, but only out of the corner of your eye. You should have 3–4 cm of thin ribbon of the light metal magnesium. Hold the metal by one end with a pair of tongs and then heat the other end of the ribbon in a Bunsen flame.

This is the metal which is used in photographers' flash bulbs. How is the metal set alight in a flash bulb? Fireworks and flares contain this metal in powder form.

What are the energy conversions here?

Experiment 3.18

Look at a light meter. The needle in this apparatus belongs to the part of it which measures electric current. Point the meter at a source of light – a lighted electric lamp or a window. What happens to the needle? What is the energy change taking place?

In the window of the apparatus is a light cell, sometimes called a photo-electric cell. Most space ships have large numbers of these, all automatically pointed towards the Sun. From these cells the electricity required to run the radio and TV sets is obtained.

Fig. 3.11 Technicians working on a new space satellite. The square panels on the satellite are covered with photo-electric cells which convert the Sun's energy to electricity

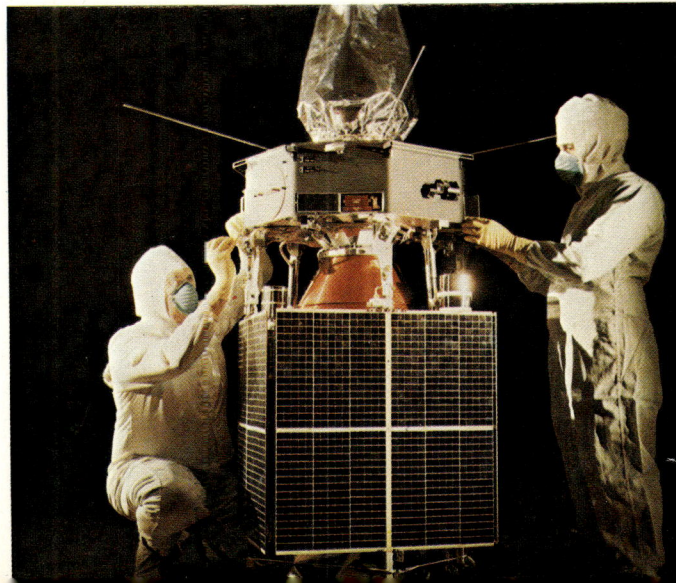

Experiment 3.19

Join a piece of fuse wire in the circuit shown in Fig. 3.12. Close the switch and send a current through the wire. What happens to the fuse wire? Can you find tiny balls of it on the

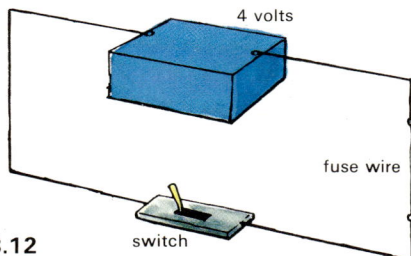

Fig. 3.12

bench? Fuse wire is sometimes made partly of lead, a metal which melts very easily. What kind of energy have you used which caused it to melt?

Fuses are used in electrical circuits at home so that if too much current is passed they melt and prevent the circuit from getting too hot.

Make a list of all the electrical appliances you know which make heat energy when the electricity supply is switched on.

Experiment 3.20

Fig. 3.13

When the switch is closed in the circuit in which the lamp in Fig. 3.13 is included, the light will be reflected from the head-lamp on to the bulb of the thermometer. Watch the reading on the thermometer. What happens to it? It is not the light energy from the bulb which causes this to happen. What other kind of energy must the bulb be giving off as well?

When you have carried out all these experiments you should have a very good idea of the ways in which energy can be converted from one form to another. There are many more examples

which you will come across yourself – keep an eye open for them in the future. It is by changing energy from one form to another that we make it available for ourselves to use in any way we wish. You will easily realize that, if it were impossible to change energy about in this way, we should not be able to live. We started off this unit by thinking of how we got the energy we need to keep us alive. It comes from the food we eat. If it were impossible to change chemical energy into heat and into kinetic energy we could not live. Similarly, all the energy we need to run our machines and all the energy we get out of them goes through a number of changes. If the chemical energy locked up in petrol could not be changed into heat and into kinetic energy there would be no motor-cars. So far you have used very simple apparatus to show how it is possible to change energy from one form to another. We are now going to look at this question on a bigger scale and see how energy conversions are used in everyday life to provide us with energy we can use in the home and in industry.

3.9 ENERGY CONVERTERS IN ACTION

Where does the electricity come from that you use in your home? It is possible that it is made at a hydro-electric power station. Let's see how one works. For this purpose we are going to set up a model of a hydro-electric scheme. In Fig. 3.14 you will see a diagram of the model, and in Fig. 3.19 there is a photograph of the actual thing.

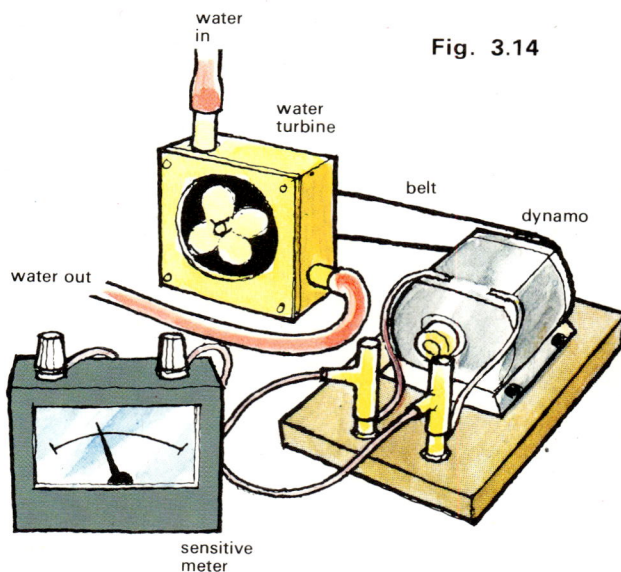

Fig. 3.14

Experiment 3.21

To work the model turn on the water tap. The water turbine then starts moving and it turns the dynamo. Look at the pointer on the meter. If we had enough power we could use the output of the dynamo to light some lamps.

Answer these questions:
1. Where does the water used in this experiment come from?
2. How was the Sun's energy used in getting it there? We have to think back to the Sun's heat energy changing some of the water in the sea, lakes, and rivers into invisible water vapour. When this air containing water vapour gets cold, it cannot hold so much water. What happens to the extra water vapour that it cannot now hold?
3. Where generally do clouds let most rain fall – on flat plains or on the hills?
4. How do we store up some of the rain which falls on the hills?
5. What kind of energy has this stored-up water?
6. In the experiment, what kind of energy does the water in the rubber tubing have?
7. Does the needle of the meter move?
8. What does this tell you about the dynamo?

Now write down a list of all the forms of energy in the order in which they appear in this model.

Find out the names of power stations which work like this, and find their situations on the map. Note down the areas from which they receive their water supply.

Why is electrical energy so cheap in places like Norway and Switzerland?

Experiment 3.22

Fig. 3.15 shows a model of another kind of machine called a pile driver. Switch on the motor until the weight comes up to the axle. Then switch off. The weight should run down again by itself, but, if it does not, slip the band off the pulley on the motor.

1. When you switch on the motor what forms of energy are present in the battery, the wires, and the pulley wheel of the motor?
2. What kind of energy does the weight have when it has been pulled up to the axle?
3. What is this energy converted into as the weight falls?
4. What does this energy do to the nail in the cork?

Make a list of all the energy conversions which take place in this model. Fig. 3.16 shows a full size machine of this kind at work. What is it used for? Have you seen one at work in your own area? What kind of industry would use a machine like this?

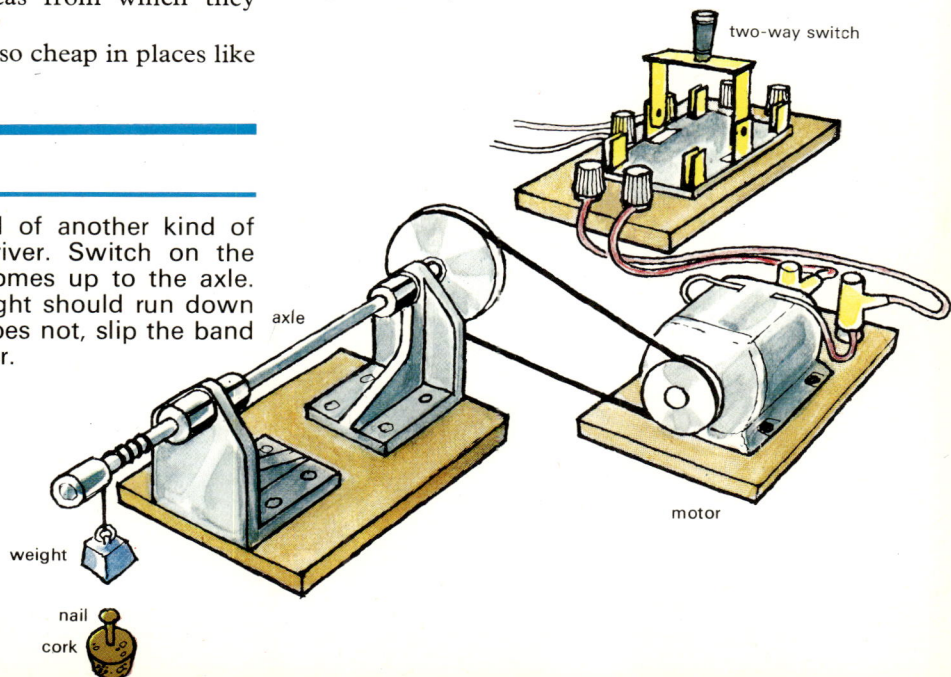

Fig. 3.16 A pile driver at work

Fig. 3.15

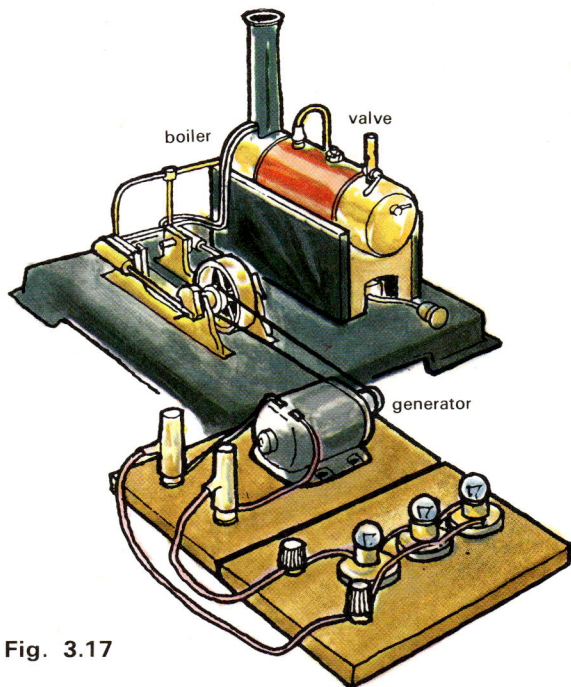

Fig. 3.17

Experiment 3.23

In Fig. 3.17 we have a model of a steam engine connected up to a **generator** or **dynamo**, and the current from this is used to light a number of lamps.

Model steam engines are fascinating and fun to play with. Some of you may have one at home. They have to be used carefully, however, or the boiler may burst. Do not begin heating the boiler in the model until you are sure that it is about three-quarters full of water. When you heat the water what happens to it?

After you have been heating the water for a few minutes a jet of water droplets should begin to come from the safety-valve. If you now give the fly-wheel a push the engine should start working. Adjust the position of the generator and the engine so that you have the right tension in the belt to make the engine turn the generator as fast as it can. Have only one lamp at first screwed up in its holder.

1. What happens to the lamp?
2. If you screw in another lamp, what happens to the speed of the engine? Which is it easier for the engine to do, light one bulb, or two?

3. Try a third lamp, and see what happens now. Does this agree with what you said in answer to question 2?
4. How does the engine run if you uncouple all the bulbs?

Now write down in order all the forms of energy which are present in the different parts of this apparatus, and show how they are converted one into another.

This is a model of the equipment that the famous American inventor Thomas Edison used to make electricity to supply New York, the first city in the world to have electric lighting.

You have now found two ways in which energy is used to make electricity on the large scale. Which of them do you think is the cheaper?

Experiment 3.24

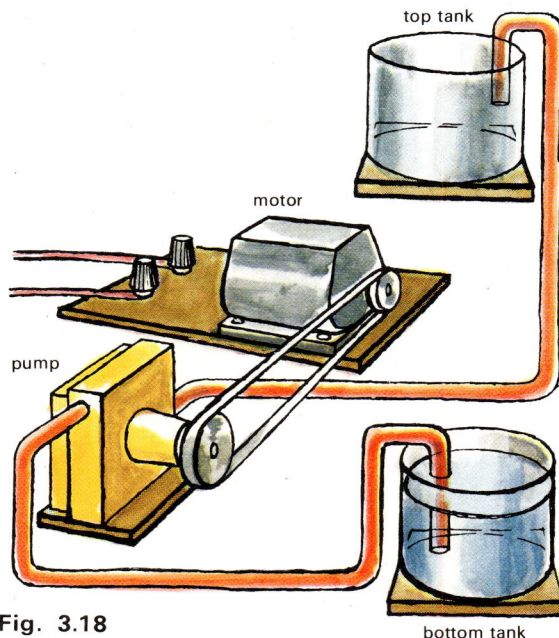

Fig. 3.18

Here we have an electric motor which drives a small pump which will make water flow from the bottom tank to the top one. If now the water in the top tank is allowed to flow fast enough down to the bottom tank through a water turbine it would turn this round, and the turbine could be used to drive a dynamo which would give electricity. It is rather difficult with a school model to make it work in reverse like this in the generation of electricity.

Fig. 3.19 This dam stores up water just like the top tank in Fig. 3.18

1. In what form is the energy in the battery which is used to drive the motor?
2. What form is it converted into by the motor?
3. In what form is the energy contained in the water in the top tank?

This model shows how some hydro-electric stations work. At peak hours when there is a great demand for electricity, water is run from a dam high up in the hills down through a turbine to drive a generator and make electricity. At off-peak times, when there is little demand for electricity, surplus electricity from other power stations is fed into a motor, which works a pump, so that water is sent back to the high loch again, ready to be used at the next peak hour.

Experiment 3.25
Storing energy with a fly-wheel

In this experiment we have a motor (which, as you have already learnt, will act as a dynamo or generator when it is turned with no battery connected to it), connected by a band to a large, heavy wheel, called a fly-wheel.

There is a two-way switch connected to the motor, which enables us to connect the motor to a battery, or with a bank of lamps. When the motor is connected to a battery and the position of the fly-wheel is adjusted to get the tension of the band right, the fly-wheel is turned by the motor. When it is going at a good speed the battery is switched off, and the fly-wheel continues to drive the motor which now acts as a generator. It supplies current which will light at least one of the lamps.

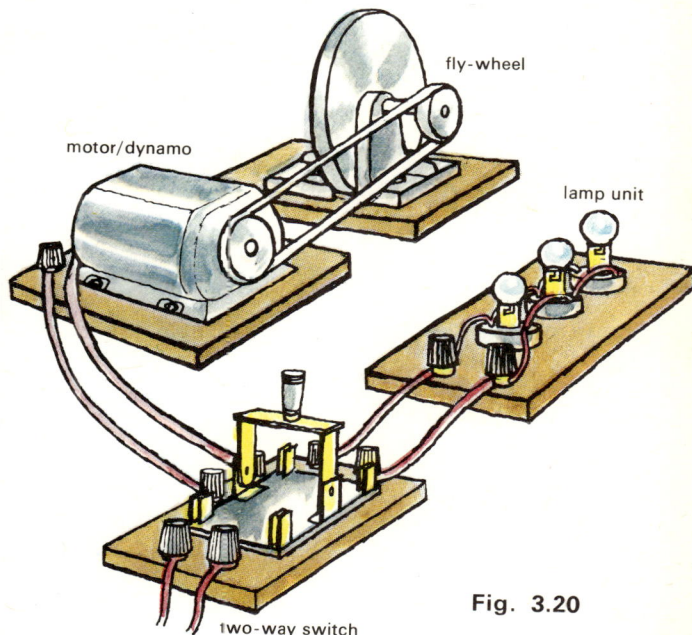
fly-wheel
motor/dynamo
lamp unit
two-way switch
Fig. 3.20

1. How is it that the fly-wheel takes some time before it gets moving really fast?
2. How long do the lamps stay alight?
3. What has happened to the fly-wheel by the time the lamps go out?
4. Where did the energy come from to keep the generator turning when the battery was disconnected?

Big, heavy objects are difficult to get moving, but once they are moving they are difficult to stop. One morning, perhaps, your father's car would not start on the battery and he asked you to help to push it. You will know how difficult it is to get a heavy thing like a car moving. But perhaps, too, you have tried to stop a car which was moving very slowly, and you will know how difficult that is.

You did a little experiment a short while ago in which a fly-wheel stored up energy; do you remember what you discovered? What kind of energy does a fly-wheel store?

Experiment 3.26
Opposing kinetic energy

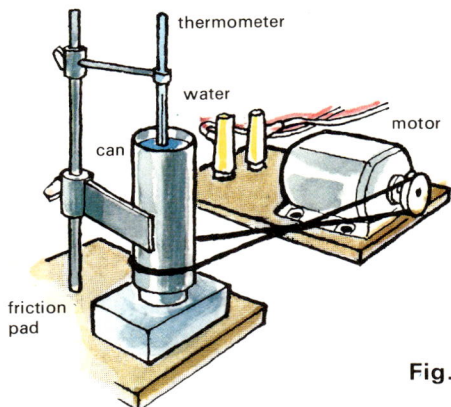

Fig. 3.21

In this experiment we have a metal can which contains water to a depth of about 1 cm. The can is rotated by connecting it to an electric motor. Inside the water is a thermometer by means of which you can find the temperature of the water. Outside the can is a friction pad made of cloth which presses against the can. The pressure is adjusted so that the motor still turns the can at a reasonable speed.

When the friction pad is moved up against the rotating can the motor slows down a little. Why?

Do you remember the very first experiment you did about energy, when you rubbed your finger along the bench? What happened? If you could see the surfaces of the can and the friction pad under a very powerful microscope, you would find that, although they appear to be smooth to the naked eye, they really have a lot of tiny projections sticking out from them. In fact they look quite rough. Perhaps you can understand why it is difficult for them to slide over one another. The motor has to use up energy to force one surface over the top of the other, and so it has to slow down.

Now have a look at the thermometer. Is its

reading the same as it was before you rotated the can? What has happened to it? What kind of energy must have produced this effect? Would you expect this when you think of that first experiment on energy that you carried out?

In this experiment the can may be supposed to be something like part of a wheel. What does the friction pad remind you of? Think of the wheel of a bicycle or of a motor-car. How do you stop your bicycle when it is moving?

Experiment 3.27

Here we have a ratchet wheel connected to a clockwork spring. It has, indeed, come out of a clock. The pulley on the axle on which the spring is wound is connected to a dynamo by means of a band, and the output of the dynamo is fed to some lamps.

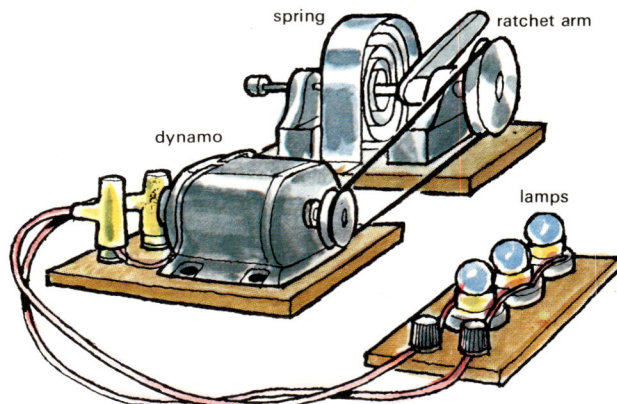

Fig. 3.22

First of all notice how the ratchet works. It is really a way of stopping a spring from un-winding once you have wound it up. When you release the ratchet arm the spring at once unwinds itself, and, of course, turns the dynamo. Watch what happens to the bulbs when you do this.

1. Where did the energy come from that was put into the spring?
2. What kind of energy did the spring have?
3. What happened to this stored up energy when you released the ratchet arm?
4. What kind of energy did the dynamo produce?
5. What kind of energy did the lamps change it into?

Now try to make up a 'flow-sheet' showing all the changes of energy that take place in this experiment.

Experiment 3.28
Making an accumulator

In this experiment you are going to use dilute sulphuric acid. This liquid is dangerous; do not get it on your fingers, or spill it on your clothes. Take a large beaker and put some of the acid into it. Get two lead plates and clean them with emery cloth so that they are of the same colour. Now put them into the acid, making sure that they do not touch. (A block of wood wedged between the plates at the top of the beaker will keep them apart.) Connect the two lead plates to the 4 volt output of a lab pack, which is a source of electricity, see Fig. 3.23. For this experiment the current must flow in one direction, and we call this **direct current** — you will learn more about this in Unit 7. Watch the plates carefully. Do you see any bubbles forming? Where do they form — on both plates or only on one? These bubbles are hydrogen bubbles — a gas you came across when you were dealing with that odd metal, calcium, in Experiment 1.21. Are both plates now the same colour? Look particularly at the plate connected to the + (positive) terminal.

After a few minutes it should have a brown colour, something like a dark coloured rust. When you have passed the current for about 10 minutes, switch it off, and connect the wires from the lead plates to a bulb in a holder. Do not let the bare ends of the wires touch together when you connect them to the holder.

What happens to the bulb?
How long does this happen?
Look at the plates in a real accumulator. Can you tell which are the positive plates?

Fig. 3.23

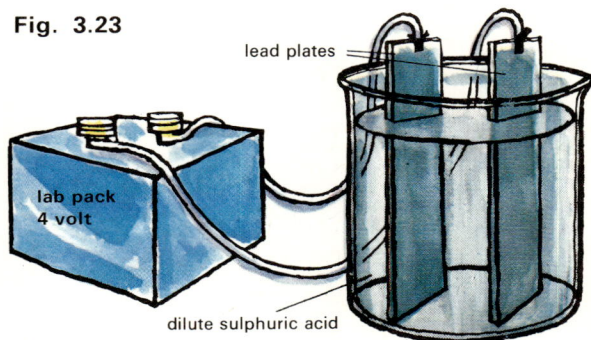
lead plates
lab pack 4 volt
dilute sulphuric acid

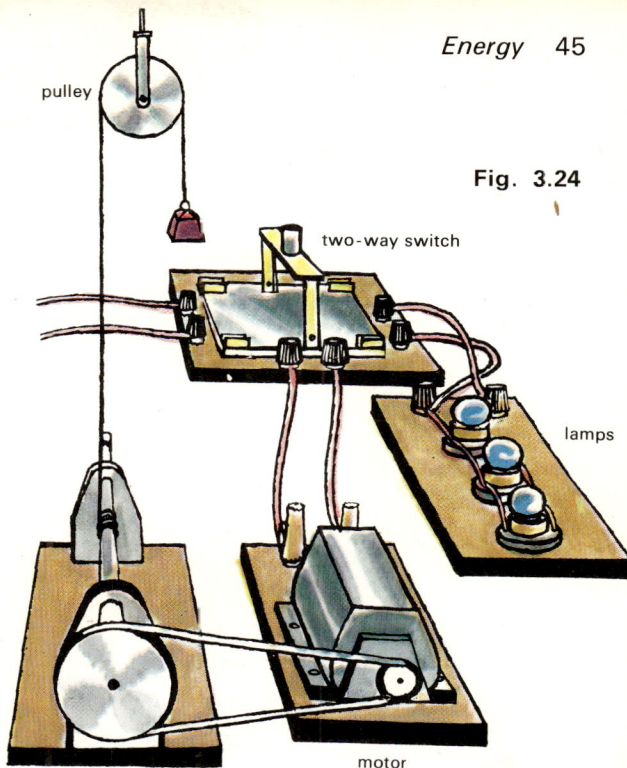

pulley

Fig. 3.24

two-way switch

lamps

motor

Experiment 3.29

This experiment is rather similar to others you have done. A two-way switch connects a motor/dynamo either to a battery or to a set of lamps. The motor is arranged to turn an axle and so to pull up a weight over a pulley. When the weight gets near the pulley, put the two-way switch over to the other side so that it connects the motor/dynamo to the bulbs.

What happens to the weight, and what happens to the bulbs?
Draw a flow-sheet to show all the energy changes in this experiment.

3.10 ENERGY AND LIVING THINGS

We started our work on energy by talking about ourselves — how we all need energy to live. When you think of all the movements we carry out day in and day out, you will understand that we must have energy for this. Even when you are asleep parts of your body are in motion all the time. You continue to breathe, and as you breathe your lungs become inflated and deflated several times a minute. To do this your rib-cage has to expand and contract. Your heart is moving all the time, pumping blood round your body. So even if you did not walk or run or wave your arms about or think, you would still require energy.

In what form do we take in energy? From where do we get this supply of energy?

If you think of the different kinds of food you eat, you will soon discover that it all comes from plants. Bread, potatoes, fruit – all come from plants. What about meat, you will say? Well, our meat comes from animals, which depend on plants for their food. If you think about this for a little while, making a list of all the things you had for your meals, say, yesterday, and noting where they came from, you will see that plants provide us with all our food, and so with all our energy. How important is the farmer's work! Without him there would be no-one to work the machines which are such an important part of our modern life. We could perfectly well do without machines – although our life would be much more difficult and uninteresting – but we could never do without plants and animals, for without them we should die.

Plants, of course, cannot grow without sunlight – and so we come back to what we said at first, that the Sun is the source of all our energy.

You will be studying the substances that make up our food later in the course, but we can say now that they are of three types – protein, carbohydrate, and fat. What about water? Well,

water is not a food, because we do not get energy from it. Nevertheless it is essential for our life. Then there are substances called vitamins, which you have heard about. They are necessary to keep us in good health, but they do not supply us with energy and are not primarily responsible for our growth, and so they are not counted as foods.

Although we get some energy from all these types of substance – protein, carbohydrate, and fat – the one that gives us most is carbohydrate. The foods which contain a lot of carbohydrate are the energy-giving foods. The carbohydrates include things like sugar, and starch, and the foods which contain these are cereals such as wheat, rice, and maize (or corn), and things made of them, such as bread and cakes; potatoes, carrots, turnips, and other vegetables; and of course sugar itself, in the form of sweets or in sweet fruits.

Make a list of all the carbohydrate-containing food you can think of. They all come from plants. How does the plant make carbohydrates? That is a question – a very important one – that we shall have to study later. We shall then carry out a number of experiments which will show us the wonderful way in which the plant does this, and we shall find again that the Sun is all-important in the process. In the meantime, however, let us look at some carbohydrates and do some experiments that will convince us that we can get energy from them.

Fig. 3.25

| Proteins | Carbohydrates | Fats |

Experiment 3.30
Energy from custard powder

Custard powder is a mixture of carbohydrates. Can you find out what they are? Set up the apparatus shown in the diagram (Fig. 3.26).

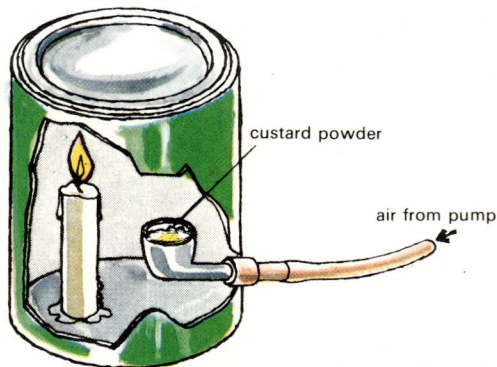

custard powder

air from pump

Fig. 3.26

The custard powder is put into the bowl of the clay pipe inside the tin. Light the candle inside the tin and press on the lid. Quickly pump some air from a bicycle pump or a pump for blowing up balloons down the rubber tubing so that the custard powder is blown out of the pipe. Then immediately close the clip on the rubber tubing. What happens?
WARNING! Don't lean over the lid of the tin.

1. What evidence is there that the carbohydrate contains energy?
2. How would you show that it was not just the air being blown into the tin that produced the result?

Experiment 3.31
Energy from sugar

Sugar is another form of carbohydrate. Your teacher will pour some concentrated sulphuric acid on to some sugar in a beaker. What happens? After a minute or so some of you might feel the outside of the beaker.

1. What do you think the black stuff is? [The first part of the name 'carbohydrate' will help.]
2. What happened to the temperature?
3. Where do you think this energy came from?

rubber tubing to oxygen source

glass nozzle

(a) sucrose

heat

(b) sucrose

heat

(c) sucrose mixed with a little potassium nitrate

heat

Fig. 3.27

Here is another experiment with sugar which your teacher will carry out. Some sugar is placed in each of three crucibles, see Fig. 3.27. Heat the first with a Bunsen. Heat the second with a Bunsen but play a jet of oxygen on to the surface of the sugar. Increase the heating as the sugar burns. Heat the third, and add a pinch of potassium nitrate to the sugar. Potassium nitrate is a chemical which contains oxygen which it can fairly easily give up.
What effect do the oxygen and the potassium nitrate have on the burning of the sugar?

These experiments help us to understand how our bodies obtain energy. Suppose you are working or running fast, what do you find happening to the rate at which you breathe? (You learnt about this in Unit 1.) Why do you think you need to do this? What is likely to be happening inside your body?
You may be a little puzzled about what we have discovered about the burning of sugar and what goes on inside your body. Quite obviously the carbohydrate that you eat is not burnt up quite like the sugar in the crucible, where there was a lot of flame and smoke. It would be disastrous if it were! The process must take place much more slowly and it clearly does not require a flame to start it off. In chemistry we often come across processes (the chemist calls them **reactions**) which take place slowly without heat being applied but much more quickly when heat is used. For example, when iron rusts we get essentially the same product as when we burn iron in oxygen. Iron rusts slowly, but when it is burnt in oxygen it rusts very quickly. This is something like what happens when the sugar is burnt inside us; the reaction takes place very slowly and no heat is required to start it off. But when sugar burns in oxygen it blazes away very quickly.

When we burnt the sugar in the crucibles we allowed the energy which is given as heat to get away and do nothing for us. We could, of course if we had wished, have used the heat to work a steam engine, which could have turned a dynamo and given us electricity. It would have been a very messy way of heating the water, though! In the body we do not allow the energy produced by burning the carbohydrate to escape – or at least not much of it. We use it to enable us to move about and do all the things that a living animal does. Some of the energy, however, is given out as heat. How do you know?

Experiment 3.32

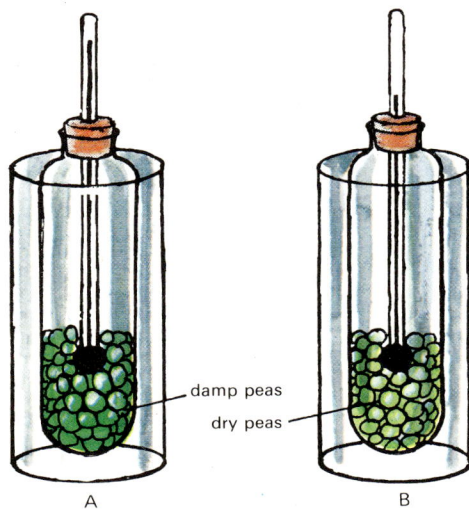

damp peas
dry peas

A   B

Fig. 3.28

Animals are not the only kind of living things. What other kind have you come across?

Take two small vacuum flasks and fit them with rubber stoppers and thermometers, as shown in Fig. 3.28. Half-fill the first flask with soaked peas, and the second with dry peas.

Leave the flasks and come back periodically throughout the day and write down the temperatures shown on the thermometers.

Can you account for any difference? What do you think the moist peas might have begun to do? They contain a baby plant and a food store containing carbohydrate.

Why did we use vacuum flasks in this experiment?

Some more questions for the energetic!

1. Does the fair (or the 'shows' if you call them that) sometimes come to your town or village?

   Write down as many energy conversions as you can think of which take place in a fairground.

2. How would you carry out the following chain of energy conversion:

   mechanical → electrical → heat → light

   electrical → chemical → mechanical

   sound → electrical?

WHAT HAVE YOU LEARNT IN THIS UNIT

1. Energy is the mainspring of all life, and of all the activity of mankind.

2. Although it is difficult to say exactly what energy is, we can say what it will do. There are so many examples of this in this unit that they cannot all be listed in this summary. Here are some of them: Energy will:

> make things get hot;
> make things give out light;
> make things give out sound;
> enable things to move in all sorts
>   of ways, e.g. upwards, sideways,
>   round and round;
> cause explosions; make things burn;
> compress things; electrify things;
> magnetize iron and steel (and
>   some other metals).

3. All energy on the earth comes, in the end, from the Sun.

4. Look at the chart in Fig. 3.1. It shows all the forms of energy that you have come across in this unit. One very important thing about energy is that it can be changed from one form to another. You should be able to say how you would convert any form of energy on the chart into any other.

5. The harnessing of energy, and the using of it for the purposes we wish, has been one of the triumphs of the scientists and the engineer. Machines make it possible for us to use energy conveniently. They often convert energy from one form to another.

6. Living things must use energy to remain alive. They obtain this energy from their food, mainly by burning up carbohydrates such as sugar and starch.

Unit Four
What are Things Made of?

4.1 SORTING THINGS OUT

We have seen earlier in the course (page 19) that one thing that scientists have to do before they can get very far is to classify things. If they can find out 'properties' which are the same for a particular group, it saves a lot of trouble in writing them all down. If, for example, I can say that all boys have hair on their heads, it saves me saying that John has hair on his head, Bill has hair on his head, Ian has hair on his head, and so on, and so on, and so on. Unfortunately it is not always easy to find a 'property' or a 'characteristic' which is true of everything in a group. For instance, in the example just quoted it might be that a very small numbers of boys do not have hair on their heads because they have had a serious illness. Yet they are still boys. The scientist is often up against this difficulty. There are usually border-line cases which are difficult to fit in. You came up against this when you were asked to classify boys and girls according to the colour of their hair. You were asked to say whether they were dark, fair, or red-haired. There was probably someone with 'mousy' hair, and you did not know where to put him. We do our best, however, and try to find properties which are as distinctive as possible.

4.2 SOLIDS, LIQUIDS, AND GASES

When thinking about bodies, the scientist finds it convenient to classify them into solid, liquid, and gas.

Write down the names of three solids, three liquids, and three gases.

What are the characteristics of solids? Are all solids hard? Are they all heavy? Are they all shiny? If you think about it you will see that none of these fit all solids. Many are hard, but some are soft and can be cut with a knife (like a piece of cheese for instance). Many sink, but some float on water (like wood or cork). Many are shiny, such as metals, but some are dull, or at least could not be called shiny. There is one thing, however, that all solids do – they 'stay put'. If you place a solid on the table it does not run away. A liquid does. You cannot heap up a liquid on a table; it always flows away and forms a thin layer. If you want to make it keep to a certain shape you have to put it in a container.

What are the characteristics of gases? You might think they are all invisible. Are they? Well, let us see.

Experiment 4.1

In this experiment a gas is given off which is dangerous if you breathe a lot of it. Do not take a big sniff! Put a few pieces of copper wire in a dish or in a flask. The teacher will come round and put a few crops of concentrated nitric acid on to it. What happens? Are all gases colourless, or invisible?

Fig. 4.1 Beware of the gas!

Whether you want to or not you will soon smell the gas you have just dealt with. Do all gases have a smell? Obviously not, because we cannot smell the air. Do all gases burn? Some do – you have come across one that does (which?); but many do not, the air for example.

What, then, do all gases do? If some town gas (or bottled gas) is allowed to escape from the tap

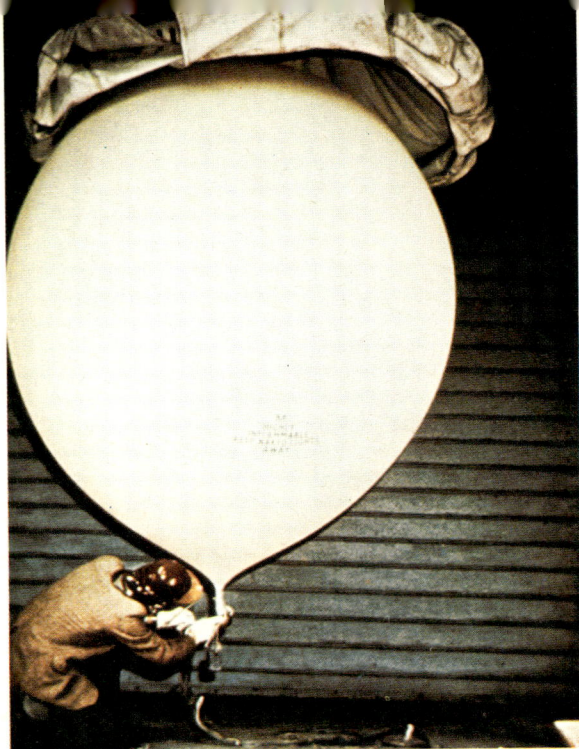

Fig. 4.2 Weather balloon being filled with hydrogen. Why is hydrogen used?

you can soon smell it all over the room. Obviously gases move about very easily. You cannot keep a gas in one place at all unless you imprison it in a bottle, or a balloon, or a tyre, or something like that. They flow even more easily than liquids.

We sum up what we have learnt about solids, liquids, and gases like this.

Solids do not flow. They stay where they are.

Liquids flow from one place to another.

Gases flow very easily indeed and in all directions, up and down, sideways, forwards, and backwards.

Because the earliest known gases were invisible and could get through keyholes and under doors, they were regarded by people who lived long ago as very mysterious, and they were confused with ghosts. In fact the word 'gas' is possibly connected with the German word 'geist' which means 'ghost'. You may still come across the use of the word 'spirit' or 'spirits' for a gas or a vapour. 'Spirits of salt', for example, is the name given to the gas given off when concentrated sulphuric acid is added to salt, and 'spirits of hartshorn' is the old name for ammonia gas, which is given off when animals' horns are heated with lime.

4.3 WHAT ARE THINGS MADE OF?

At the start of this course, it was pointed out that the scientist is always asking questions and trying to find the answers. One of the most important questions to ask is what are things made of? This has occupied the minds of scientists for a long time – more than 2000 years in fact – and we now think that we have solved the problem at any rate as far as the main points are concerned.

Let us do some simple experiments and see how we can explain them.

Experiment 4.2

Blow up three balloons as nearly as you can to the same size, one with air, one with carbon dioxide, and one with coal gas or hydrogen. Tie the necks securely so that gas cannot get out. Now tie them up somewhere where they can be left. Come back tomorrow and see what has happened to them.

Fig. 4.3

While this experiment is going on let us carry out some others. If you put a few drops of perfume in a dish on the front bench, it is not very long before you can detect it all over the room. We have already seen that gases move about easily from one place to another. How does that happen?

4.4 THE DETECTIVE AT WORK!

'Ah!' you may say, 'that is because of air currents'. Perhaps it is, and so we had better find out.

When a scientist suspects that some factor is the cause of something happening, like all good detectives he tries to eliminate the suspect. He does this by seeing if the thing still happens when the suspected cause is taken away. I want to find out if the ghost I see in my bedroom at midnight is really my young brother Charlie creeping about in his pyjamas, and so I tie him to his bed so that he cannot get out. If I still see the ghost I know it cannot be Charlie!

I want to see if it is air currents that cause the perfume to move across the room, and so I prevent air currents from happening and see if it still gets across the room. It is obviously very difficult to prevent air currents in a room, but I can do this in something smaller, such as a corked flask. The difficulty then is that I cannot get my nose inside! But I could try it with something I can see instead of smell. Bromine is a dark brown (and very dangerous) liquid which gives a heavy brown vapour, and this is a substance that can be used for this experiment.

Experiment 4.3

Your teacher will put a drop of bromine at the bottom of a flask, using a funnel with a long stem. He will then cork the flask. What happens to the bromine vapour?

We call the movement of one substance through another **diffusion**.

Experiment 4.4

Another experiment that your teacher will show you is rather more startling. Two flasks are connected together by glass tubing with taps as shown in the diagram. A few drops of bromine are placed in flask A and the tap C is

Fig. 4.4

closed. Tap D is opened and the tube is connected to an air pump which sucks most of the air out of flask B. Tap D is then closed and C is opened.
What happens?
Why is diffusion so much faster this time?

We can now return to our experiment with the balloons. What has happened to them? Have they all shrunk in size? Have they all shrunk by the same amount?

4.5 WE CAN MAKE A GUESS

Here is an observation that we have made. How can we explain it? A possible explanation is that there must be some holes in the balloons and the gases are escaping. Think of a way of checking this and try it out. You should find that the balloons are not broken and yet it is obvious that the gases are getting out. We must search for another explanation.

Suppose the balloons were really acting like sieves with very tiny holes so small that you cannot see them or detect them in the ordinary way, and suppose that the gases were made of tiny particles which could get through the holes; this would give us a reasonable explanation of what has happened. If this guess is right, it would of course explain other things too. Can it explain how perfume gets across to the other side of the room? Yes it can, because if the perfume is made up of tiny particles and they are moving, and if air too is made up of particles, the perfume particles can find their way in between the air particles, and so get to the other

Fig. 4.5 Does this help you to find out how the gases escaped from the balloons?

side of the room. We have now had to extend our guess to suppose that the particles are moving.

Can you explain on this guess why bromine diffuses much more rapidly into a vacuum than it does in air?

4.6 PERPETUAL MOTION?

Experiment 4.5

Put a crystal of copper sulphate at the bottom of a test-tube and almost fill the tube with water, without shaking. Let the tube stand for a time and note what happens.

You can try the same thing with a crystal of iodine. Do not pick up iodine with your fingers; it will turn them brown, and may burn you. Slide a small crystal of iodine from a spatula into a test-tube. Add some water. Does it dissolve? Now drop in a crystal of potassium iodide and let the tube stand for a time.

Does our guess about substances being made up of particles explain these observations too?

Do you think that the copper sulphate solution diffuses through water as fast as bromine or perfume diffuses through air? If not, can you suggest a reason why?

Experiment 4.6

This time we are going to see if substances will diffuse through jellies. Boil up some agar with water, and pour the solution into a glass dish and let it set. Put a crystal of copper sulphate on the surface. What happens?

You can do the same experiment in a test-tube. Almost fill the tube with hot agar. Allow it to set and put a crystal of a coloured substance on top. Copper sulphate or potassium permanganate will do. Let it stand for a week and see what has happened.

You might object that this effect is caused just by gravity. How could you show that it was not?

Is the rate of diffusion through a jelly faster or slower than through water? Can you explain this on your guess that matter is made up of particles which can move?

We now turn to a different idea. Suppose you keep on diluting a coloured solution by adding more and more water to it. What will happen? Well it is obvious from our experience that the

colour will get lighter and lighter until you cannot see it at all. It is interesting to find out just how much you have to dilute a highly coloured liquid until you cannot see the colour.

Experiment 4.7
Where does the colour go?

Take a test-tube rack with six test-tubes in it. As we are going to use these as measures, they must all be the same size, say 12.5 cm long. Stick a piece of label on each tube one-tenth of the length of the tube up from the bottom — in our case 12 mm up — this will be near enough. Fill up one tube to the label mark 12 mm from the bottom with a concentrated solution of potassium permanganate. You will see that this is an almost black (actually deep purple) liquid. Then fill up the tube with water. How many times have you diluted it?

Now put 12 mm of this liquid into the next tube and fill up to the top with water. Is the liquid still coloured? How many times has the original solution been diluted now?

Repeat this procedure with the next tube, and go on doing this until the colour has disappeared. How many times was the liquid diluted when this happened?

Using the idea that matter is made up of particles, can you explain why the colour disappears?

Experiment 4.8
How far does an oil film spread?

Take a large glass or metal tray and put some water in it so that the bottom of the tray is completely covered. Shake a little chalk dust or talcum powder on to the water. You will be provided with a very dilute solution of an oil in alcohol. Put one drop of this liquid on to the water from a teat pipette. Because the oil was diluted so much only a very small amount of oil was added to the water. Does the oil drop spread out to cover the whole surface of the water? Can you explain your result from your guess that oil, like everything else, is made up of tiny particles?

Put some lead shot into a wooden tray or a glass dish. Does this help you?

We have been talking about spreading things out. Did you know that we can spread out some metals into such thin sheets that we can see through them?

Experiment 4.9
Seeing through metals

You will be given a piece of gold leaf held between two glass plates. Look *at* it and it looks like gold. Hold it up to the light and look *through* it. What colour do you see now?

The fact that we can spread things out in this way – coloured substances, oil, metals – can be easily explained if we suppose that they are made up of tiny particles. Of course, other explanations are possible. Can you think of one?

What about matter being something like a rubber sheet that can be stretched?

Would this explain diffusion? Perhaps you think it might.

Well then, let us look at a few more experiments and see what conclusion we come to.

Experiment 4.10
Where does the alcohol go?

Here is something of a mystery. Take two measuring cylinders. In one put exactly 50 cm³ of methylated spirit (impure alcohol) and in the other exactly 50 cm³ of water. Pour the water into the alcohol. Wait for a moment or two until the mixture gets cold and then read the volume.

What volume would you expect the mixture to have?

Does it actually have this volume?

Can you explain your result?

If you are baffled try this experiment. It might give you a clue. Put about 50 cm³ of dried peas in a measuring cylinder. Then add

Fig. 4.6 A thin film of oil on water

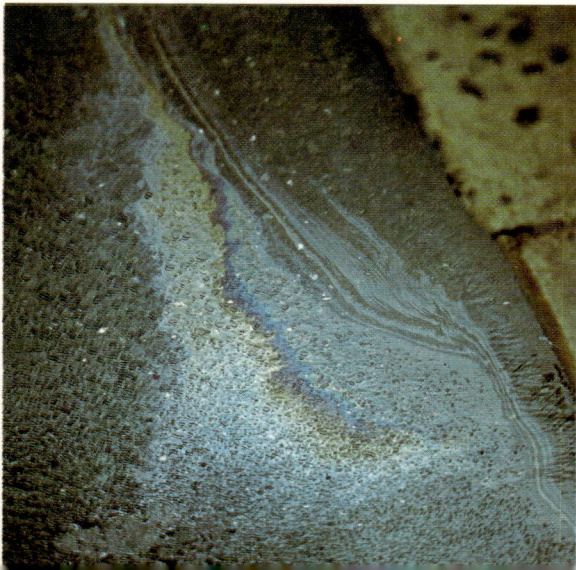

from another cylinder about 50 cm³ of barley.

Guess what must have happened to the alcohol and water.

Where does the salt go?

You can try this experiment on your own at home. Fill a glass to the brim with water. Add some salt to it slowly. Does the water overflow? If not, where is the salt going?

Is it still there? How do you know?

4.7 IS IT A GOOD GUESS?

You have now done quite a number of experiments, the results of which all fit in with the guess that matter is made up of tiny particles. In fact there seems to be no other reasonable way of explaining them all. If *you* can think of one, tell your teacher at once – you might be another Isaac Newton! Yet this idea is not an easy one to grasp because no-one has ever seen one of these tiny particles even with the most powerful microscope. Why then do we believe that our guess is the right one? Well, we must say straight away that *it might not be* the right one, but it is the *only* reasonable way of explaining all the observations we have made so far, and hundreds of others. In addition, scientists have planned experiments assuming that this guess is right, and they have always worked. The best example of this is the production of atomic power. Assuming that matter was made up of tiny particles, scientists worked out that it ought to be possible to release energy from them. They set to work to do this – and they succeeded! Now we cannot believe that this would have been possible if it were based on wrong ideas. If the particle guess is wrong, the production of nuclear energy must be a most remarkable fluke!

4.8 GUESSES, HYPOTHESES, AND THEORIES

Scientists call a guess a **hypothesis**; if the hypothesis explains things so well that it is thought to be true it is called a **theory**. We believe, as a result of our experiments, that matter is made up of particles, so we could call the theory the 'particle theory of matter'. The tiny particles of which everything is composed are called **atoms**. Sometimes a number of these are joined together to make larger particles which are called **molecules**. We shall discuss this again later (page 58). Of course, this atomic theory remains a guess, but it is a jolly good guess.

Fig. 4.7 Robert Brown

4.9 A MYSTERY

About 150 years ago, when the atomic theory was not well established, a Scottish botanist, Robert Brown, was examining under the microscope some pollen grains floating in a drop of water. Pollen grains are found on the stamens of plants, and are small particles which take part in the formation of seeds; if you walk through a field of buttercups in the summer you will find that your shoes get·covered with a yellow dust. These are pollen grains. Many types of pollen consist of such small grains that they are invisible to the

Fig. 4.8 Pollen grains like these studied by Robert Brown

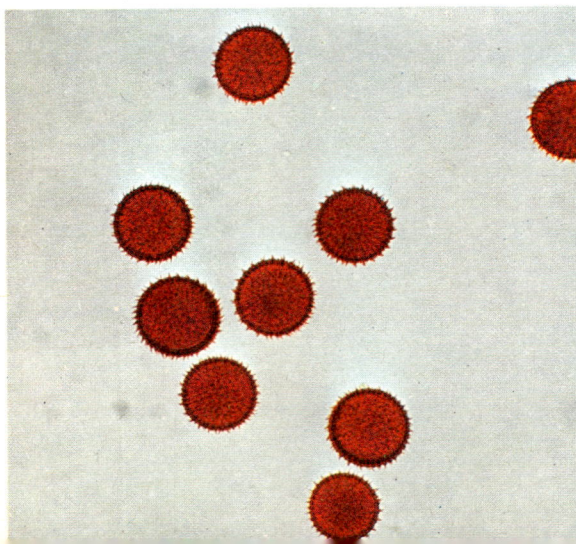

unaided eye, but some of us know they are there because they give us hay fever! When Robert Brown looked at his pollen grains he saw that they were moving about slightly, more or less as if they were vibrating. He had seen something that he had not noticed before, and like all true scientists he wondered why it should happen. So he began to make guesses, and test them. First he thought they might possibly be alive; after all they had come from a living plant. How could he find out if this was why they were moving? You will remember that a scientist would tackle this question by removing the suspected cause and seeing if the effect still happened (page 51). So he could kill them (if they were alive) and see if the particles still moved about. He therefore boiled the grains with water and found that they still jigged about as before. Then he thought there might be currents in the water that caused the movement, but, when he made certain that there could not be any by keeping the temperature constant, he found that the pollen grains still moved. It did not occur to him that atoms could have anything to do with it, and he gave up trying to explain the movement – which is called after him, the **Brownian movement**.

4.10 – AND ITS SOLUTION

We now believe that we have solved this problem, and this is the explanation we have thought of. The pollen grains are small and light. They are surrounded on all sides by water which is made up of tiny particles which are always on the move. They buffet the pollen grains making them move a little one way, then they are knocked in another direction, and so on. Have you ever played a game with a large beach ball, where a crowd of children try to push it over a goal line? The ball is first pushed one way, then the other, but it never moves very far unless a whole lot of children push one way together. The beach ball is like the pollen grain, and the water particles are like the children. Another way of looking at it is to see what happens to a table tennis ball when marbles hit it from all directions. A group of you could try this. Use a tray to stop the marbles rolling off the bench. A game of football is something like this too, but here the ball is small and the kickers are large, so the ball travels long distances.

You can see the Brownian movement yourselves.

Experiment 4.11
Atomic pushball or the Brownian movement

Your teacher will set up a small box into which smoke can be puffed. It has a glass top and glass sides. A beam of light is passed sideways through it and you look through the top with a microscope. You will see little spots of light. These are smoke particles reflecting the light which is shining on them. Look carefully and notice what the particles are doing.

Remember that in this experiment you are *not* seeing the particles of which matter is composed, only the effect which they produce on grains which themselves consist of thousands of atoms.

4.11 THE 'BLACK BOX' OF MATTER

Do you remember the experiment you did some weeks ago when you tried to guess what was inside a tin without opening the lid? The atomic theory is a good example of how scientists have found out what is inside a black box without opening it. Of course you could not be quite sure you were right about the contents of the box, and so the scientist cannot really be *quite sure* about atoms; but, because everything we have investigated fits in with this guess, we are now reasonably certain that we are right. In addition, as you will learn later on, we have had a go at trying to get the 'box' open and we have been able to knock atoms out of matter, but we still suffer from the disadvantage that, even when we have succeeded in doing this, we cannot see them. It is as if the tin in your experiment contained only very fine dust; if you got an air gun and shot at the tin the dust would come out and you would not see it! However, you would know it was there because it tickled your nose!

4.12 ELEMENTS

There are some substances which contain only one kind of atom. These are called **elements**. Ninety-two of these occur by themselves or linked up with other elements in the earth. We have been able to make some new elements in very small quantities artificially in atomic reactors, so that altogether we now know something like 108 of them.

Symbols consisting of one or two letters are used

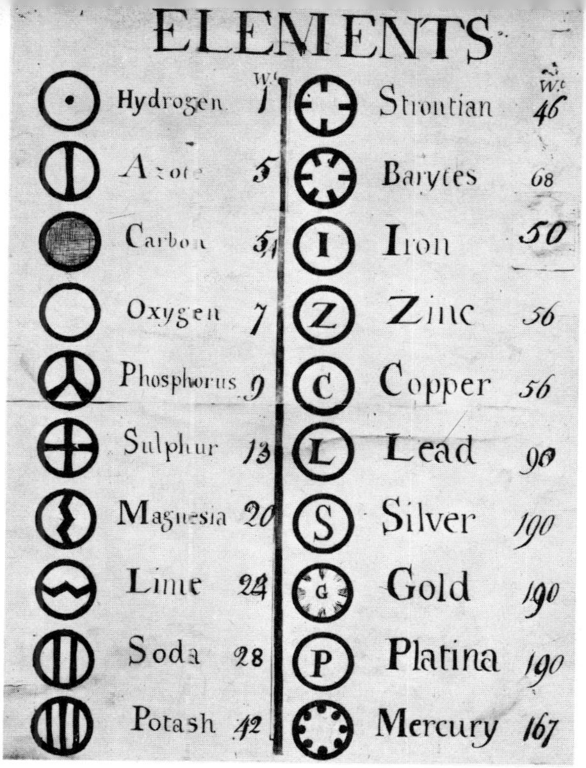

Fig. 4.9 A list of symbols for some of the more common elements, prepared by John Dalton in 1806

instead of the names of the elements. Here are some of them.

Element	Symbol	Element	Symbol
oxygen	O	sodium	Na
hydrogen	H	copper	Cu
nitrogen	N	gold	Au
phosphorus	P	silver	Ag
chlorine	Cl	calcium	Ca
sulphur	S	lead	Pb

You may think it odd that we do not always use the initial letters of the names of the elements as abbreviations for them. This is because there would not be enough letters to go round. When two letters are used they usually come from the Latin names for the elements. Thus the Latin word for sodium is natrium, so we use Na to stand for it. The Latin word for lead is plumbum, and in this case we use Pb to stand for it.

Can you see how the plumber got his name?

You are not expected to learn the symbols for the elements at present, but if you frequently look at a chart of elements you will gradually pick them up.

4.13 SORTING THINGS OUT AGAIN

At the beginning of this section we said that scientists often needed to classify things in order to save time in describing their properties. If we look at the list of elements we could classify them in two ways. First we could sort them into solids, liquids, and gases. You will be surprised to find that out of the ninety-two natural elements only two are liquids at room temperature. You have already come across them. They are mercury (used in thermometers) and bromine. Of course we can melt the solid elements if we heat them strongly enough, and we can liquefy the gases by cooling them enough.

Another way of classifying the elements which we often find to be useful is into metals and non-metals.

Pick out from the list of elements six metals and six non-metals, and write them down in your note book. Some common metals you will not find among the elements – brass, bronze, pewter, steel, and solder for example. This is because they are made up of a number of elements; brass for instance contains copper and zinc, and bronze contains copper and tin. The above metals are called **alloys**. All our coins are alloys.

4.14 COMPOUNDS

What happens when we mix elements? Sometimes nothing at all, but sometimes something very dramatic. Sometimes nothing happens in the cold, but if we warm some elements together a very great and sometimes spectacular change takes place. Obviously if we mix copper and oxygen together in the cold nothing happens, otherwise we could not keep 'copper' coins in our pockets. If we mix copper and hydrogen nothing ever happens, no matter what we do to them. But if we mix copper and chlorine they get very hot and both substances are completely changed. Your teacher will show you what happens if a thin sheet of a copper alloy, called Dutch metal, is dropped into a jar of chlorine. Other very spectacular changes occur when a small piece of phosphorus is placed in a jar of oxygen, or when a piece of magnesium ribbon is heated and held in a jar of oxygen. Your teacher will show you these. If you are lucky he might also mix some hydrogen and oxygen in a plastic bag and put a lighted match to it. You will probably be surprised at what happens!

In all these cases the elements have changed completely; the product is quite different from the elements we started with. We say that they have **reacted** together, and the product is called a **compound**. We can also say that the elements have **combined** together. In all the examples we have given so far the reaction has been violent, but you must not think that all reactions are like that. Some of them are very slow and quiet, like the combination of iron and oxygen to form iron rust, for instance. In all the reactions you saw, a new substance was formed, but at the same time something was given out. What was it?

4.15 CHEMICAL MAGIC

Now you can make a compound for yourself.

Experiment 4.12
Chemical magic

Put a little sulphur in the bottom of a test-tube. Coil up a length of thin copper wire and slip it into the tube so that it is just above the sulphur, as shown in Fig. 4.10. Now heat the sulphur carefully and watch what happens to the copper.

Does it get hot?

Does the wire look like copper when you take it out of the tube?

Quite clearly something drastic has happened to it. It is no longer copper. It has combined with the sulphur to form the compound copper sulphide.

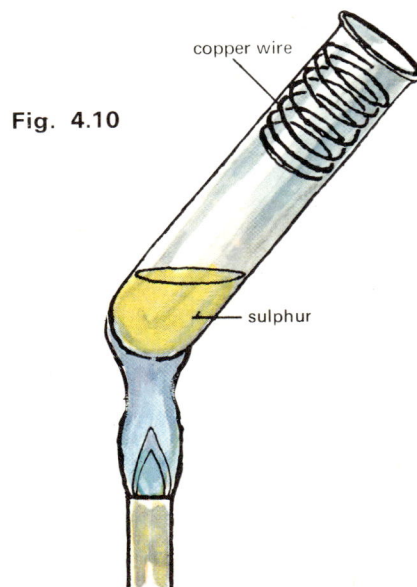

copper wire

Fig. 4.10

sulphur

Here is an additional experiment that you can do if you have time. Mix some iron filings and sulphur together (a spatula full of each will do). Put the mixture into a small test-tube and heat it.

What happens?

Get the product out of the tube. You will probably have to break the tube to do this. How could you find out if it is still iron? Try it and see.

Here again, something new has been formed. Does this still contain iron? If not, where has the iron gone? What would you call the new substance?

4.16 MAKING AND BREAKING

It is not easy to get the copper and the sulphur back again from the copper sulphide, although it can be done. We shall therefore look at another compound, copper chloride. You will remember that copper and chlorine combine very vigorously when the copper is very thin, so this time we shall use copper turnings or copper wire.

Experiment 4.13
Making and breaking a compound

Your teacher will set up the apparatus shown in Fig. 4.11. The chlorine is made in a generator, of which you do not need to know the details, and it is passed over the copper turnings in a hard glass tube which is heated gently. The extra chlorine which passes over is absorbed in the liquid in the jar, as chlorine gas is poisonous and we do not want it to escape into the laboratory.

Fig. 4.11 Making a compound!

4.17 ENERGY COMES INTO PLAY

The chlorine passes over the copper, which gets red hot, even though it is being heated only gently. Hence quite a lot of energy is given out in the form of heat when copper chloride is formed.

If we want to separate the copper chloride into copper and chlorine again we shall have to put this energy back. You might think that you could do this just by heating it strongly; sometimes we can break up compounds that way, but not very often. You cannot use this method with copper chloride. We can, however, supply energy, in another way – for example in the form of electricity.

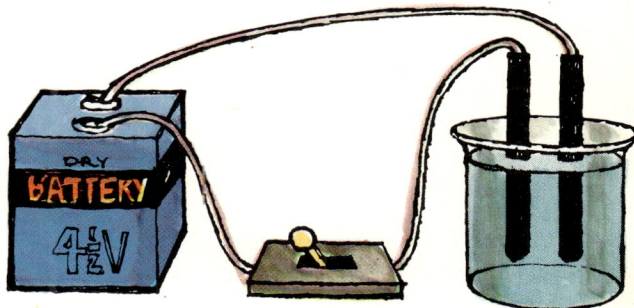
Fig. 4.12 Breaking a compound!

Dissolve in water the copper chloride that was made from copper and chlorine. Put the solution in a beaker. Connect two carbon rods (these are called **electrodes**) to a battery or to the low voltage supply on the bench or to a power pack and dip them into the copper chloride solution. What happens? Can you smell the chlorine as it bubbles off from one of the electrodes? Look at the other electrode. What has happened to it?

We can get copper from copper chloride another way. Dip a steel pen-knife blade or old razor blade into a solution of copper chloride. What happens?

This second experiment, unfortunately, does not give us the chlorine back again.

Obviously the copper chloride still contains the copper and the chlorine we started with, as we were able to get them back by passing electricity through the solution. Yet the copper chloride is quite different from both copper and chlorine. Something must have happened to both of them when they combined, and this must have something to do with the energy that was given out. We shall not pursue this point further just now, but it is certainly something that we must find out about later on.

Compounds, then, are very different from the elements that make them up. They are obviously not just mixtures. When we mix iron filings and sulphur and look at the mixture with a magnifying glass, we can see the iron and the sulphur, and we can pick out the iron with a magnet. But we cannot see the iron and the sulphur in the iron sulphide, and we cannot pick out the iron with a magnet. Also when we mix iron and sulphur they do not get hot, whereas when we make the compound a lot of energy is given out.

When you burnt magnesium in oxygen you got a white ash of magnesium oxide. It is difficult to believe that this ash contains magnesium and oxygen. However, it is obviously not just a mixture of magnesium and oxygen, because magnesium is a shiny metal and oxygen is a gas, while magnesium oxide is a white powder.

4.18 MOLECULES

The smallest particle of a compound is called a **molecule**. A molecule is a cluster of atoms. In the case of magnesium oxide the molecule contains one atom of magnesium and one atom of oxygen combined together.

Water is a compound of hydrogen and oxygen. There are two atoms of hydrogen and one atom of oxygen in a molecule of water.

We can never talk of an atom of a compound. This term can only be used of elements. There are **atoms** of gold and **atoms** of chlorine, but not of gold chloride. There are **molecules** of gold chloride, each of which contains three atoms of chlorine to one of gold.

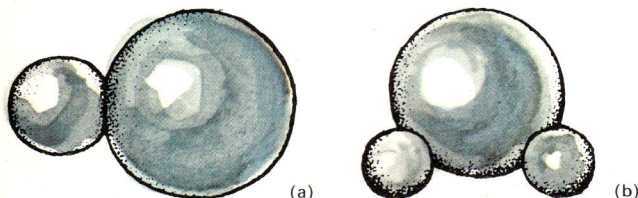

Fig. 4.13 Molecules of (a) magnesium oxide and (b) water

You will see that all this is based on our guess that matter is made up of atoms. No-one has ever seen an atom, and no-one has ever seen a molecule; but if we believe in atoms we must also believe in molecules.

4.19 SOLIDS, LIQUIDS, AND GASES AGAIN

To sum up, we *believe* that matter is made up of atoms. Some substances are composed of molecules which are clusters of atoms; these substances are compounds. Those which consist of only one kind of atom are elements.

Why do we believe in atoms and molecules when we cannot see them? You will remember that our answer to this question is that we can only explain the behaviour of matter reasonably by supposing that substances are made up of these particles. If this is so, our atomic theory must give a sound explanation of why solids, liquids, and gases behave as they do.

Solids are rigid and they retain their shape – or they 'stay put'. If this is so the particles which make them up must be arranged in a definite order – in ranks and files. Just imagine that there are twenty-five pupils in your class, and that you arrange yourselves in a block of five rows with five pupils in each row. Those in each row link arms, and wooden poles are slipped through the arms so as to link the five rows together, as in the picture. The boys and girls in this block can now no longer move about separately. The block must move as a whole. It could not for example get out of the door, just as a lump of ice in a bottle cannot get through the neck of the bottle. This seems to give a reasonable picture of a solid – it is a model of a solid.

Now suppose we heat a solid. You know what will happen. The solid will melt and become a liquid. It loses its shape and it can flow. In a liquid it seems that the particles are more free than they are in a solid. They are not linked together. This is not, however, a perfect picture of a liquid. Can you see where it is at fault? A liquid has a surface, even if it spreads out as a film, and so at the surface there must be something holding the particles together.

What happens when we heat a liquid? It boils. It changes into a gas. We know from our Experiments (4.3 and 4.4) with bromine that a gas will fill any space into which it is put. It does not have a surface at all. It can get under doors and through keyholes and even through the walls of a balloon. The particles in a gas must be very free to move indeed.

This again is a theory, because no-one has ever actually seen the particles of a gas moving. We guess that this is so because of the way in which gases behave. We call this theory the **kinetic particle theory**. You met the word 'kinetic' before on page 32.

We see then, that we can explain very simply the important differences between solids, liquids, and gases on the basis of the theory that matter is made up of particles, and that these particles can move more easily in some states of matter than in others.

How did we make a solid into a liquid and a liquid into a gas? That is a simple question to answer. What do we have to do to ice to make it into water, and to water to make it into steam?

4.20 PUTTING IN ENERGY

When we warm things, what are we putting into them? What is heat? When we put energy into things, one thing that may happen is that they may move. When we put energy into an array of particles in ranks and files they will start to move. The more energy we put in, the more violently they will move. Let us go back to our model of a block of boys and girls. Suppose they all start shaking. At first the block gets slightly bigger.

Eventually, *if they shake hard enough*, they will have to unlink their arms, and the wooden poles will drop, and they will be free. They now look like our model for a liquid.

You will notice that they will not break their bonds *unless they shake hard enough*. In other words, a certain amount of energy has to be put in before they break apart. This agrees with what we found in experiments where each particular solid had to be heated to a certain temperature (its 'melting point') before it changed to a liquid. Why, do you think, do different solids have different melting points?

Water melts at 0 °C and iron at about 1500 °C. What can we say about the strength of the bonds between the molecules of water and between the atoms of iron?

Why do we have to put energy into a liquid to make it into a gas?

When you boil 1 cm³ of water you get about 2000 cm³ of steam. How does the theory explain this?

4.21 A SOLID-LIQUID-GAS MODEL

With the simple apparatus shown in the diagram below it is possible to illustrate what happens when energy is put into a set of particles. A loud-speaker cone has a perspex or glass tube round it.

perspex or glass cylinder

beads

loud-speaker

Fig. 4.15

Some beads rest on the cone. The loud-speaker is connected to a low voltage a.c. supply which will make it vibrate. The strength of the vibration is controlled by altering the current flowing

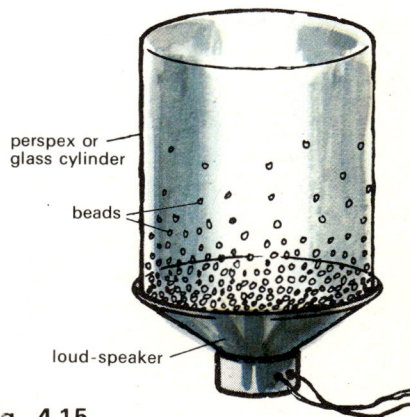

Fig. 4.14 The block must move as a whole!

through the loud-speaker. When the vibration is increased the beads move about more and more and become further and further apart, thus illustrating the change from solid to liquid to gas.

Another way of doing this without using a loud-speaker is shown in Fig. 4.30.

4.22 HOW DO SOLIDS HOLD TOGETHER?

This sounds all very well, but if you are thinking about it carefully you will probably have some questions to raise. If we are right in saying that in solids the particles are arranged in a definite order and are fairly closely packed together, why does not a solid just fall to pieces, like a heap of sand? In trying to argue this one out, the only conclusion we can come to is that the particles are attracted together by quite strong forces. A penny does not crush when we put our foot on it, so in the case of copper the forces must be very strong indeed. Other solids, like copper sulphate crystals, can be crushed with a hammer, but even so we can never crush them so finely that we break them down into atoms. All we do is to make small copper sulphate crystals.

What forces of attraction do we know about? You know about gravitation; all bodies are attracted to the earth by this force. However you must not think that gravitation comes into play only between the earth and neighbouring bodies. In fact there is a gravitational force between any two bodies – between you and your desk, and between you and your neighbour, for instance. You will hear much more about this later on.

Fig. **4.17** Magnetism – the magnet will pick up only certain types of nails

Quite clearly the force between you and your neighbour must be very small. If it were as great as the force between you and the earth, you can imagine what would happen. We should all go about as one lump, and that would give rise to some very awkward situations. But this is just what the atoms in a penny do. However, we can calculate the gravitational force between the atoms in copper, and we find that it is much too small to account for holding them together. If gravitation were the only attractive force there would be no solids; everything would be a gas!

There must be some other forces of attraction. You know of one straight away – magnetism. But not all substances are attracted by a magnet – copper certainly is not – and so we have to rule this one out.

Do you know what happens if you rub a plastic ball-point pen on your coat sleeve and then put it near some small pieces of paper or some chalk dust (as in Fig. 4.18)? Try it and see. What force is this?

As this is the only other force of attraction we know about at present it seems likely that it is this that holds particles together. Thus, we believe that the force which keeps a solid rigid is an electrical force. This is as far as we can go at present. You will learn much more later about the important part that electricity plays in the structure of matter.

Fig. **4.16** This astronaut is floating in space in zero gravity and is connected to the space craft by a line to prevent him drifting away

Fig. **4.18**

4.23 COMPRESSIBILITY

What would your theory about the make-up of solids, liquids, and gases lead you to expect about their 'squeezability'? Let's try to see how well the theory works.

How easy is it to compress solids, liquids, and gases? It does not require much experimenting to answer this question. You are sitting on a chair or a stool. Does it get smaller when you sit on it? If you were to sit on a strong rubber bag full of water, would it get smaller?

What happens, though, when you sit on an air-cushion?

Try the following experiment.

Experiment 4.14
Can we compress water?

Fill an old bicycle pump with water. Hold your finger tightly over the end and try to force the plunger of the pump in. Can you do it? Probably your finger will be forced away, and a jet of water will squirt out. You had better do this experiment in the open air!

The fact that liquids are difficult to compress is used in cars where the brakes and the clutch are operated 'hydraulically'. The brake pedal is connected with the brake mechanism itself by a tube containing brake fluid – an oil. When you put your foot on the pedal the movement is transmitted to the brake drum by the fluid, which acts as if it were a solid rod. If liquids were easily compressed, would this mechanism work?

Experiment 4.15
Can we compress air?

Put your finger over the end of a bicycle pump and try to force the plunger in. How does the result differ from that of Experiment 4.14?

It is clear from these simple experiments that while gases can be fairly easily compressed, liquids and solids cannot. How well does this agree with our ideas about the particles in solids, liquids, and gases?

Of course, you know from experience that gases can be easily compressed or forced into a smaller space. When do we do this in everyday life?

Why is it important that there should be no air bubbles in the hydraulic brake system of a car?

4.24 HEATING SOLIDS, LIQUIDS, AND GASES

What again? Yes, because there is something else to discover here. You will say that you know already what happens when solids and liquids are heated – solids melt and liquids boil. Yes, but now look at this.

Experiment 4.16
Heating a metal rod

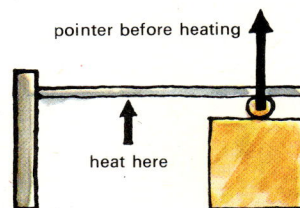

Fig. 4.19

Set up a retort stand and a wooden block as shown in Fig. 4.19. On the top of the wooden block is a cotton reel with a straw or a piece of wire stuck on to it with a piece of plasticine. Heat the rod of the retort stand. What happens to the pointer? What must have happened to the rod? What happens to the pointer when the rod cools down?

Experiment 4.17
Heating a liquid

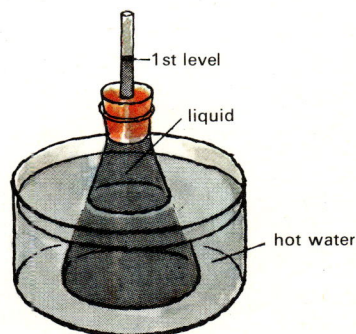

Fig. 4.20

Fill up a flask to the brim with water, and then put in a cork with a glass tube passing through it, as shown in Fig. 4.20. Some of the water will be forced into the tube. Note its level. Now put the flask in a beaker or dish of hot water. What happens?

Experiment 4.18
Heating a gas

Take an 'empty' flask. Really, of course, the flask is full of air. Put in a cork with a glass tube, and support the flask by a stand so that the end of the glass tube dips below water in a dish. Put your warm hands round the flask. What happens? You can try warming the flask even more by a small Bunsen flame. Now let the flask cool while the glass tube is still below the surface of the water. What happens now?

You will find that in all these cases the substance – solid, liquid, or gas – gets bigger when it is heated. We say it **expands**. When it cools down again it goes back to its original size; it **contracts** on cooling.

From the results of these experiments which do you think expands the most – solid, liquid, or gas?

Can you explain these observations on the basis of the particle theory? Write a note in your note book giving your explanation. Remember that when you heat anything you are pumping energy into it. This will have an effect on the particles.

There are many other ways of showing that substances expand when they are heated. Here are some other experiments you might do very quickly.

Experiment 4.19

When an electric current is passed through a wire it gets hot. You will know about this as it is the way in which electric lamps and electric fires work.

Stretch about a yard of fine constantan wire between two glass rods held by retort stands as shown in Fig. 4.21. Put a heavy nut on the wire somewhere about the middle. Connect the wire to a low voltage supply and pass a current through it. What happens?

What happens when you switch the current off?

Experiment 4.20

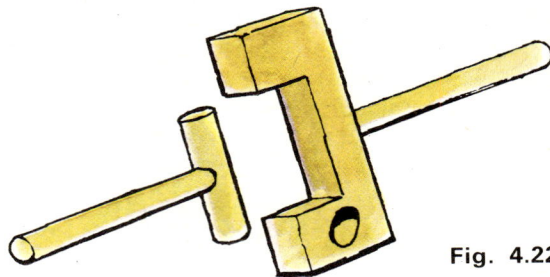

Fig. 4.22

This is known as the bar and gauge experiment. You will have a rod mounted on a handle, and a gauge. Check that the rod just fits into the gauge when it is cold. Heat the rod, and then check if it fits when it is hot. There is a hole in the gauge into which the end of the rod just fits when it is cold. Does it fit when hot?

Experiment 4.21

Fig. 4.23

This is another experiment similar to 4.20. A metal ball just fits into a ring when it is cold. Heat it. Does it fit now?

Experiment 4.22

When a hot body cools it contracts. The force exerted when it contracts is very great, as this experiment shows.

A steel bar is held in a strong iron frame. One end of the bar is threaded and has a wing-nut on it. There is a hole at the other end of the bar through which passes a cast-iron pin. The bar

Fig. 4.21

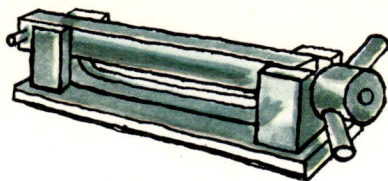

Fig. 4.24

is strongly heated and then the nut is screwed up so that the bar is held rigidly in the frame. What happens as it cools down?

4.25 SOME QUESTIONS

Why are the ends of metal bridges supported on rollers rather than on rigid mountings?

Why does an electric fire or gas cooker or an electric cooker make creaking noises when it cools down?

Why does a thick glass bottle or jar crack when boiling water is poured into it?

Why are sections of concrete roadway separated by thin strips of tar (or sometimes wood)?

Why are fire grates fitted so that they are loose?

In what laboratory instrument do we make use of the expansion of a liquid?

4.26 FURTHER INVESTIGATIONS

It is interesting to find out whether all metals expand by the same amount per cm when they are heated through the same temperature range. Here is a simple experiment which will answer this question.

Experiment 4.23

You will be given a bar made of two different metals riveted together. They may be copper and iron, brass and iron, invar (an alloy of nickel and iron) and copper, or any other pair. Hold the bar in the Bunsen flame. What happens to it?

What conclusion can you draw from this experiment? To help you answer this think of two athletes running on a circular track. Who has to run the further, the one on the inside of the curve or the one on the outside?

The fact that a bi-metallic strip curves when it is heated is used to switch off things like electric irons or cookers when they reach a certain temperature. This gadget is called a **thermostat**. If there is an old electric iron at school you should be able to see this. When the temperature rises, the bi-metallic strip bends

upwards and breaks the circuit, so stopping the electricity from flowing. When the iron cools down it bends back and completes the circuit again. By turning the knob on top of the iron the gap width is altered and the strip has to bend more, or less, before it breaks the circuit.

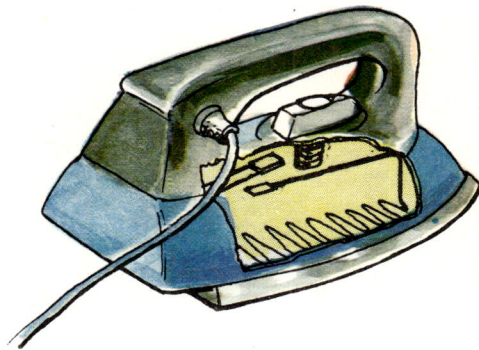

Fig. 4.25

The idea is also used in some kinds of thermometers, where the bending of the strip makes a pointer move over a scale.

When a body expands, does it get any lighter?

Would you expect a copper bar 50 cm long to expand by the same amount as a bar 100 cm long when heated through the same temperature range?

If you wanted to compare the amount of expansion of several metals, what would you have to keep constant?

How, on your theory of matter, could you explain the fact that copper and iron, for instance, do not expand equally?

4.27 LIGHTNESS AND HEAVINESS

For our next piece of work we want to be able to say how heavy one kind of thing is compared with another. Obviously 1 kg of feathers is heavier than 0.5 kg of gold, yet everyone would say that feathers are 'lighter' than gold. It is clear that we can only compare 'heaviness' if we weigh the same volume of each substance. Thus if we weigh a litre of gold and a litre of feathers, it is obvious that the gold will weigh much more than the feathers. We call the weight of 1 m^3 of anything its **density**, or its **relative weight**. As we more often deal with smaller volumes than 1 m^3 you will find that densities are usually expressed in g cm^{-3}, as in the list on page 64.

Substance	Density (g cm^{-3})
brass	8.5
bromine	3.1
carbon dioxide	0.002
carbon (graphite)	2.3
copper	8.9
copper sulphate	2.28
cork	0.25
glass	2.5
gold	19.3
hydrogen	0.000 09
iron	7.9
lead	11.3
lubricating oil	0.9
mercury	13.6
methylated spirit	0.8
milk	1.03
oxygen	0.0014
paraffin	0.8
petrol	0.7
sand	2.6
silver	10.5
tin	7.3
turpentine	0.9

Do you remember finding the weight of 1 cm^3 of water (Experiment 1.12)? What is the density of water?

Rearrange this table putting all the solids in one column, all the liquids in another, and all the gases in a third.

The weight of 1 m^3 of a substance will depend on:

1. the number of particles there are in 1 m^3, and
2. the weight of each particle.

The first of these depends on how tightly the particles are packed.

Would you expect the density of a solid to be generally greater than that of a liquid, and that of a liquid to be greater than that of a gas? Is this borne out by your table?

Can you suggest why the density of mercury (a liquid) is greater than that of iron (a solid)?

When a body is heated it expands. Does this make any difference to the number of particles present or to the weight of each particle? Obviously not. But it does make a difference to the volume, which increases as the body is heated.

Suppose we have ten particles each weighing 1 g originally in 10 cm^3. Suppose the volume becomes 11 cm^3 when the substance is heated. We still have 10 particles weighing 1 g each but they are now in 11 cm^3. Has the density increased or decreased?

As almost everything expands when it is heated, heating a substance will almost invariably decrease its density.

What happens when we put together liquids of different density which do not mix? Let's find out.

4.28 FLOATING AND SINKING

Experiment 4.24

Take a tall jar — a measuring cylinder will do — and put in it a little mercury, some dibromoethane (ethylene dibromide) coloured with iodine, some water and some ether. What happens?

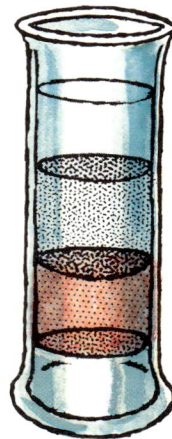

Fig. 4.26

The density of dibromoethane is 2.2 g cm^{-3}. and that of ether is 0.7 g cm^{-3}. Are the various layers in order of density?

You do not need to be told that cork floats on water. What is the density of cork (see the table on this page) and that of water?

Write down a general rule about the connection between floating and density.

We have seen that when anything is heated it expands and its density gets less. Explain the fact that the water in the hot-water tank is hotter at the top than it is at the bottom.

Why does hot air rise?

Fig. 4.27 The ascent of the Montgolfier brothers' balloon in 1783

4.29 THE FIRST AERONAUTS

One of the first men to 'fly' went up in a hot-air balloon. About 200 years ago two brothers, Joseph and Etienne Montgolfier, knowing that hot air rises, made a hot-air balloon and a friend of theirs ascended a height of about twenty-five metres in a basket attached to the balloon. You can make a model of this by getting a large circular sheet of thin paper about two metres in diameter. You may have to stick some smaller sheets of paper together and cut out the shape. Tie some cotton threads to a number of points round the circumference of the paper and attach them to a small tin lid. Soak some cotton wool in methylated spirit and put it in the lid. Take the 'balloon' into the playground and get your friends to hold it up while you light the methylated spirit. If there is not too much wind the 'balloon' will rise as it becomes full of hot air.

Instead of methylated spirit on cotton wool you can use 'meta' fuel.

Fig. 4.28 A modern hot-air balloon

4.30 PRESSURE

If you shoot peas from a pea-shooter against a small blind, it will move. A force is exerted on it. If your particle theory is correct, the walls of a vessel containing a gas will, in the same way, have a force exerted on them because they are being continually bombarded by the moving particles. The force on a certain area of the walls is called the **pressure**.

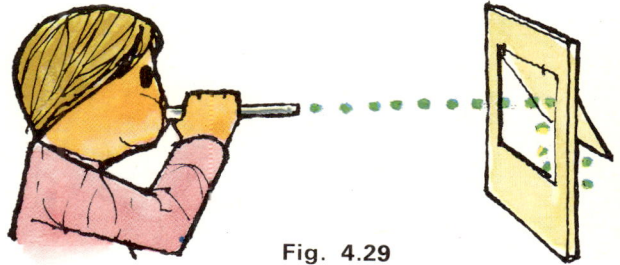

Fig. 4.29

We can use our loud-speaker model to imitate this or we can make the membrane vibrate as shown in Fig. 4.30. Cut a disc of balsa wood which will fit into the glass (or plastic) 'chimney' of the model. When we set the particles vibrating they hit the balsa wood 'piston' and push it up.

When we push air into a container, such as a car tyre, we are pumping in more air particles, and so the number of particles colliding with the walls of the container in one minute increases. Thus the force on the walls increases. If we pushed in as many air particles as were there to start with the force would be doubled. The pressure is the force exerted on a unit area. The tyre pressure gauge measures not the total force on the whole tyre but the force on unit area of it. At present the units are pounds per square inch, but different ones will be used when we 'go metric'.

How can we increase pressure without putting in more particles?

double piston made of balsa wood

glass beads

Fig. 4.30

cam on electric drill

4.31 AIR PRESSURE

As we live in a 'sea of air' we are being bombarded all the time by air particles. In other words we are living under pressure. Why don't we feel this pressure? To find out the reason we can do a simple experiment.

Experiment 4.25
The collapsing bottle

Get a large plastic bottle which has a rubber bung with a tube passing through it. This bung must be quite air-tight, as we are going to take all the air out of the bottle, and we do not want any to get back in. Connect the tube to a vacuum pump – that is a pump which will suck air out of things. What happens to the bottle?

(If you use a metal can for this experiment and you do not have a pump, there is another way of getting the air out of it. Your teacher will show you.)

Why does the bottle collapse?

Fig. 4.31

Why does a glass flask on the laboratory shelf not collapse? Well, in this case there are air particles bombarding it on the inside and air particles bombarding it on the outside. The two pressures are opposite and cancel each other out.

If we take all the air particles out of the flask, as we did with the plastic bottle, the bombardment is all on the outside and there is nothing to balance this on the inside. The result is as if you had put a heavy weight on it. The flask would be crushed in the same way as the bottle was. What about us? Well, we are really like a hollow tube.

We have air inside us, as well as outside, and so the two pushes balance and we do not feel anything. If we could take all the air out of our bodies, we should be squashed by the great pressure of air that would be exerted on us. The effect on us would be the same as that on a worm when we step on it!

Experiment 4.26
How to blow up a balloon without really blowing

Fig. 4.32

Set up the apparatus shown in Fig. 4.32. The balloon in the jar is not blown up. Take the air out of the jar with a vacuum pump.

What happens to the balloon? Why?

People first began to find out about air pressure when the vacuum pump was invented. The first of these pumps was made about 300 years ago by the Mayor of Magdeburg, in Germany. He used it to remove the air from two steel hemispheres which were fitted together to make an air-tight sphere. Although they could be easily separated when there was air inside them, once the air was taken out they could not be pulled apart even by two teams of eight horses pulling in opposite directions.

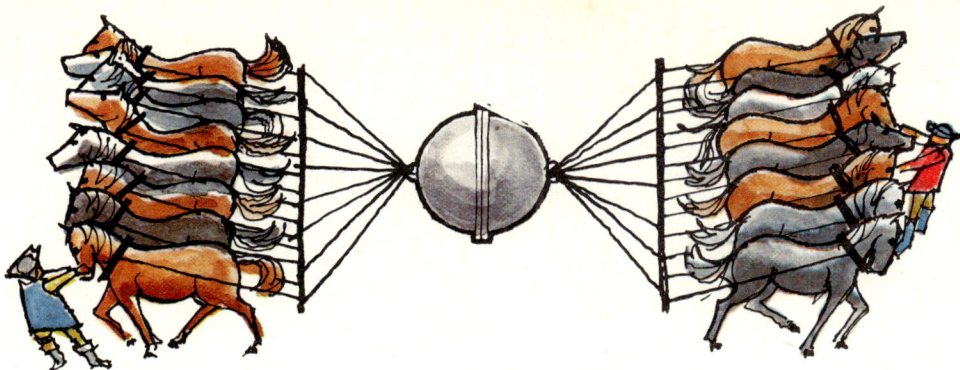

Fig. 4.33 The Magdeburg hemispheres or the horses tug-of-war!

You can try a similar experiment on a smaller scale. Instead of using horses you can use boys!

Why is it so difficult to separate the hemispheres?

Rubber 'suckers' are sometimes used to hold things on to the wall. How do they work?

4.32 SOME QUESTIONS FOR YOU

Does the force which the air exerts depend on the size of the body? Would it, for instance, be more difficult to separate large Magdeburg hemispheres than small ones? Consider this from the point of view of the number of bombarding particles.

If we want to compare the pressures of two different gases, would it do to find the force they exert on bodies of different sizes, or must they be the same size?

4.33 HOW DOES A SYRINGE WORK?

Experiment 4.27

Put the end of a syringe under water with the plunger pulled out as far as it will go. Push down the plunger. What happens and why? What happens when you pull out the plunger with the end of the syringe still under water? Why?

Fig. 4.34

For the thinkers

Where does the force come from to drive the water into the syringe?

We can easily find out the answer to this question if we have suckers of different sizes and a spring balance, as in Experiment 4.28.

Experiment 4.28
What force is needed to pull different suckers off the wall?

Get two suckers, one large and one small, and tie a thread round each one with a loop on the end. Put the hook of a spring balance through the loop and pull gently. Note the reading on the balance when the sucker comes away from the wall. Repeat two or three times. Why are the results for a particular sucker not always the same? Work out the average pull for each sucker. Are they the same?

4.34 PRESSURE MEASURERS

We discovered that when a plastic bottle was evacuated (i.e. had all the air taken out of it) it collapsed. Could this give us an idea about how to find the pressure of the air? An instrument which does this is called a **barometer**. The barometer consists of a metal box from which a good deal of the air has been taken out. The box is corrugated to make it stronger and springy. (You remember what happened to the plastic bottle or the tin can.) The pressure of the air forces the lid of the box in. The air does not always press with the same force, partly because the air does not always have the same composition. Some days it has more water vapour in it

Fig. 4.35 A barometer

than others. At some time the lid of the box will be forced in further than at others. By attaching a system of levers to the lid of the box any movement of it can be made to move a pointer over a dial. So we can find out if the pressure of the air changes, and if we put a scale on the dial we can find out what the pressure actually is.

Fig. 4.36 An aneroid barometer. See if you can find out what the word aneroid means and what it is derived from

This kind of barometer can be used for measuring heights. It is then called an altimeter. Will the pressure of the air increase or decrease as you rise? Can you explain why? What would happen to the reading of a barometer if you took it down a coal mine?

What would happen to a blown-up balloon if you took it up a mountain?

Can you devise a gadget using a balloon (or perhaps a piece of a broken balloon) to show changes in the pressure of the air?

Experiment 4.29
A new type of pressure gauge

Partly fill a U-shaped glass tube (commonly called a U-tube) with water. Connect a rubber

tube to one side and blow gently. What happens? If you blow harder can you blow the water out of the tube?

If you had a very long U-tube do you think you would be able to blow it out then? Try this with the 3-metre long U-tube on the laboratory wall.

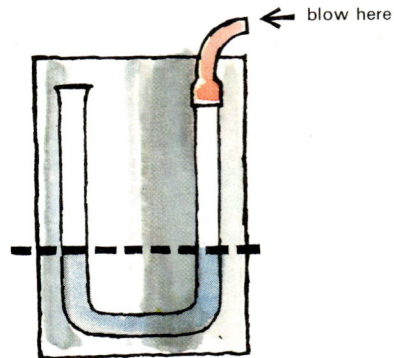

blow here

Fig. 4.37

When you blow into a tube like this you are forcing more air into one side – in other words, you are increasing the number of particles of air there and are therefore increasing the pressure. You can try the experiment if you like with a bicycle pump instead of blowing; you know what the pump does. You do the same when you blow.

We can use an apparatus like this to measure pressure. When you pour water into a U-tube open at both sides, does the water stand at the same level on both sides? Why?

When you blow down one side you force the liquid on that side down. The difference in levels is a measure of how hard you blow – or, in other words, of the pressure you are exerting.

Experiment 4.30
How hard can you blow?

Set up the long U-tube with water in it again. Try blowing down one side, and this time measure the difference in level of the water. This shows you the pressure you can exert with your lungs. Is it the same for all members of the class? Why?

Do you think you could blow the water round further if the tube were narrower so that there was not so much water to blow round? Try it and see.

That's odd, isn't it; you probably did not expect this result. Can you explain it?

This U-tube apparatus is called a **manometer** – which just means pressure measurer (it comes from the Greek word *mano*, which means thinness, and *meter* meaning measurer – something that measures the 'thinness' of a gas; it has nothing to do with measuring a man!).

Experiment 4.31

Use a water-filled manometer to find the pressure of the gas supply.

4.35 THE BOURDON GAUGE

The U-tube manometer is not the sort of thing you would use to find the pressure in your car tyres, is it? It would be far too inconvenient. Pressure gauges used for this kind of purpose, and for finding the pressure of gas in a gas cylinder, are based on the idea used in a very simple party toy. Have you come across a paper tube with a springy wire inside it? The wire coils

Fig. 4.38

itself up into a spiral, and, of course, winds up the paper with it. When you blow down the paper tube it unwinds. We can use this to find the pressure of a gas by seeing how far it can make the spiral of wire unwind.

The kind of gauge which uses this idea is called the Bourdon gauge.

Experiment 4.32

Fig. 4.39

Use a Bourdon gauge to find your lung pressure, and the pressure you can get with one stroke of a bicycle pump.

WHAT YOU HAVE LEARNT IN THIS UNIT

1. Matter can be sorted out into solids, liquids, and gases, and these can be very easily changed into one another merely by heating or cooling (putting in energy, or taking away energy).

2. You carried out a number of experiments which gave you clues about the way in which matter was constructed. When you pieced these clues together you arrived at the conclusion that matter was made up of very small particles, which are moving about. This was the only reasonable guess which would agree with all your observations. No-one has ever seen these particles, yet we believe our guess is the right one.

3. When we applied our guess (which is called a **theory**) to such things as the melting of solids and the boiling of liquids, we found that it gave a good explanation of them.

4. You have discovered the following facts.

(a) Solids and liquids are difficult to compress, but gases can easily be squeezed into a smaller space.

(b) Solids, liquids, and gases expand when they are heated, solids not very much, liquids rather more, and gases quite a lot.

(c) Substances vary in heaviness or density, depending on the weight of the individual particles which make them up and on how tightly they are packed together. The density of anything is the weight of a certain volume of it. To compare the densities of different substances we must choose the same unit of volume, and this is the cubic centimetre. So density is measured in $g\ cm^{-3}$.

(d) A less dense liquid floats on a more dense one if it does not mix with it. A solid floats on a liquid if it is less dense than the liquid.

(e) When chemicals are mixed they sometimes react together to form a new substance. Sometimes we have to warm them together to start off the process. Energy changes occur when reaction takes place. Heat is usually given out.

(f) Elements are substances which cannot be broken up into anything else. The smallest particles of elements are **atoms**. Certain elements combine together to form compounds. The smallest particles of a compound are called **molecules**.

(g) Compounds are altogether different from the elements which make them up.

(h) If energy is given out when a compound is made, it has to be put back to break up the compound again.

(i) A gas which is imprisoned in a container (e.g. air in a tyre) exerts a pressure on the container.

(j) Pressure can be explained as being due to the bombardment of the walls of the container by the gas particles. The more particles which hit the sides of the container in a certain time, the greater is the pressure of the gas.

(k) The atmosphere exerts a pressure on things. This is measured by a barometer. The existence of air pressure explains why syringes work, why rubber 'suckers' stick to a wall, and why a plastic bottle collapses when the air is taken out of it.

(l) Pressure can be measured by a pressure gauge. A liquid in a U-tube can be used. The difference in level of the liquid in the two limbs is a measure of the pressure. A more useful kind of pressure gauge is the Bourdon gauge in which the pressure of the gas is made to uncoil a wound-up tube.

Unit Five
Solvents and Solutions

5.1 REMEMBER?

What happens to water in a dish if it is left out in the open for some time? It dries up. We say 'the water evaporates', which just means that it turns into vapour. How does this happen?

You will remember that in the last unit we came to the conclusion that matter was made up of particles, and that in solids the particles were packed in an orderly fashion in ranks and files. In a liquid they are somewhat further apart and are not in any order. In a gas they are still further apart and are now free to move in whatever way they like. When a solid is heated it melts and when a liquid is heated it boils. The vapour *always* takes up more space than the liquid it comes from.

The three ways in which matter can exist are called states of matter. We talk of the solid state, the liquid state, and the gaseous state. When a solid melts we say that it changes its state from solid to liquid, and when a liquid boils it changes its state from liquid to gas. These changes of state take place at definite temperatures called the melting point and the boiling point. You found the melting point of ice in Unit 1, but we shall revise this work now.

water

ice

Fig. 5.1

Experiment 5.1
Finding the melting point of ice and the boiling point of water

Put some crushed ice into a small beaker and put a thermometer into the ice. What temperature does it read?

Take out the thermometer and warm the ice. What happens to it?

If you continue to heat the liquid, what happens? Put the thermometer in the liquid and when it is boiling take the temperature. What does the thermometer read now?

Put the thermometer in the steam coming from the boiling water. What does it read this time? The temperature of the steam from boiling water is the boiling point of the water.

Hold a cold dish in the steam coming from the beaker. What do you notice forming on the dish? How did it get there?

Write down a list of the changes of state of the water that you have seen taking place in this experiment.

Having observed what happens, we now have to explain it if we can. This should not be difficult, as we discussed it in the last unit. When we heat a body we are imparting heat energy to it. Energy makes the particles vibrate more, until eventually they break away completely from the ranks and files they occupy in the solid state. If still more energy is put in, they vibrate more and more until the force which keeps them together in the liquid is overcome and the particles are now completely free and in the form of a gas.

5.2 HIDDEN (OR LATENT) HEAT

You may say that this sounds simple enough – in fact a little too simple. We noticed that, when we had the thermometer in the boiling water or in the steam, the temperature did not go up, but remained the same at about 100 °C although we were still putting heat energy into the water. Where is the heat energy going to?

The heat energy is being used to release all the water molecules from the liquid state and free them as gaseous molecules. Although it is true that as more heat energy is added to the liquid molecules they vibrate more, a definite amount of energy is required to enable them to break away altogether and become vapour or gas. We call this energy the **latent heat of vaporization** of the liquid. Of course, when steam is changed back into water, as in the experiment with the dish held in the steam, we get all that energy back.

If you scald yourself with steam you get a worse burn than with boiling water. Why?

Similarly when ice changes into water the reading on the thermometer remains at 0 °C until all the ice has melted. This is because all the heat energy that is being put in is being used to break up the crystals of ice. When this has happened the temperature will begin to rise again. The heat that has to be put into a solid to melt it at the melting point is called the **latent heat of fusion** of the solid.

Here is an additional experiment if you have time.

Instead of using crushed ice in your test-tube in Experiment 5.1, add some salt to the ice. Put a thermometer in the mixture. Does it read the same as it did when you used ice alone?

Now boil the salt water and find its boiling point. How does it differ from the boiling point of water?

Put sand in the ice instead of salt, and repeat the experiment.

What conclusions can you draw from this experiment?

5.3 EVAPORATION

We opened this section by asking what happened to water when it was left out in a dish for some time. How can we explain that it dries up (or evaporates) although we are not heating it?

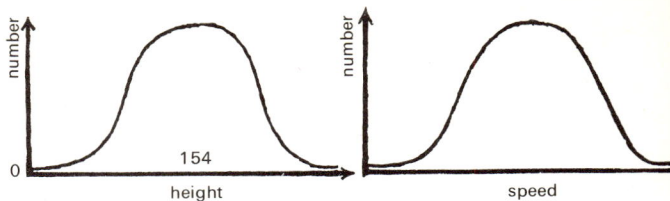

Fig. 5.2

Fig. 5.3

Well, you will remember that in Unit 1 we found that all members of the class did not have the same height. When we plotted a graph of the number of boys and girls against height it was like the one in Fig. 5.2. A very few were extra tall and a very few were extra short. Most were round about average.

It is just the same with the speed of molecules in a liquid. All the molecules do not move at the same speed. At a certain temperature a few will be moving very quickly, and a few very slowly. Most of them have speeds somewhere about the average. Some of those moving very quickly are, in effect, at a higher temperature than the others; those that are moving slowly are at a lower temperature. The thermometer indicates the average temperature of all the molecules. Those that are moving really fast can escape from the surface of the liquid and so the liquid evaporates. It evaporates much more slowly at room temperature than when it is heated with a burner because so few of the molecules have the necessary energy to escape.

Of course, these 'hot' molecules had all been counted in by the thermometer when it gave us the average temperature of the water. When they are lost the liquid ought to get colder, and so it does. We would not notice this because the water would immediately take in energy from the air round about it and heat up again. You know from experience that water colder than the air round about will gradually heat up until it is at the same temperature as its surroundings, and on the other hand your hot bath water gradually gets colder until it is at the same temperature as the room. However, if we could stop heat from getting into the water from the warm air round about it, it would indeed get cooler as the 'hot' molecules evaporate from it.

How do you think we could help a liquid to evaporate so rapidly that it did not have time to get warmed up by the surrounding air?

Here is an experiment that your teacher can do.

Experiment 5.2

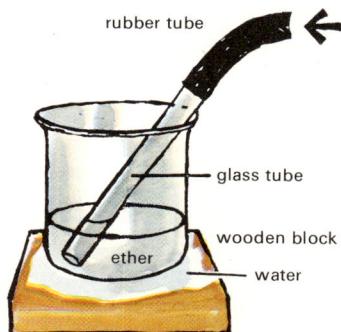

Fig. 5.4

In this experiment the teacher will be using ether. Ether vapour is very inflammable, so there must be no flames anywhere in the laboratory when this experiment is done. Ether is a liquid which evaporates very rapidly; when air is blown through it it evaporates so quickly that it does not have time to warm up again.

Some ether is placed in a small beaker standing in a pool of water on a block of wood. Air is blown into the ether through a rubber tube. A pair of bellows or a balloon pump is useful for doing this. After a few minutes see if you can lift the beaker off the block.

What has happened? Can you explain it by using your theory of the nature of matter?

When we heat a liquid we put more energy into all the molecules. Some of those which had only average speeds are now 'gingered up' so that they are moving really fast and can escape. The more heat energy we put in, the more of these hot molecules there will be and the faster the water will evaporate.

Experiment 5.3
What are the best conditions for evaporation?

Cut several pieces of blotting paper all five centimetres square, and soak them in water. Put them in different places and find how long each takes to dry. Find suitable places as follows.

1. A cold flat surface free from draughts.
2. A cold flat surface with cold air blowing over it from a fan or a vacuum cleaner.
3. A cold flat surface with warm air from a hair drier blowing over it.
4. A warm surface free from draughts.
5. A warm surface, the moist paper being wrapped in a polythene bag.
6. A warm surface free from draughts, the paper being folded into small squares.

In which of these situations does evaporation take place most freely? On a hot or a cold surface? With a large or a small surface area? In still or moving air?

Try to explain your answers by using your ideas about particles and energy.

In everyday life we use some of the facts we have discovered. Why do we use hot air from a hair drier and not cold air? Why do we spread out our wet swim suit when we want it to dry, and not just leave it in a heap? Why does the washing dry more quickly when it is windy than when there is no breeze?

Fig. 5.5

Why do people feel more 'sticky' in a hot, humid atmosphere than they do in an equally hot dry one?

5.4 CONDENSATION

If, as we said above, water is all the time evaporating, where does it go to, and why is there any water left? Well, there is only one place it can go to and that is into the air. We know that there is water vapour in the air because on a cold day moisture condenses on the inside of the cold glass windows. This water must have been in the air in the room. It is clear from this observation that cold air cannot hold so much water vapour as warm air. We can show this even better by leaving out in the air some substance that absorbs water, such as ordinary salt, which will get damp after a time. (Specially prepared table salt has some chemicals added which prevent it getting damp and clogging up the salt shaker.)

If you are interested, and have a good enough balance in the laboratory, you can weigh the water vapour in the air.

Experiment 5.4
Weighing the water vapour in the air

We can do this by weighing a substance which will absorb water vapour, then exposing it to air for a time and weighing it again. As the water taken up does not weigh very much, you will need a special balance for this experiment, such as a single-pan automatic balance. A suitable substance to use is silica gel. This should be heated before the experiment to make sure that it is dry before you start.

5.5 CLOUDS AND RAIN

What about our second question – why is there any water left? Well, that is easy to answer. We all know that it rains! How are clouds formed?

For one thing we have discovered that cold air does not hold as much water vapour as warm air, so that when air is cooled the extra water that it can no longer hold condenses. Let us see how we can make clouds artificially.

Experiment 5.5
Making clouds

A large bottle has a little water at the bottom. Air is pumped into it by a bicycle pump, as shown in Fig. 5.6. The clip is suddenly opened to let the air escape. What happens? It is interesting to have a thermometer inside the bottle. What happens to the temperature? Does this explain why the cloud forms?

Fig. 5.6

Air may become full up (or saturated) with vapour by passing, for example, over the sea. If it is forced to rise by coming into contact with a range of hills, it becomes colder, and then cannot hold so much water vapour. The extra water condenses as a cloud. Sometimes, however, the water vapour does not condense and the air is then said to be 'supersaturated'. In this condition it does not take much to make the water condense. Dust particles may cause it to do so. The tiny particles of dust act as 'centres' around which the water vapour can condense. This is why fogs more often form in smoky districts than in smokeless zones. Vapour trails from aeroplanes are clouds formed by the plane passing through air which is supersaturated with water.

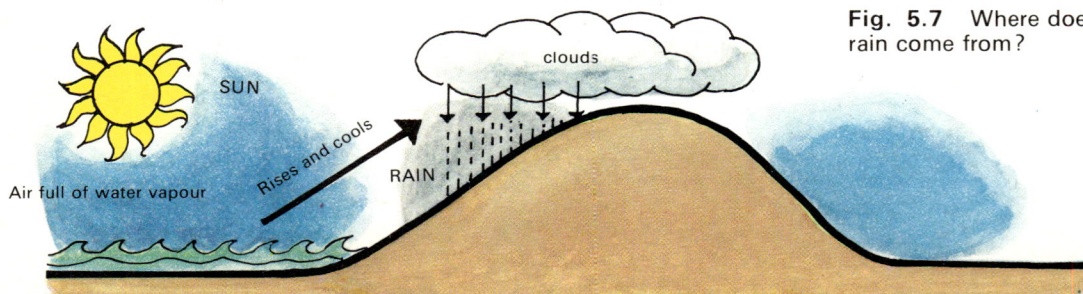
Fig. 5.7 Where does the rain come from?

Fig. 5.8 Making rain clouds. (*top*) Typical cloud just before seeding and (*bottom*) a growing rain cloud photographed 37 minutes after seeding

Where does the energy come from to evaporate the water from seas and lakes? Fig. 5.7 on page 74 shows how this cycle of events takes place. It is a continuous cycle which is always going on. Water which evaporates at one part of the earth may be deposited as rain a long way away.

What happens to the water that falls on the earth? It obviously soaks into the earth, or else falls on our buildings and streets and flows away into the sewers. Rain water is not pure to start with, although it does not contain very many impurities.

Fig. 5.9 Vapour trails produced by the Red Arrows aerobatic team

Experiment 5.6
How pure is rain water?

Collect some rain water and evaporate it. Is there any solid material left?

Warm some rain water in a beaker. Small bubbles appear some time before the water boils. What are they?

Rain water, then, contains some dissolved gas. As the only gas through which the rain has passed is air we might expect this dissolved gas to be made up of gas from the air.

Sometimes, after a thunderstorm, rain water may be very slightly acid. This is due to the fact that, when an electric spark (the lightning flash) passes through the air, a little of the oxygen and nitrogen combine to make a gas which dissolves in water to form nitric acid. This acid solution is of course very weak indeed – but it is very important to agriculture, as you will learn later on. In industrial towns rain water may become slightly acid because of impurities in the air arising from the waste gases from factories. When coal is burnt, acid gases are usually given off, the quantity depending on the kind of coal used. When these gases dissolve in rain water, they form acid solutions which can eat away the stone of buildings. If you live in an industrial area you will be able to find many examples of this.

Fig. 5.10 A flash of lightning during a storm

5.6 POND WATER — AND THE BEASTIES IN IT!

Rain water eventually finds its way into rivers or lakes or ponds. Water which collects in ponds and ditches is usually stagnant – that is, it does not move. It becomes muddy, and small organisms thrive in it.

Experiment 5.7
Looking at pond water

Put a drop of pond water in a small glass dish (called a Petri dish) and look at it first with a hand lens. You might possibly see some living organisms in the water as well as some small green particles which are very small plants. If you do not see anything with a hand lens, use the low power of a microscope. Your teacher will show you how to do this.

Water is essential for all life, our own included. It is also of prime importance in industry. Make a list of the industries in your neighbourhood which use large quantities of water.

We get most of our water for drinking purposes from lakes or rivers. In a few places in the country we may still get it from springs, but these are too small to satisfy the needs of large communities. Sometimes lakes are made artificially by, for example, damming a river and so preventing the water from running away. These lakes are called reservoirs. Where would it be best to dam a river to make a reservoir – near its source, or near its mouth?

Experiment 5.8
Looking at river water

Collect some water from a river or lake, and look at it under the low power of the microscope. It is not as dirty as pond water, but it will still probably contain some particles of mud and some plant material, and possibly a few 'beasties'. To make this water suitable for drinking it must be purified.

5.7 PURIFYING WATER

Some time ago you found out how to separate solid particles from water by filtering with a filter paper. Why would this method be unsuitable for purifying large quantities of water for drinking?

To remove solid particles, the water is filtered through a gravel bed. We can imitate this process in the laboratory, and for this purpose we shall take some really dirty pond water and show how the mud and other solid matter can be removed from it.

Experiment 5.9
Filtering pond water

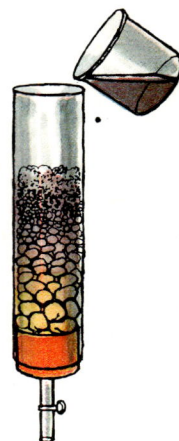

Fig. 5.11

Your teacher will set up for you a filtration column packed as shown in the diagram. Pond water is trickled slowly through the column and collects in the beaker at the foot. Does it look cleaner?

Look at some of the water first through the low power of the microscope. Can you see anything?

Now put a drop of the filtered water on to a microscope slide and look at it under the high power of the microscope. You may see some rod-shaped particles. These are bacteria. Draw a diagram of what you see.

Evaporate a little of the filtered water on a watch glass, or in a small glass dish resting on an aluminium beaker containing water which is kept boiling. Is there any residue?

Our drinking water is filtered in this way, but is also treated with chemicals to kill off living organisms, such as bacteria, which may be harmful. Not all bacteria cause disease; in fact some are essential for healthy living, but there are some which can be very dangerous indeed, giving rise to such illnesses as typhoid.

You have probably come across one substance with which water is often treated in order to kill bacteria. This is chlorine gas, which is used to purify the water in swimming baths, and is sometimes used to purify drinking water too. We can see what effect chlorine has on the living organisms in pond water.

Experiment 5.10

Look at some pond water under the microscope. Can you see some living organisms in it? Your teacher will now bubble some chlorine into it. What do you see when you examine the chlorinated water under the microscope?

Try to find out where your house water supply comes from and what is done to purify it. If possible visit the water works and see for yourself.

5.8 TAP WATER

Is tap water pure? Does it contain any dissolved solids? You know how to remove solid particles from a liquid, but dissolved substances cannot be removed in the same way. We have also learnt how to get the dissolved substances from a solution, but how would we get pure water from a solution?

5.9 DISTILLATION

Experiment 5.11
Making pure water

Do you remember how you condensed steam and obtained water from it? Does this give you a clue? See if you can devise an apparatus to obtain pure water from salt water. For possible answers look at the end of this unit (page 92), but do not do so until you have actually tried out methods for yourself.
How would you find out if the water was pure?

This process of getting pure water from water containing dissolved substances is called **distillation**.
If you were asked to get pure water from muddy water containing dissolved solids, would it be necessary to filter it first?

5.10 SEPARATING TWO LIQUIDS

We have seen how we can obtain a pure solvent from a solution by distillation. Is it possible to separate a liquid from another one in this way?
Suppose we have a mixture of alcohol and water and we want to separate the alcohol from it. Alcohol boils at 78 °C and water at 100 °C. Can

Fig. 5.12 A malt whisky distillery at Muir-of-Ord, Ross-shire

you guess what will happen if we gradually heat a mixture of alcohol and water?
Let's put your guess to the test.

Experiment 5.12

Take about 20 cm^3 of water in a dish and add 10 cm^3 of alcohol to it. See if it burns when you put a lighted match to it.
Now pour your alcohol-water mixture into your distillation apparatus and boil it. Collect about 5 cm^3 of distillate.
Does the distillate burn easily?
Does the liquid left in the distilling flask burn?
Explain what has happened. Was your guess right?

This method of separating liquids is widely used in industry. All the petrol used in cars and aeroplanes is obtained from crude oil in this way. You will come across this process again later on.
Perhaps you now know why a place where whisky is manufactured is called a distillery (Fig. 5.12).

5.11 SEA WATER

Experiment 5.13

Evaporate some sea water on a glass slide. Is there anything left? Does 1 cm^3 of sea water weigh more or less than 1 cm^3 of tap water?

The residue when sea water is evaporated is mainly salt. Altogether the sea contains an enormous amount of salt.

Salt is a very important substance. As we all know, it is used to flavour food; but this is not just a fad. Salt is necessary in order to help produce a substance required for the digestion of food. Not only is food without salt insipid, but we are unable to use it properly.

Salt is also the raw material in the manufacture of a large number of chemicals. All the salt that is used comes either from the sea itself or from dried-up salt lakes. These are often covered with other layers of rock, and the salt then has to be mined, as in Poland. In Britain an ingenious way of bringing the salt to the surface is used. A pipe

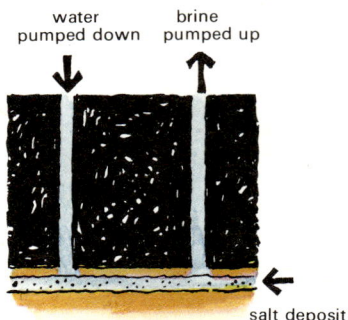

water pumped down   brine pumped up

salt deposit

Fig. 5.13

is sunk to the salt deposits and water is pumped down it. The water dissolves some of the salt and some distance away salt solution is pumped up. The solution is then evaporated.

In some parts of the world where there is plenty of heat from the Sun, sea water is evaporated by making use of this heat. Large concrete pans fill up with sea water at high tide. When the water recedes the salt solution starts to evaporate and by the next high tide it has all 'dried up'. Then the pan fills up again and the same process goes on. After a time, when sufficient salt has collected, it is scraped out. Although the body must have salt, we find it very objectionable to drink salt water, such as sea water. It makes us very thirsty and may even make us sick. The preparation of pure water from sea water is therefore of great importance in some countries where there is very little rain and it is difficult to get drinking water.

Would distillation be a suitable method to use?

Of course it would give the required result, but it is expensive because it requires fuel to boil the water. Many countries which are very dry are short of fuel too. Can you guess why? So other processes have been devised for getting pure water from sea water. The general name for them is 'desalination' processes. This simply means

Fig. 5.14 Piles of sea salt produced in salt pans on the coast of Majorca

methods of removing salt. Can you devise a simple way of getting drinking water from sea water in a hot country?

Sketch in your note book the apparatus you invent.

5.12 DISSOLVING

Water dissolves a large number of substances; a liquid which dissolves other things is called a **solvent**.

Experiment 5.14
Making a solution

Shake up some salt with water. It disappears. Where has it gone to? Is it still there although you cannot see it? How do you know? How could you get it back?

You will think that this is a simple experiment but in fact there are really some pretty important things going on here. Can you explain, using the particle theory, what has happened to the salt when it disappeared?

To get the salt back you evaporate the solution in an evaporating dish.

Experiment 5.15
Does sand dissolve in water?

You will say that of course it does not, but if someone asked you to prove it how would you satisfy them? Think it out for yourself and then try your experiment.

Perhaps you have wondered why some things dissolve in water and others do not. This is a very difficult question to answer, but you may have your own ideas. Try to write them down.

5.13 SATURATED SOLUTIONS

Can we dissolve any amount of salt we wish in water, or can a certain volume of water hold only a limited weight of salt?

Experiment 5.16
How much salt will dissolve in 20 cm³ of water?

Measure out 20 cm³ of water into a large test-tube. Have ready some little packets or heaps of salt each weighing 1 g. Add one of these to the water and shake the tube. Repeat with another 1 g measure. Go on doing this until some salt remains undissolved. How many grammes of salt will dissolve in 20 cm³ of water?

You have answered the question you set yourself.

We call a solution which will not dissolve any more solid a **saturated** solution. The solid which is dissolved is called the **solute**. A saturated solution is one which is full up with the solute.

Experiment 5.17
Does a given quantity of water dissolve the same weight of all solutes?

To find the answer to this we can try Experiment 5.16 with different solutes. Different groups in the class can try copper sulphate, potassium nitrate, alum, ammonium chloride, sodium sulphate.

What conclusion does the class come to?

Experiment 5.18
Does hot water dissolve more of a substance than an equal weight of cold water?

Heat 20 cm³ of water in a test-tube to about 70 °C. Now repeat Experiment 5.16 with the substance you used before.

Does temperature make any difference to the weight of solute that dissolves?

Is the effect the same for all substances?

Can you put forward a theory that might explain your results?

What will happen when your hot saturated solution cools down? Look at your test-tubes and see if your guess was correct.

5.14 SPEEDING UP SOLUTION

What factors control the rate at which a substance dissolves? You can probably think of some things right away. Does the size of the crystal have anything to do with it? Does stirring make a substance dissolve more quickly? What about the temperature of the liquid? We have already found out that a certain weight (or volume) of hot water dissolves more solid than does the same weight of cold water, but does it dissolve any more quickly? We can design some experiments to find out the answers to these questions.

Experiment 5.19
Factors affecting speed of solution

(a) Choose two crystals of copper sulphate as nearly as possible the same size. Crush one of them to fine powder in a mortar. Put 100 cm³ of water into each of two beakers. Take the temperature of the water in the two beakers and check that it is the same. Add the whole crystal to one and the powder to the other. Which dissolves more quickly?

Is it permissible to shake the beakers while the substances are dissolving?

(b) For experiments (b) and (c) you should use some powdered copper sulphate.

Again take two beakers each containing 100 cm³ of cold water. Test the temperature as before. Weigh out two lots of 1 g of the powder, and add one lot to each beaker. Leave one alone, and stir the other vigorously with a glass rod. Which one dissolves first?

(c) This time we want to find out whether the powdered copper sulphate dissolves more quickly in cold or in hot water. You should be able to design this experiment for yourself.

Sum up the results of your experiments by saying what are the best conditions for rapid dissolving.

1. Large or small crystals,
2. With or without stirring,
3. Hot or cold water.

Explain your results in terms of the kinetic theory of matter.

This experiment, although quite simple, illustrates a very important principle of scientific investigation. We have three factors which we suspect might be concerned with quickness of solution; they are size of crystal, stirring, and temperature of the solvent. If we want to find out if each of these is effective we have to try them out one at a time. Thus, if we want to find if the size of crystal has anything to do with it we try experiments with different sizes of crystal but we must keep all the other conditions the same. In this case the temperature of the water must be the same (that is why we tested it), and the liquid must either not be stirred at all or, if it is, it must be stirred at the same rate in both beakers. If this were not so, we should be unable to pin down the effect we observed to the size of the crystal alone; some other factor might be influencing the result too.

To sum up, if there are several variables which can influence the results of an experiment and we want to find out the effect of one of them, we must keep all the others constant during the experiment.

5.15 ENERGY AGAIN!

When you were making solutions in Experiment 5.17, did you happen to feel the test-tube? Did it get warm, or cool? If you did not notice this at the time, it is worthwhile doing the following test.

Experiment 5.20
Energy changes when substances dissolve

Dissolve some of each of the following in some water in a test-tube — calcium chloride, ammonium nitrate, and sodium hydroxide. (Sodium hydroxide is dangerous stuff to deal with. Do not touch it. Your teacher will provide you with the chemicals in test-tubes. All you have to do is to add water. Do not close the tube containing sodium hydroxide solution with your thumb when shaking it. Use the cork supplied.) Do the tubes get hot or cold? If you are not sure, use a thermometer to help you.

This experiment shows that in the cases you have chosen, heat is either given out (i.e. the tube gets hot), or is taken in (i.e. the tube gets cold) when a substance dissolves. It does not follow, of course, that this *always* happens; you have tried only three substances. In science we must be careful not to say that something happens every time when we have tried only a few examples; in other words we cannot make a general rule on the basis of a few observations.

A process in which heat is given out is called an **exothermic** process; one in which heat is taken in is called an **endothermic** process. What term would you use for the dissolution in water of (i) calcium chloride, (ii) ammonium nitrate, (iii) sodium hydroxide?

5.16 CRYSTALS

When you made a hot saturated solution of a substance in Experiment 5.18, you noticed what happened when the solution cooled. We are now going to look at this more closely.

Experiment 5.21
Making crystals

You will be given various substances to experiment with: copper sulphate, alum, and potassium nitrate are suitable. Make a *saturated* solution of each substance in about 50 cm³ of water at the boiling point. Pour off the hot saturated solutions into other beakers, leaving behind any undissolved solids. Put a drop of each solution on separate microscope slides and watch what happens. Look at the residue with a hand lens. Draw what you see.

Leave the rest of the solutions to cool slowly until the next science lesson.

What has formed in the beakers? Are the crystals all the same shape? Are they larger or smaller than those on the microscope slides?

To prepare small fine crystals, would you cool the saturated solution slowly or quickly? What would you do to obtain large crystals?

Experiment 5.21(a)
Making large crystals

To make really good specimens of large crystals you should make a cold saturated solution of the substance. Alum or copper sulphate are good ones to try. Pick a good small crystal from the bottle and tie it securely to a fine nylon thread.

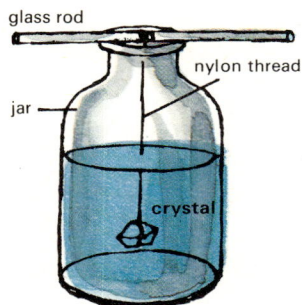

Fig. 5.15

Tie the other end of the thread to a glass rod or a piece of wood that will rest on top of the beaker of solution so that the crystal hangs in the saturated solution. Put the beaker in a place

Fig. **5.16** Alum crystals produced by the method of Experiment 5.21(a)

where the temperature is fairly constant, and let it stay there for a long time. Every few days look at the crystal. It should grow quite large. If it seems to be growing small crystals on the outside, cut them off with a sharp knife or a razor blade. You should be able to grow a very large, fine crystal this way. Other members of the class might try other substances such as chrome alum or potassium nitrate.

Preserving sugar has much larger crystals than castor sugar. How do you think the methods of making these two kinds of sugar differed?

The same is true of salt. Salt used for preserving or for putting on icy roads has large crystals. Table salt has tiny crystals. Why do we not use large crystals for table salt? Would it be more or less expensive to make large crystals?

Crystals are not always obtained from solutions. Sometimes when solids are melted and the liquid is cooled, crystals separate.

Experiment 5.22
Making crystals of sulphur

(Care is required in this experiment. Molten sulphur can cause a nasty burn.)

Melt some sulphur in a dish. Do not heat it too strongly, but only until it just melts. Then take the flame away and let the liquid cool until a solid crust forms. Make a hole in the crust and pour out the liquid inside. Cut out the solid from the dish and look at the crystals. What do they look like?

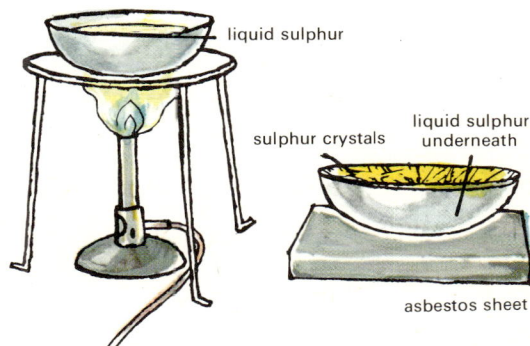

Fig. 5.17

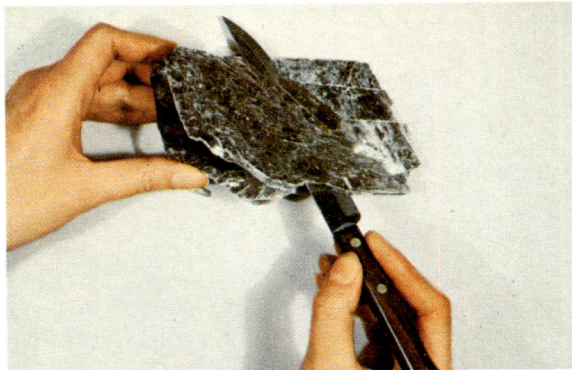

Fig. 5.18 (*left*) Quartz, (*top right*) mica showing its flat-sheet crystal structure, and (*bottom right*) iron pyrites

Experiment 5.23
Making crystals of salol

Melt a little salol on a microscope slide, and let it cool. Use a microscope to watch what happens, or project the slide with a film strip projector.

Sometimes when metal breaks you can see crystals in the broken portion. If possible examine a broken brass handle or other metallic object and look at the crystals. Sometimes you can see very thin crystals of zinc on a piece of galvanized iron. Crystals, some of them very beautiful, often occur naturally. Look at specimens of quartz, calcite, galena, iron pyrites, amethyst, rose quartz and any other crystalline minerals you may have at school. Are all the crystals the same shape?

Experiment 5.24
Cutting crystals

Take a large crystal of galena or of calcite. Hold a penknife along the length of the crystal and give it a sharp tap with a hammer. The crystal breaks into smaller ones. Do the small crystals have the same shape as the original large one? We say that the crystal cleaves. Try putting the knife across the crystal, and then striking it with

a hammer. Does the crystal cleave this time? If it breaks, does it break as easily as before?

We have noticed that crystals of a particular substance, such as quartz, or salt, or sugar always crystallize in the same shape, and cleave more easily one way than another to form smaller crystals which have the same shape as the original large crystal. This suggests that the particles which make them up are arranged in a definite way which gives the crystal its shape. This shape will obviously depend on the size of the particles since this determines how they pack together. Fig. 5.19 shows how the particles which make up sodium chloride (common salt) crystals are packed together to make a cubic crystal.

Fig. 5.19 A model showing the structure of sodium chloride (common salt)

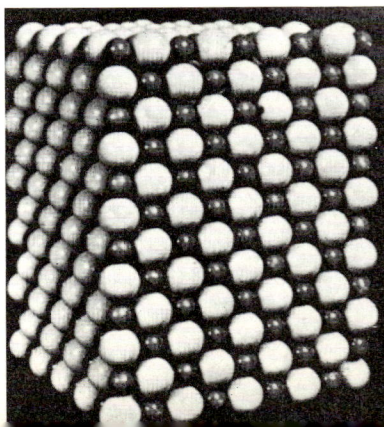

5.17 SOLUTIONS IN SOLVENTS OTHER THAN WATER

So far we have been concerned only with solutions in water. Do other liquids dissolve things?

Experiment 5.25
Does sulphur dissolve in toluene?

N.B. *Toluene is a flammable liquid and care must be taking in using it.* Put about 50 cm³ of toluene in a flask and add about 5 g of powdered sulphur. Have a metal can large enough to hold the flask and boil some water in it. *Turn out the flame,* and see that no other burners are alight round about. Put the flask into the hot water. Does the sulphur dissolve?

If it all dissolves, add a little more until a saturated solution is formed. Now let the hot saturated solution cool. You should obtain good crystals of sulphur. What shape are they?

Fig. 5.20

Experiment 5.26
Dissolving iodine

Take five test-tubes and put in each a small crystal of iodine. To the first add water, to the second a solution of potassium iodide, to the third methylated spirit (impure alcohol or ethanol), to the fourth a little acetone, and to the fifth paraffin. In which of the liquids does the iodine dissolve? Write up your results in the form of a table.

A solution of iodine in alcohol is called tincture of iodine; this name is also given sometimes to a solution of iodine in potassium iodide solution. It was used a great deal as an antiseptic, but its place has largely been taken by other solutions which are equally good killers of bacteria but do not cause as much pain when they are put on to an open wound.

It is obvious from our experiments that many other liquids besides water can dissolve substances, and that sometimes things which do not dissolve in water will dissolve in other solvents. On the other hand things which dissolve in water may be insoluble in other liquids.

As additional experiments find out if sugar dissolves in paraffin, or salt in acetone.

Dissolve some shellac in methylated spirit. This solution is used as French polish.

Experiment 5.27
Experiments with nail varnish

You are provided with some strips of glass (microscope slides) which have been painted with nail varnish and put aside to dry. Which of the following liquids will dissolve the nail varnish and remove it from the slide? Water, methylated spirit, acetone, ethyl acetate.

Smell these liquids. Which one do you think the manufacturer used to make nail varnish?

Experiment 5.28
'Dry' cleaning

You will be given some rags which have oil or grease stains on them. Find out which of the following liquids is most effective in removing the stain: water, methylated spirit, dichlorethylene, turpentine.

In those cases when the stain was removed, where has the oil or grease gone?

We see then that many liquids can act as solvents, and that very often the solutions are useful in everyday life. Make a list of important solutions in solvents other than water that have not been mentioned above.

5.18 SEPARATION OF SUBSTANCES

Experiment 5.29

If we are faced with the problem of separating one substance from another we can often solve it if we can find a liquid which will dissolve one of the substances and not the other. You know how to proceed after that.

Try to obtain pure samples of both the components of one or more of the following mixtures.

1. Salt and chalk
2. Wax with iron filings embedded in it
3. Iron filings and copper filings (You do not need a solvent for this one.)
4. Sugar and sand

5.19 CHROMATOGRAPHY

Have you noticed that when you spill some plum juice on the tablecloth a stain is found with a red part in the middle with a colourless ring round it? It looks as though the water in the plum juice travels further on the cloth than the dye in the juice does. You can sometimes see the same thing with an ink spot on a piece of blotting paper. We can make use of this to separate things and to tell us what substances are present in a mixture. Here is an example.

You might think that ink is simply one dye dissolved in water. Let us see if it really is.

Experiment 5.30
An investigation of ink

Take a filter paper and cut it so that you can bend down a piece of the paper to form a sort of tail (Fig. 5.22). Put a spot of ink at the centre of the paper and then rest it on top of a Petri dish containing water so that the tail is in the water. The water is soaked up by the filter paper and reaches the ink spot. Draw a diagram to show what you see.

Using a pure dye, such as methyl orange or methylene blue, repeat the experiment and compare the results.

What can you say about the ink?

Can you guess at a reasonable explanation of how this separation works?

Devise an experiment to find out if inks of the same colour but made by different manufacturers contain the same dyes.

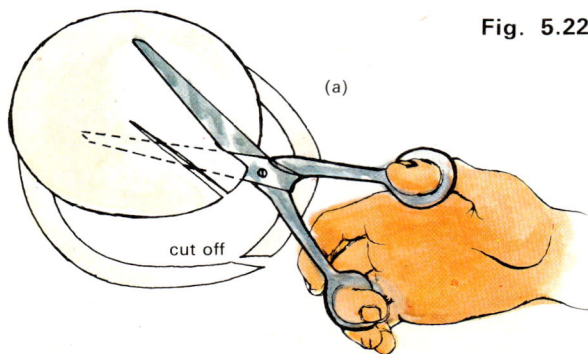

Fig. 5.21 Chromatographic patterns produced by a variety of inks and dyes

We call this process **separation by chromatography**. It is very useful indeed for finding out the constituents of complex mixtures, such as the compounds which make up our hair or our finger nails or the green colour of plants.

5.20 THE IN-BETWEENS

Experiment 5.31

Pass some carbon dioxide gas into some lime water in a gas jar, as in Fig. 5.23. Label this jar A.

In a second gas jar dissolve about 5 g of sodium thiosulphate in about 500 cm^3 of water and add about 5 cm^3 of dilute hydrochloric acid. Label this jar B.

In a third gas jar full of water add a little concentrated iron (III) chloride solution. Label this jar C.

In a large beaker heat some water almost to boiling and add about 5 cm^3 of concentrated iron (III) chloride solution. Cool the beaker in a trough of cold water and label this D.

Which of the jars contains a solution? If the others are not solutions, what are they?

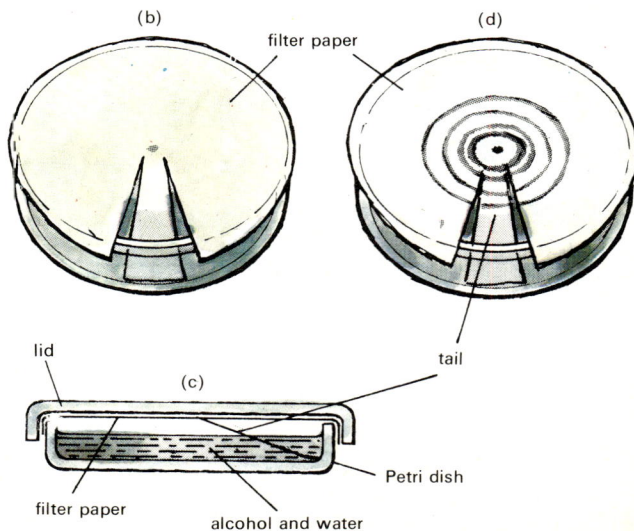

Fig. 5.22

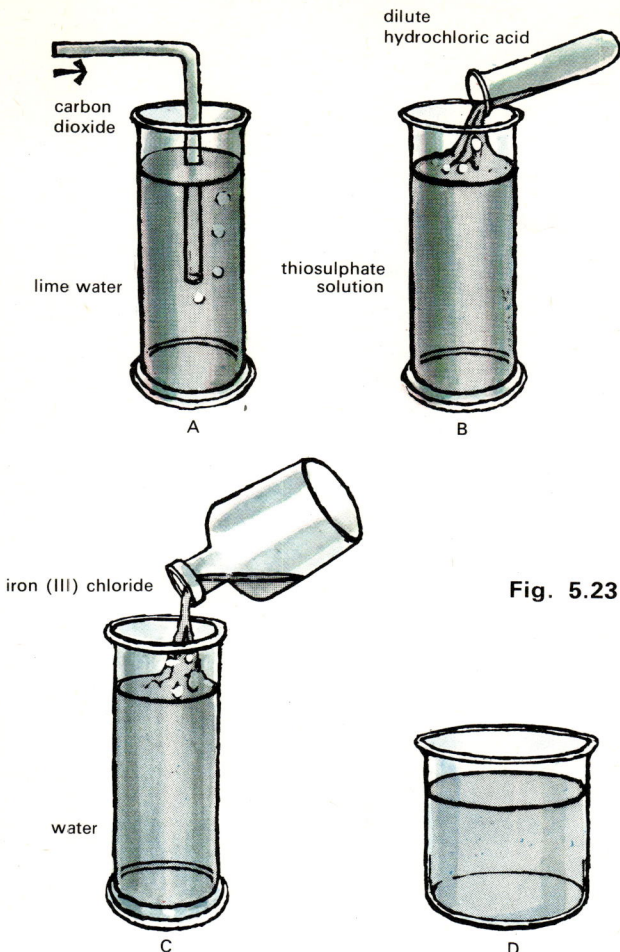

carbon dioxide

lime water

dilute hydrochloric acid

thiosulphate solution

A   B

iron (III) chloride

water

Fig. 5.23

C   D

You may have some difficulty in saying whether the liquid is clear or not. Here is a way of finding out. You have probably noticed that the air in a room may seem to be quite clear, but when a beam of sunlight comes in through the window it shows up particles of dust in the air. You can see this better in a cinema, when the beam from the projector passes through air containing very fine particles of tobacco smoke. You may also see it in the laboratory when a film is being shown or when the film-strip projector is used and there is chalk dust in the air. You would not see the beam of light at all if there were no particles in the air; so we can use a strong beam of light to tell us if there are particles of dust in the air, or if there are tiny particles in a liquid. This beam of light is called the 'Tyndall beam'; you came across it before when you were observing the Brownian movement (page 54).

Try passing a strong beam of light through the liquids in the gas jars. The film-strip projector can be used to provide the light. It is a good idea to pass the beam of light first through a solution of potassium dichromate. This is an orange coloured solution which filters out some of the colours in the light from the lamp and so gives a better effect. The jars are then placed in the beam. Which of them is clear?

To answer the first question we must ask ourselves how we recognize a solution. You have already done some experiments which might help you. First, you know that in solutions the particles are so small that they will pass through a filter paper. Second, a solution is transparent or clear. You can see through it. Third, in a solution the particles are evenly spread through the solvent. There is nothing settling out.

A liquid which contains a solid which settles after a time, is called a **suspension**.

A liquid which contains particles of solid which are so fine that they do not settle, but show up in a Tyndall beam, is called a **colloid**.

A liquid which contains particles which are so fine that the liquid is perfectly clear is called a **solution**.

A colloid is in between a suspension and a solution. It is not one thing or the other. That is why we have headed this section 'the in-betweens'.

Fig. 5.24

The Tyndall beam

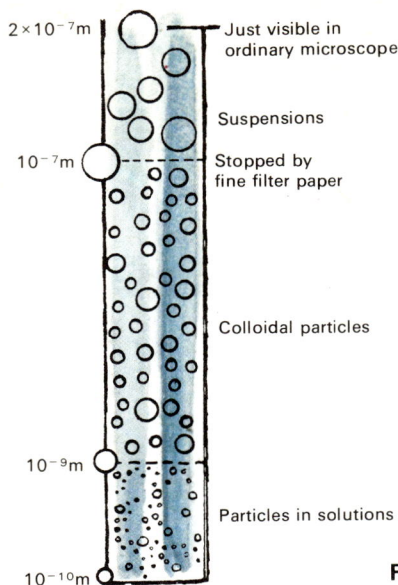

2×10⁻⁷m — Just visible in ordinary microscope

Suspensions

10⁻⁷m — Stopped by fine filter paper

Colloidal particles

10⁻⁹m

Particles in solutions

10⁻¹⁰m

Fig. 5.25

Fig. 5.25 shows the relative sizes of these particles.

Which of your jars contains a solution, which a suspension, and which a colloid?

Here is an experiment for you to do at home. By passing a beam of light from a strong torch through jam jars containing various liquids find out which are true solutions, which are suspensions, and which are colloids. Fill the jam jar about three-quarters full of water and add some of the liquid you are testing to it. Here are some you can try: tea, instant coffee, vinegar, detergent, toothpaste, ginger beer.

Experiment 5.32

Boil a little water in a beaker and add a pinch of powdered starch to it.
Find out for yourself if it has formed a true solution or a colloidal solution.

Does sugar form a true solution?

Why is it that the very fine particles do not separate out from a colloid? To answer this you should recall your work on the Brownian movement in Unit 4.

Experiment 5.33

Shake up some olive oil with vinegar in a test-tube and allow the mixture to stand. What happens?

Now add a pinch of dry mustard to the mixture and shake again. Allow to stand. What happens this time?

Olive oil and vinegar do not mix, but when the mustard is added the droplets of oil do not separate out. As in the case of the solid particles of a colloid, the droplets are so small that they do not fall to the bottom of the tube.

These mixtures are called **emulsions**.

Experiment 5.34
How does a detergent work?

Shake up 1 cm³ of oil with 5 cm³ of water. Allow the mixture to stand. What happens? Now add a few drops of detergent, and shake vigorously again. What do you see now?

The detergent evidently prevents the small droplets from joining together to make larger ones. It keeps the oil and water in the form of an emulsion. A substance which does this is often called an emulsifying agent. This is how the detergent removes grease and dirt from our hands.

Emulsions are used often in everyday life. You made a type of salad cream in Experiment 5.33. Other types of cream such as hair cream and vanishing cream are emulsions, and so is milk. Milk has very tiny globules of butter fat suspended in water. Some of this separates out as cream when the milk is allowed to stand, but when the cream is skimmed off there are still some fat globules suspended in the water. Will these globules be smaller or larger than those which have separated out? Homogenized milk has been treated in such a way as to make the fat globules even smaller, so that they do not separate out as cream. The smaller globules make it easier for a baby to digest.

Some of you take cod liver oil emulsion when you have a cough. This consists of cod liver oil in very fine drops emulsified in water to which some other chemicals have been added. Some of these are chosen for their medical use, but others are emulsifying agents.

You have heard of emulsion paints. These contain colloidal particles of coloured solids and droplets of oil emulsified in water.

You will find out soon that emulsions play a part in the process of digestion and absorption of food in our bodies.

So far we have dealt with solid particles dispersed (i.e. spread out) in a liquid, and with liquid particles dispersed in a liquid. There are other important types of colloids too. Smokes are fine particles of solid dispersed in a gas, usually air.

Experiment 5.35

Your teacher will put a few drops of a concentrated solution of ammonia in a small glass dish, and in another dish next to it a few drops of concentrated hydrochloric acid. What happens?

Aerosols are tiny droplets of liquid dispersed in air. You can easily make an 'atomizer' to produce an aerosol. The apparatus is shown in Fig. 5.26.

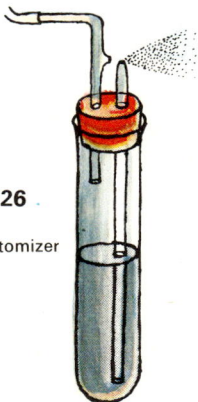

Fig. 5.26

A home-made atomizer

Experiments 5.36
Aerosols

Make an 'atomizer' and spray water from it through a beam of light from a projector. What do you see?

Try spraying some water from your atomizer on to a blackboard at a distance of about 0.5 m. What area did it cover, and how much liquid did it take to cover this area?

What advantages does paint spraying have over painting with a brush?

Something to do at home

Make a list of colloids you can find in the kitchen, the larder, and the bathroom.

You do not blow into the can of an aerosol. What makes the spray come out of the can?

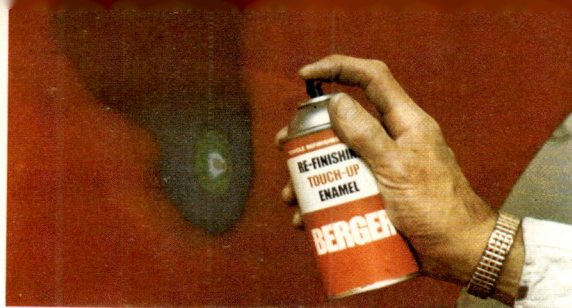

Fig. 5.27 Aerosol car spray

Look at the warning on an aerosol can about its disposal when empty. Why does it give this warning?

Although colloids have many uses in everyday life, they are also sometimes a nuisance; for instance, there is smoke in the air. How can we get rid of it? It is obvious that we cannot filter the air by the usual methods because the smoke particles are so small that they pass right through filters.

Particles of colloids often have electrical charges on them. We can make use of this fact to separate smoke particles from air.

Experiment 5.37
Getting rid of smoke

We shall do a very simple experiment first; it is like one that you have done before.

Rub a plastic rod (a plastic ball-point pen, or a fountain pen will do) on your coat sleeve, and then hold it near some chalk dust on the bench. What happens?

By rubbing the plastic rod you have charged it with electricity, and it is now capable of picking up small particles.

We are going to use this fact to take smoke particles out of smoky air. Set up the apparatus like that shown in Fig. 5.28.

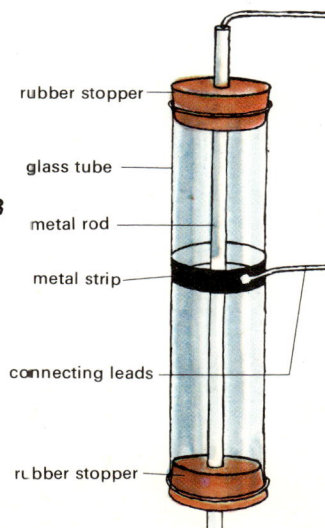

Fig. 5.28

rubber stopper

glass tube

metal rod

metal strip

connecting leads

rubber stopper

87

A glass tube has a metal rod running through it, held in position by rubber stoppers. A metal strip is wrapped tightly round the tube about half-way down. The rod and the strip are connected to a Van de Graaff generator – a machine for producing high voltage electricity. Before switching on the generator, puff some smoke into the tube. Now switch on the machine.

What happens?

In some areas factories are forbidden to pour out smoke into the air, and one way of preventing it is by using an electrostatic precipitator of this kind. In some chemical manufacturing plants it is essential that the gases used should be free from dust, and it is often removed in this way.

5.21 COLLOIDS AND US

In Experiment 5.32 you found out that starch does not make a true solution but is a colloid; sugar however does form a true solution. As we saw in Unit 3, these substances are very much alike; they are both carbohydrates, they both form part of our food, and they give us energy. Why should one form a true solution and the other not?

We have discovered that, when a substance dissolves, it breaks down into such small particles that we cannot see them. In a colloidal solution these particles are still very small and we cannot see them with the naked eye, but they show up when a beam of light is passed through. The particles in a colloidal solution are larger than those in a true solution.

Can it be that a molecule of starch is so much bigger than that of sugar – and that this is the reason why the starch forms a colloidal solution while the sugar forms a true solution? This would certainly seem a reasonable explanation. How can we find out if it is true when we cannot actually see the molecules themselves? This experiment may suggest a way.

Experiment 5.38
Sifting soil

Put a handful of dry soil in a sieve and shake. Some particles come through and others do not. Which particles fell through the sieve? Compare these with the particles remaining in the sieve.

5.22 STARCH AND GLUCOSE

You are going to find out whether a starch molecule is bigger than a sugar molecule. There are actually quite a lot of substances that we call sugar. There is the sugar you put in your tea or on your corn-flakes, and this we call cane sugar or beet sugar (according to whether it comes from sugar cane or sugar beet); there is milk sugar (which as its name implies is found in milk); there is fruit sugar (found in many fruits); and there is glucose (found in some plants and animals). Here are the proper chemical names for these sugars.

cane sugar or beet sugar	**sucrose**
milk sugar	**lactose**
fruit sugar	**fructose**
glucose is just **glucose**.	

If we wish to compare the sizes of starch and sugar molecules we must find tests for them so that we can recognize them. In our experiments we shall use the sugar that is simplest and most easy to test for. This is glucose. It also happens to be the sugar that is most important for us as far as the working of our bodies is concerned, as you will soon see.

Experiment 5.39
Tests for starch and glucose

Make some starch 'solution' by adding a pinch of starch to a beaker of boiling water. Let it cool.

Also dissolve some glucose in water in another small beaker.

Take a little of your starch 'solution' in a test-tube, and add a drop of iodine solution. What happens?

Try the same test with your glucose solution. What happens?

How can you tell whether a solution contains starch or glucose?

Here is another test.

Take two test-tubes A and B. Add some glucose solution to A and some starch 'solution' to B. Add 3 cm³ of *Benedict's solution* to each tube, and let both of them stand in a beaker of boiling water. What do you observe?

Glucose is called a **reducing sugar** because it 'reduces' a copper compound in the Benedict's solution. When this happens, the colour of the solution changes. It was blue to start with.

Afterwards you will find a brown powder in it.

Referring back to Experiment 5.38, can you think of a way of finding out whether the starch molecule is larger than the glucose one? If you poured a mixture of starch and glucose through the sieve used in Experiment 5.38, what would happen? They would not, of course, be separated. The mesh of the sieve is too large. In order to separate the mixture you would have to find a sieve with extremely small holes in it – so small that they would let only one of the substances through. Would a filter paper do? If you are not sure, try filtering solutions of glucose and starch separately through a filter paper.

Visking tubing acts as a sieve which will let only small molecules through. Visking is a material something like cellophane. It is used in kidney machines.

Experiment 5.40
Movement of starch and glucose through a 'molecular sieve'

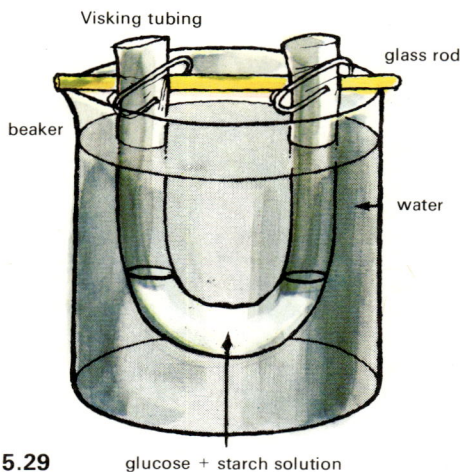

Fig. 5.29   glucose + starch solution

Cut a piece of Visking tubing about 15 cm long. Soak it in water to soften it. Pierce a small hole about 2 cm from each end of the tube, and push a glass rod or a pencil through these holes.

Put two dropperfuls of glucose solution and two dropperfuls of starch 'solution' into the Visking tube. Rinse the outside of the tube, and then support it over a small beaker half full of water, so that the tube is covered with water.

After 10 minutes, using a clean dropper, remove a sample of liquid from the beaker, and test it for glucose and for starch, using the tests you discovered in Experiment 5.39.

Test the liquid in the beaker again after 30 minutes, and then after one or two days.

From your results answer the following questions.

1. Which molecules have passed through the Visking tubing?
2. Which molecules have not passed through?
3. Which molecule do you think is larger – starch or glucose?

5.23 THE PROCESS OF DIGESTION

When you swallow food it passes into a tube called the **alimentary canal**. The walls of this canal behave like Visking tubing in that they allow only small molecules to pass through them. Large molecules cannot pass through the walls into the body.

Experiment 5.41

Bread, potatoes, and rice form the staple diet for millions of people in the world. Do these foods contain large or small molecules? Test them for starch and for reducing sugars. Enter your results in a table like the one shown below.

You have found that foods contain large, complex molecules. But these cannot get through the walls of the **intestine** (part of the alimentary canal) because they are too big. They cannot be used by us for food to supply energy unless they are changed into small molecules. This is just what **digestion** is – the breaking up of large, complex molecules like starch, into simpler

Food	Is starch present?	Is glucose present?	Are the molecules large or small?
Bread			
Potatoes			
Rice			

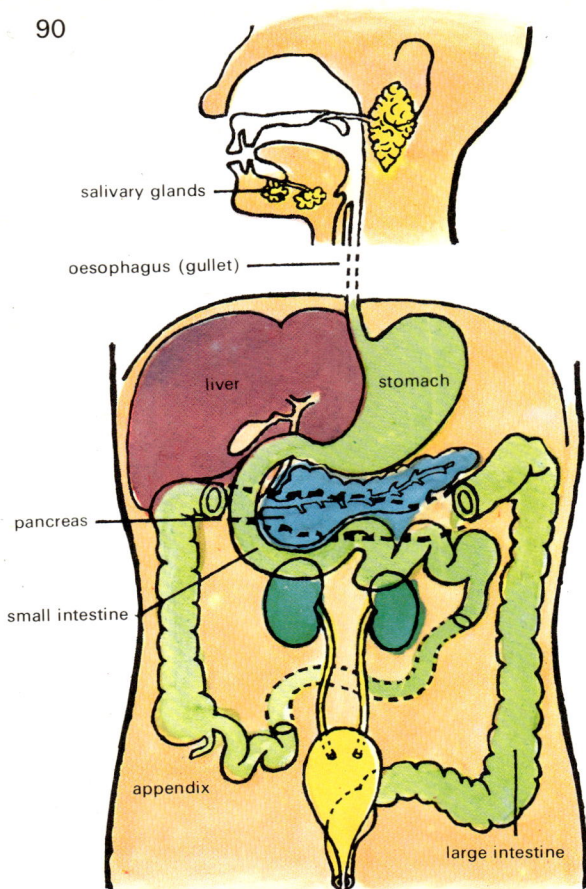

Fig. 5.30 The organs concerned with digestion

smaller molecules which can pass through the walls of the intestine into the blood stream.

How is digestion brought about?

Experiment 5.42
Breaking down starch molecules

One way of breaking down starch molecules is to boil them with acid. Take a little of your starch 'solution' in a small beaker and add an equal volume of dilute hydrochloric acid. Boil the contents of the beaker for about 15 minutes; add a little water if the liquid evaporates too much. Now let the liquid cool.

We want to test the liquid for reducing sugar, but before we do this we have to destroy the acid present. We can do this by carefully adding sodium bicarbonate until there is no more fizzing.

Now try the Benedict's solution test. What happens?

Starch is broken down into reducing sugars by boiling with acid. But this is obviously *not* the way this happens in the body: we do not have a stomach full of boiling hydrochloric acid. Moreover can you imagine what it would be like if all the foods containing starch had to be boiled in acid before being served up and eaten? Clearly the body must do this in a different way.

Experiment 5.43
Digestion of starch

Place four separate drops of iodine solution on a white tile. Label two test-tubes A and B. Put 3 cm^3 of starch in each tube. Add about 1 cm^3 of saliva to test-tube A; then place both tubes in a water bath at which the water is at a temperature of 37 °C. Why do we choose this temperature?

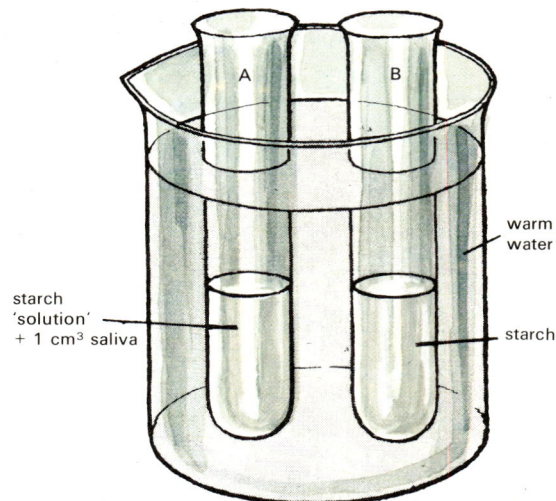

Fig. 5.31

After 2 minutes take one drop from each test-tube and add each to a drop of iodine solution, using a clean dropper for each test.

After 30 minutes test a second sample from each tube with iodine solution.

After 30 minutes is there any starch left in A?

After 30 minutes is there any starch left in B?

Test the liquid in both tubes for reducing sugar.

What has happened to the starch in A?

What does tube B show? Test-tube B and its contents is called a **control**. Why do we have to carry out a control experiment?

The starch in tube A has been broken down by saliva – but how? Saliva contains a complex chemical which speeds up the conversion of starch to a reducing sugar. This special chemical is one of a large group found in the body, called **enzymes**. Enzymes are very important substances. They speed up chemical reactions in organisms, but they themselves remain unchanged. We should be very different persons – even if we could live at all – if there were no such things as enzymes. Each particular enzyme has a special job to do, and there are certainly plenty of jobs to be done in the human body!

It would be interesting to find out if enzymes are able to work at any temperature, or if they work best round about one particular temperature.

Fig. 5.32 Enzymes play an important part in wine making. Here the grapes are being turned over at the start of the fermentation process

Experiment 5.44
Do enzymes work at different temperatures?

In Experiment 5.43 you put the test-tubes into a water bath at 37 °C. Does the enzyme in saliva digest starch at other temperatures? Find this out for yourself. Use temperatures both below and above 37 °C.

Do plants contain enzymes which digest starch? Here is an experiment you could do to find out.

Experiment 5.45

Your teacher will give you a sterile Petri dish containing agar jelly and starch. Cut some germinating pea seeds or barley grains into two and place each on the surface of the agar so that the cut surface is in contact with the agar. Cover the dish and leave it at room temperature for one or two days. Now remove the seeds and pour iodine solution over the surface of the agar.

Do any regions of the agar remain clear? What has happened to the starch in these regions? Do plants contain enzymes?

WHAT YOU HAVE LEARNT IN THIS UNIT

1. Matter exists in three states – solid, liquid, and gas.

2. Changes from one state to another take place at definite temperatures, called the melting point and boiling point, e.g.

$$\text{ice} \xrightarrow{0\ °C} \text{water} \xrightarrow{100\ °C} \text{steam}$$
$$\text{solid} \qquad \text{liquid} \qquad \text{gas}$$

3. As heat energy is put into a liquid, such as water, its temperature rises, and then remains steady while the liquid boils. This temperature is 100 °C for water but it is not the same for all liquids. A definite amount of energy is required to allow the particles to break free from the liquid. This is called the **latent heat of vaporization**.

Similarly the heat that has to be put into a solid to enable the particles to break away from the ordered arrangement in the solid when it melts is called the **latent heat of fusion**.

4. Liquids evaporate even without heating. This is because they contain a few particles which are moving at higher speeds than the others, and which can escape easily from the surface.

5. The best conditions for evaporation are: (a) warmth; (b) large surface area; (c) moving air; (d) a dry atmosphere.

6. Air can hold only a certain amount of water vapour at a certain temperature. When it is 'full up' with water vapour it is said to be saturated with it. If air saturated with water vapour is cooled, the extra water vapour that it cannot now hold will be 'squeezed out' in the form of tiny drops of water. This is how clouds are formed.

7. Rain water contains some dissolved gas, but should not contain any dissolved solid. Pond water contains, as a rule, dissolved substances, particles of soil and small organisms.

8.   Solid particles can be removed from water by **filtration**. This will not, however, remove dissolved substances; nor will it remove small organisms such as bacteria. These are killed by treating the water with chlorine.

9.   Many substances dissolve in water. They break up into very tiny particles which are too small to be seen, and which mix completely with the water.

10.   A liquid which dissolves a substance is called a **solvent**. The substance dissolving is called the **solute**, and the mixture of solvent and solute is called a **solution**. So

solvent + solute = solution

11.   The solute can be got back from a solution by **evaporation**, the solvent by **distillation**.

12.   Only a given quantity of solute will dissolve in a given quantity of solvent at a fixed temperature. A solution which is 'full-up' with solute is called a **saturated solution**.

13.   The factors which determine the speed with which a substance dissolves in a solvent are:
(a) stirring; (b) size of crystal – small crystals dissolve more rapidly than large ones; (c) temperature – usually the hotter the liquid the more rapidly does a substance dissolve.

14.   When substances dissolve there is usually an energy change. A change in which heat is taken in is said to be **endothermic**, and one where it is given out is called **exothermic**.

15.   When a saturated solution is cooled crystals separate out. Crystals of one substance are usually of the same shape, but may differ in size. To get large crystals the saturated solution is allowed to cool slowly. To get small crystals it is cooled quickly. Crystals are also formed when liquids are cooled. When crystals are broken they always break into smaller crystals of the same shape. Crystals can be cleaved in certain directions only.

16.   Water is not the only solvent. Sulphur will dissolve in toluene, iodine in alcohol, oil and grease in liquids used for 'dry' cleaning.

17.   Another method of separating substances is by **chromatography**.

18.   Some substances, such as starch, do not dissolve in water to form a true solution. All of a 'solution' of starch in water passes through a filter paper. When a strong beam of light is passed through the 'solution' it appears cloudy. This is called the **Tyndall beam**.

A liquid which contains a solid which settles out after a time is called a **suspension**.

A liquid which contains particles of solid which are so fine that they do not settle is called a **colloid**. It looks cloudy when a beam of light is shone through it.

A liquid which contains particles which are so fine that the liquid is perfectly clear is called a **solution**.

A liquid containing very fine drops of another liquid which do not settle out is called an **emulsion**.

19.   Detergents prevent oil drops from joining together. Substances which do this are called **emulsifying agents**.

20.   **Smokes** are fine solid particles in a gas, such as air. They do not settle out. **Mists** are fine drops of liquids in a gas, for example water droplets in air. An **aerosol** is like a mist; it is a cloud of fine droplets of liquids.

21.   Colloids are of great importance to animals. The food that we eat has to get into the blood stream through the walls of the intestine, before it can be used to give us energy or make us grow. Much of the food that we eat is either insoluble in water or forms a colloidal solution. In order that it may pass through the walls of the intestine, it has to be broken down into simpler substances which form true solutions. This is what happens in **digestion**.

22.   Starch turns iodine solution blue; sugar does not. Glucose and some other sugars (not cane sugar) turn Benedict's solution brown. They are called **reducing sugars**. Starch does not do this.

23.   Sugars and starch belong to the same class of substances called **carbohydrates**.

24.   Starch is digested (changed into glucose) in the body by means of **enzymes** in saliva. Enzymes are substances which help to bring about a chemical change without being used up in the process. They work best at a particular temperature. Plants also contain enzymes.

Obviously if you have mastered this unit you have learnt a lot!

Unit Six
The Units of Life

6.1 UNITS OF LIFE

Animals and plants vary in shape. They also vary in size. They range from the very large, (some trees are over 80 m high), to the very small. Some animals and plants are so small that they cannot be seen with the naked eye. In order to study them you must magnify them, and to do this you use a **microscope**.

6.2 THE MICROSCOPE

To get the best use from your microscope you must learn how to adjust it.

1. Stand the bench lamp about 12 cm in front of the mirror.
2. Rotate the nosepiece until the low or medium power objective is above the hole in the stage.

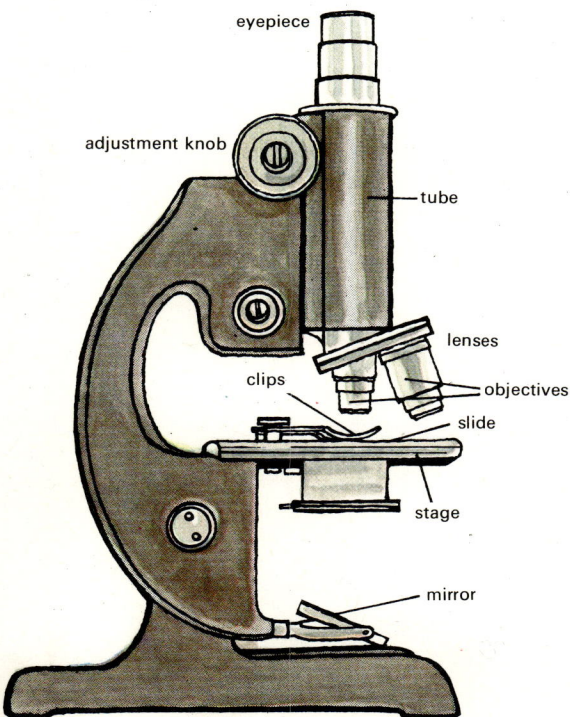

eyepiece

adjustment knob

tube

lenses

clips

objectives

slide

stage

mirror

Fig. 6.1

3. Look down the tube and move the mirror until you see most light coming up the tube.
4. Place the slide so that the material to be examined is in the middle of the hole in the stage.
5. Place your eye level with the stage and lower the objective until it is about 5 mm above the slide. (If your microscope has the adjustment knob below the stage, turn the knob until the stage is about 5 mm from the objective.)
6. Look down the eyepiece and slowly screw the objective *up* until the material is in focus. (If your microscope has the adjustment knob below the stage, look down the eyepiece and slowly screw the stage down until the material is in focus.)

Experiment 6.1
The eye, the lens, and the microscope

Look at a piece of tissue paper, look at it using a lens, and then look at it through a microscope.

6.3 THE STRUCTURE OF LIVING THINGS

Experiment 6.2
Looking at an onion

Cut an onion into two. You will see that it is made up of a collection of thick leaves. Remove one of these leaves. If you look carefully at the inside of this leaf you will see a white skin. With a mounted needle remove part of this skin and place a small piece on a microscope slide. Add a drop of water and place a cover slip on the specimen. The diagram on the next page will show you how to do this.

Examine the onion skin under the microscope. You will see that the skin looks rather like a brick wall. Each of the brick-like units is called a **cell**. (Find out who first called these units cells, and why he gave them that name.)

Draw some onion cells.

Cut onion in half. Remove one of the thick leaves.

Remove part of the inside skin.

Place a piece of skin about 10 mm long onto a slide.

Cover the skin with a drop of water.

Slowly lower a cover slip over the water.

Examine under the microscope.

Fig. 6.2

Fig. 6.3 Onion cells

Covering the onion skin with iodine instead of water, repeat the above experiment. Draw some onion cells that are mounted in iodine. Your drawing should include a round structure in each cell. This is called the **nucleus** (the plural of this word is nuclei). The nucleus controls the behaviour of the cell. On your diagram label the nucleus.

Note carefully that although you can see cells under the microscope you *cannot* see atoms or molecules. Each cell contains millions of molecules. Also, do not confuse the nucleus of a cell with the nucleus of an atom.

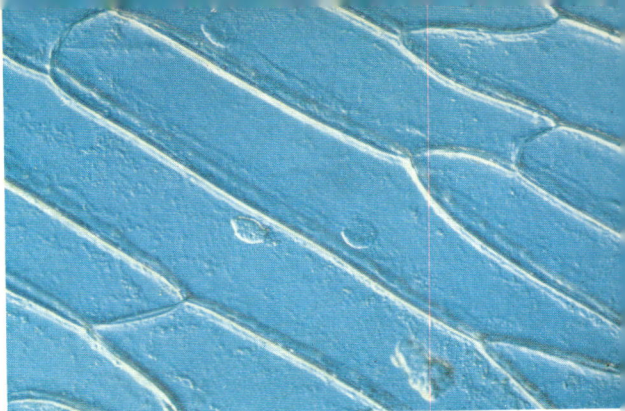

Experiment 6.3

Look at the other plant material provided. Are all plant cells alike?

Experiment 6.4
Are you made of cells?

We do not need to cut you up to find this out. There is a very easy way to remove part of you.

Place one drop of iodine solution or methylene blue solution on a slide. Scrape the inside of your cheek with the blunt end of a clean scalpel or with your finger nail, if this is clean. Touch the surface of the iodine solution with the scalpel or your nail. Cover the iodine solution with a cover slip as you did in the previous experiments. Examine the cells under the microscope, first under low or medium power, and then under high power. Draw some cheek cells. Do cheek cells contain nuclei?

Experiment 6.5
Are cells alive?

Your teacher will have some slides under microscopes for you to examine. These slides contain the leaf of a water plant. Look at the cells. Can you see small green circles in them? These are called **chloroplasts**. What is happening to the chloroplasts? Are the cells living? Give a reason for your answer.

The living things you have looked at so far have had many cells. Some living things consist of one cell only. Most of these organisms are found in water.

Experiment 6.6
Looking at single celled organisms

Your teacher will give you a liquid which contains single celled organisms. Look at a drop of it under your microscope. What do you notice about these cells? Do you think all the organisms are animals? Give a reason for your answer. Does your drinking water contain organisms? Find this out for yourself.

Experiment 6.7
Other plant cells

Look at the flower provided. With the help of the diagram below, find a stamen. Carefully

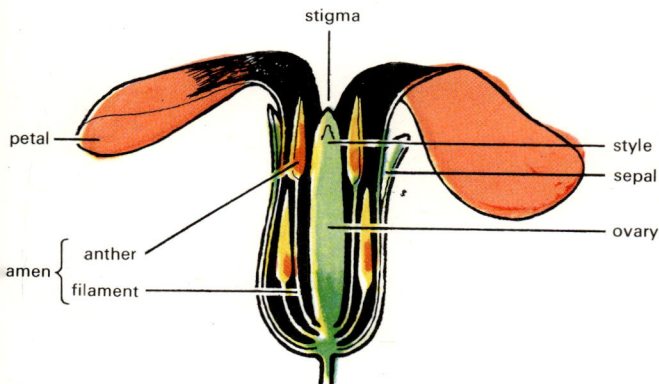

Fig. 6.4

remove the stamen. Each stamen is made up of a stalk or filament and a head or anther. Put the anther on a slide and burst it with a mounted needle. Under the microscope examine the yellow dust produced. This yellow dust is called **pollen**. Draw some pollen grains.
  Pollen grains contain special cells called **sex cells**. The sex cells in pollen are male.
  Remove the ovary from the flower. Cut across it with a knife. Using a hand lens look for small spherical structures in the ovary. These are **ovules**, and they contain female sex cells.

Experiment 6.8

Look at the pollen grains produced by different flowers. Are they all identical? Draw the different grains.

Experiment 6.9
Growing pollen

You will be provided with slides which have a thin coat of a sugary jelly on one side of them. Shake some pollen on to this jelly. Place the slide on moist filter paper in a closed Petri dish. Put the Petri dish in a warm incubator. After about 2 hours remove the slide and examine the pollen grains. Look at slides prepared in a similar way one day previously. What has happened to the pollen grains? Draw a few of them. The tubes produced by the pollen grains grow down the style to the ovules. When the nucleus of the male cell enters an ovule it unites with the nucleus of the female cell. This process is called **fertilization**.

6.4 SEX CELLS IN ANIMALS

The sex cells of animals are usually difficult to obtain, but they can be got fairly readily from the marine worm *Pomatoceros*. Have you ever picked up a stone from the beach and found it covered with thin, white tubes? These tubes may contain *Pomatoceros*. Your teacher will give you a stone with a number of these tubes on it. Look carefully at the tube and you will see that one end is open, the other is closed. Touch the open end with the point of your pencil. If you see a quick movement in the tube it means that there is a worm inside. In order to examine the worm you must remove it from its tube.

Experiment 6.10
Looking at Pomatoceros

The diagrams show you how to remove the worm.

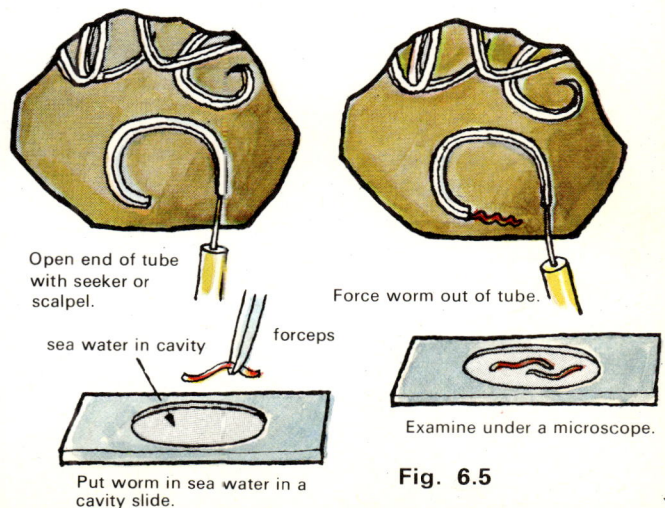

Fig. 6.5

Some worms have pink tentacles; they are female. Those with yellow tentacles are male.

Mount a female worm in sea water on a cavity slide, and examine it under the medium power of your microscope. Move the slide until you see the side of the worm. Look for round, brownish pink cells. These are egg cells or **ova**. In the same way look at the side of a male worm. Can you see any signs of movement in the liquid around the worm? This movement indicates that there are male sex cells or **sperms** present. You will probably have some difficulty in seeing the sperms because they are so small.

Notice the difference in size between the ova and the sperms. How does the shape of the sperm differ from that of the ovum? Can you suggest a reason for the difference?

Experiment 6.11
Mixing eggs and sperms

Your teacher has already removed some *Pomatoceros* from their tubes. The males and females are in separate dishes. With a clean pipette, put a drop of liquid containing egg cells on to a slide. Using another pipette, add a drop of liquid containing sperms to it. Can you see the sperms moving around an egg cell? There are probably thousands of sperms bombarding it, and one will actually enter the egg cell. The sperm nucleus fuses with the egg nucleus and the ovum is fertilized. After fertilization has taken place a clear zone appears round the egg. This prevents any more sperms entering.

Experiment 6.12
What happens to an egg after fertilization?

Look at the slide containing ova of *Pomatoceros* which were mixed with sperms earlier in the day. Draw a fertilized ovum. What difference is there between this ovum and the one drawn earlier?

After an egg has been fertilized it splits to form two cells. Each of these cells divides into two so that four cells are formed. This process is repeated until a new organism which is made of millions of cells is formed.

Fig. 6.6 Toads mating

6.5 FERTILIZATION IN WATER

Sperms from *Pomatoceros* are shed into the sea. They swim towards the female cells. Many of the sperms are swept away by the water and die. Millions of sperms are produced by each male worm and some will survive to fertilize the ova.

Most fish use this method of fertilization in water. In order to improve the chances of the ova being fertilized, the fish pair off before spawning takes place. The female trout for example digs a hole in the gravel on the river bed and lays her eggs in this. The male then covers the eggs with sperms. A large percentage of the eggs will thus be fertilized.

Amphibians, such as frogs and toads, also depend on water for fertilization to take place. Pairing takes place before the female lays her eggs. The male, which is smaller than the female, sits on her back. She lays her eggs in the water and the male secretes sperms over them. This ensures that a large number of eggs are fertilized.

Fig. 6.7 Locusts mating

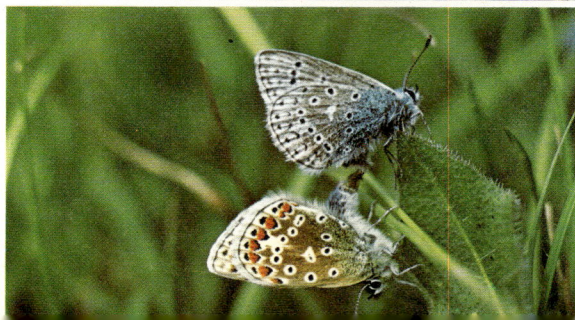

Fig. 6.8 Common blue butterflies mating

6.6 FERTILIZATION WITHOUT WATER

How do animals that live on land achieve fertilization? There is no water through which the sperms can pass to reach an egg. If fertilization is to be achieved, sperms must be deposited beside the egg, inside the body of the female. Look at Fig. 6.7. The male locust is sitting on the back of the female. Look closely and you will see that the end of the male's abdomen is inside the body of the female. The male injects sperms into her body and fertilization takes place. This is called **internal fertilization**. As well as overcoming the need for water, internal fertilization ensures that no sperms are wasted. As there is a better chance of eggs being fertilized, fewer eggs are produced at one time by land animals than by aquatic animals.

Sperms are made by the male reproductive organs, the **testes**. Sperms leave the body of most land animals through a special part of the male abdomen, the **penis**.

6.7 FERTILIZATION IN MAN

When a baby girl is born her ovaries contain many egg cells. When she is about twelve years old certain changes take place inside her body and these cause an egg cell to leave an ovary and pass into an oviduct. This process is called **ovulation**. Ovulation occurs about once every 28 days and it occurs regularly until the woman is about fifty. Most of the egg cells produced are not fertilized and these cells break up and pass out of the body.

A man starts to produce sperms when he is about twelve or thirteen years old, and does so for the rest of his life.

Fertilization occurs when sperms meet an ovum as it passes down an oviduct. To achieve this the penis is inserted into the vagina of the female and sperms are deposited near the neck of the uterus. The sperms swim up the uterus to the oviduct. If an ovum is in the oviduct, fertiliza-

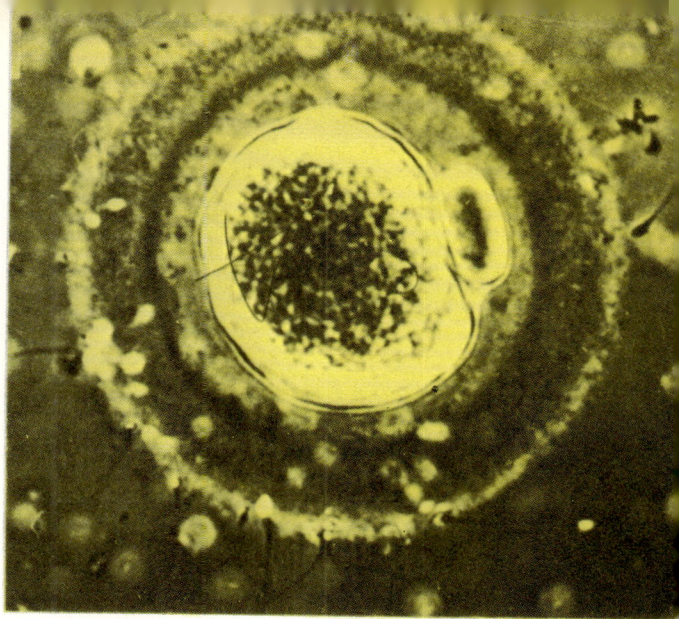

Fig. **6.10** A human ovum. Can you see the sperm swimming about around it?

tion takes place. Although many millions of sperms may be present, only one will fertilize the egg. The fertilized egg passes into the uterus and becomes embedded in its wall. There the egg cell starts to divide and an **embryo** is formed.

Each time ovulation occurs the wall of the uterus changes to receive the fertilized egg. It becomes spongy and rich in blood vessels. If the egg passing into the uterus has not been fertilized, the lining of the uterus is not required. It breaks away and passes, together with some blood, out of the body through the vagina. This process is called **menstruation**, and like ovulation it occurs regularly about once every 28 days.

6.8 HOW DO PLANTS ACHIEVE FERTILIZATION?

For fertilization to occur in a flowering plant, pollen must be transferred from an anther to a stigma. This transfer of pollen is called **pollination**. Look back at Fig. 6.4. The anthers are

Fig. **6.9** Human male and female reproductive organs

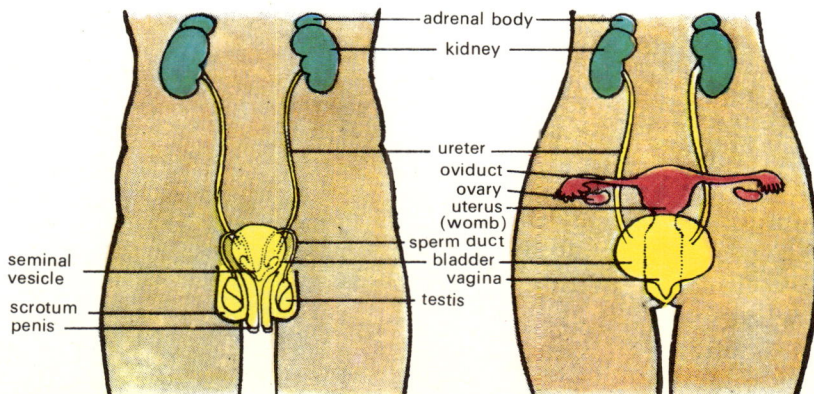

adrenal body
kidney
ureter
oviduct
ovary
uterus (womb)
sperm duct
bladder
vagina
testis
seminal vesicle
scrotum
penis

Fig. 6.11 Wind and insect pollinated flowers

Plant embryos

Fig. 6.12 Broad bean seed opened to display embryo

arranged above the stigma and so pollen can fall on to it. However, in some plants pollen is carried from the anthers of one flower to the stigmas of a similar flower. It may be carried by insects or by wind.

The pollen grains produce tubes after they land on the stigma. These grow down into the ovary, where they penetrate an egg cell or ovule, and the male cell passes down the tube into the ovule, as was explained on page 95. If you touched the surface of a stigma, what would you expect to feel? Give a reason for your answer. Look at Fig. 6.11 above. Which flowers are pollinated by insects and which are pollinated by wind? Suggest reasons for your answers.

6.9 LOOKING AT EMBRYOS

Animals and plants develop from a single fertilized egg. After fertilization the egg divides repeatedly. The developing plant or animal is called an **embryo**.

Open the soaked broad bean seed and separate the two halves carefully. With the aid of Fig. 6.12 find the embryo. The two large cream-coloured structures contain food. Put a few drops of iodine solution on to one of these structures. What happens? What is in the seed? (If you cannot remember this test, turn back to page 88.) Does the embryo contain food? What will happen to the size of the food store as the embryo grows? Give a reason for your answer.

Experiment 6.14
The growing embryo

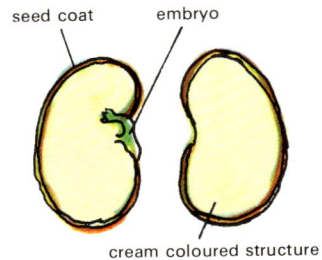

You have been given a number of plants. These are of different age, from one day to ten days from germination. Examine the plants and complete a table like the one opposite.

Measure the shoots and leaves of each plant and draw a graph.

	Age in days									
	1	2	3	4	5	6	7	8	9	10
Are there roots present?										
Is the shoot visible?										
On which day does the shoot appear above the ground? (Mark with X)										
Are green leaves visible?										
How many leaves are visible?										
In what ways are the first leaves different from the later ones?										
Can you suggest where the first leaves came from?										

6.10 ANIMAL EMBRYOS

The embryos of most mammals develop inside the mother's body. The embryos of birds and most other vertebrates develop in eggs outside the mother's body. You are going to watch the development of the chick embryo. Examine the incubator in the laboratory, and feel how warm it is. What is the temperature of the incubator? Why is it set at this temperature? Look for a tray of water at the bottom. The air inside must be moist. Can you think why? You may be able to answer this one later.

A number of hens' eggs are marked, possibly with the date. Place the eggs in the incubator so that the mark on each can be seen. Turn the eggs twice a day. Choose two pupils from your class to do this. They must also check that there is water in the tray.

Experiment 6.15
Looking at chick embryos

To examine an embryo you must first remove it from the shell. Fig. 6.13 shows you how to do this.

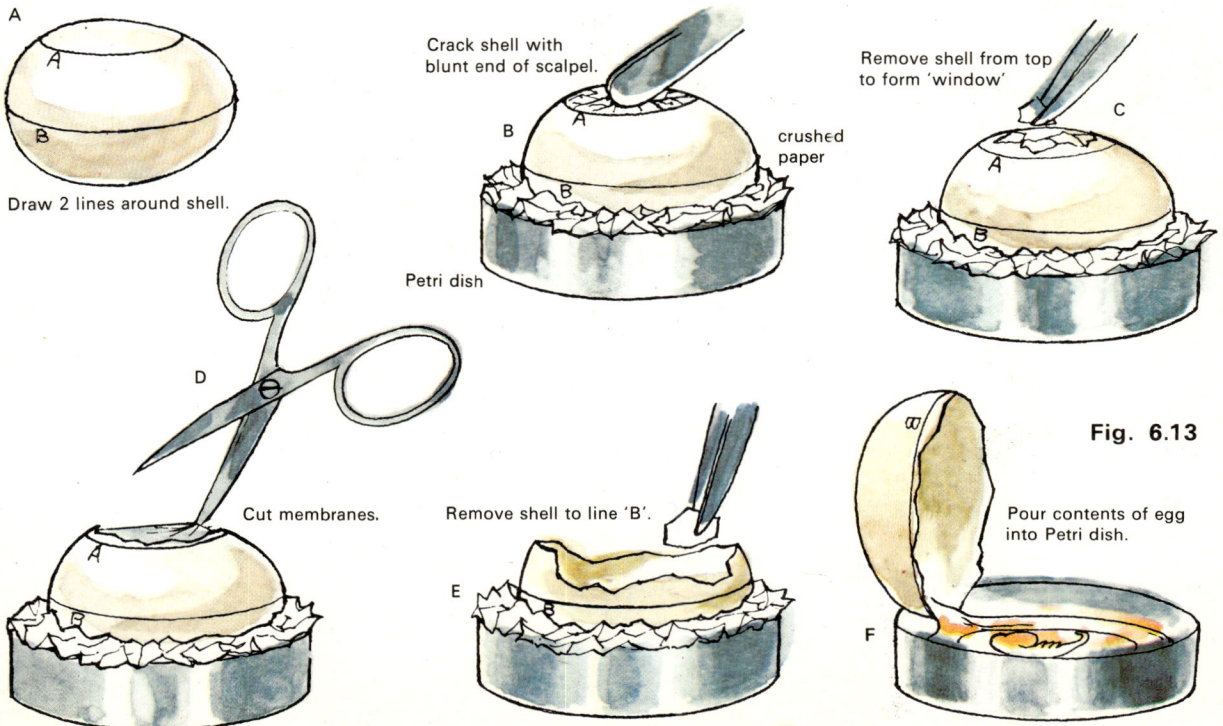

A — Draw 2 lines around shell.

Crack shell with blunt end of scalpel. / crushed paper / Petri dish

Remove shell from top to form 'window'

D — Cut membranes.

E — Remove shell to line 'B'.

F — Pour contents of egg into Petri dish.

Fig. 6.13

Structure observed	Age of embryo in days	Age of embryos in days						
Blood vessels on yolk								
Heart								
Head distinct from body								
Eyes present								
Beak formed								
Egg tooth present								
Wings forming								
Legs forming								
Feathers developing								
Digits on wings								
Digits on feet								

Remove the embryos from eggs that have been 3½, 5, 7, and 10 days in the incubator. Look at the embryos and complete a table like the one above. Complete your table when you have gathered the necessary information from other members of the class. Look at the amount of yolk attached to each embryo and the number of blood vessels covering the yolk.

Measure each embryo and plot this information in the form of a graph.

Experiment 6.16
An experiment for those of you who can observe and record

For this experiment you need an egg which has been in the incubator for 3½ days. Prepare a table for your results in your note book. Make a window in the top of the shell. Fill a dish three-quarters full with water at 38 °C. Slowly lower the egg into the dish. If the water does not cover

Fig. 6.14 Stages in the development of a chick embryo
(*top left*) 72 hours,
(*top centre*) 5 days,
(*top right*) 7 days,
(*bottom left*) 10 days,
(*bottom centre*) 15 days,
(*bottom right*) 21½ days — the chick is 12 hours old

the egg, carefully pour some in until the egg is just covered. Take the temperature of the water. Look for the embryo heart beating. With the aid of a stop clock, count the number of times the heart beats in one minute. In the table record the number of heart beats and the temperature of the water. Using a syringe withdraw some of the warm water, and then add some cold. Take the temperature of the water, then count the number of times the heart beats in one minute at this temperature. Repeat this until the temperature of the water is about 28 °C. For every new temperature count the heart beats. Try warming the water up again. Make a graph like the one below. What is the connection between the rate at which the heart beats and the temperature of the surroundings? If you remove an egg from the incubator and leave it in the laboratory, what will happen to the embryo? Give reasons for your answer.

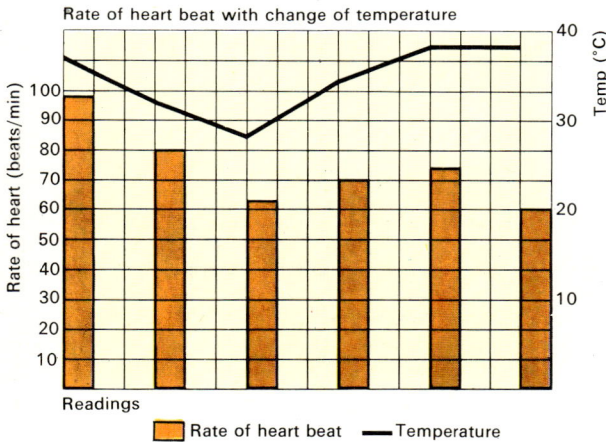

Fig. 6.15

Some questions for you to answer

1. Below is a diagram of a section through a hen's egg.

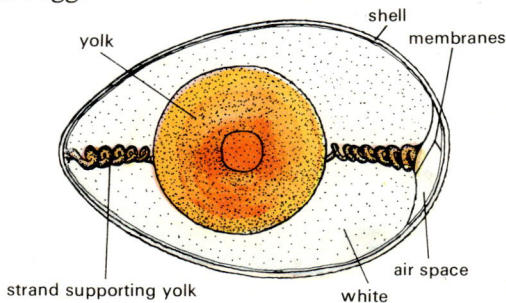

What is the purpose of
  (a) the shell
  (b) the air space
  (c) the membranes
  (d) the white
  (e) the yolk?
Give reasons for your answers.
2. Why should the eggs be turned each day?
3. When you take an egg from the incubator, why should you hold it the same way up as it was in the egg tray?
4. How did the food get into the chicken?
5. An egg which has been in the incubator for ten days is opened. No embryo is found inside. Why has an embryo not developed inside this egg?

Leave about six eggs in the incubator and allow these to hatch. If you can, watch the chickens coming out of their shells and answer the following questions.

1. What is the function of the egg tooth?
2. What does the chicken look like when it comes out of its shell?
3. Can you see any yolk?
4. What does the membrane inside the shell look like?

When the chickens are dry and fluffy, weigh them. Do this every day for two or three weeks. Put this information in the form of a graph.

Looking after your chickens

Until the chickens are about four days old they will need to be kept warm. After that they can be put into a brooder, which can be made from a large box. Give them food and water each day. When they are about three weeks old, try to find a good home for them on a farm or give them to someone who keeps hens.

6.11 MAMMALIAN EMBRYOS

To see mammalian embryos we shall have to look inside the body of the mother. We shall open up a killed pregnant rat. Look at the rat. How can you tell that she is pregnant?

When the skin and muscle layer have been opened and pinned back, look inside. Using Fig. 6.16 find the liver. What colour is it? Why is it this colour? The liver is an **organ**. Organs are made up of groups of cells, which do different jobs. A group of similar cells doing the same job

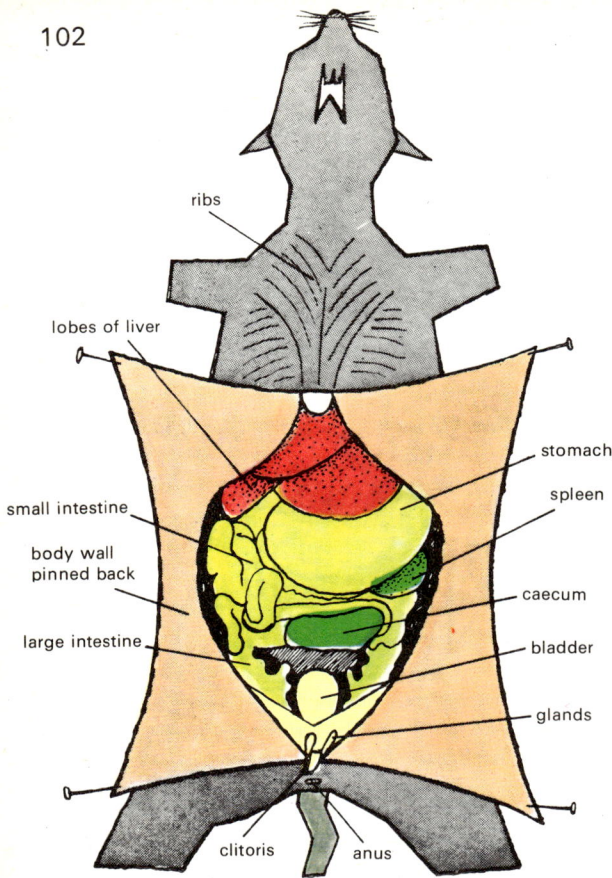

Fig. 6.16 (*above*) Rat opened to show internal organs and (*below*) pregnant rat opened to show embryos

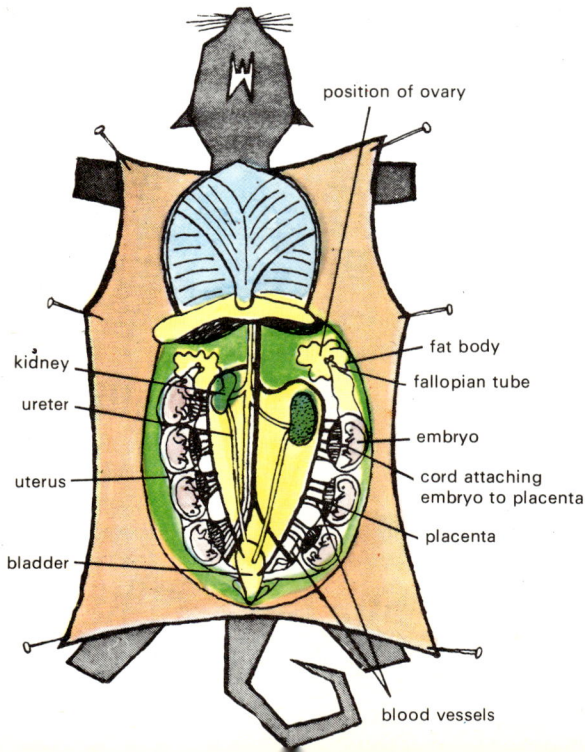

is called a **tissue**, and so organs are made up of tissues. Substances made by the liver pass into a tube called the small intestine, which is part of the digestive **system**. A system is made up of a number of organs. Can you name another system found in the body? Unravel the intestine and remove it. How long is it? When the intestine has been removed you should be able to see the reproductive system. There will be a number of embryos in each uterus. How many are there? How many eggs have been produced at one time from the ovaries?

Experiment 6.17
Looking at the embryos

Remove an embryo from the uterus. The red disc attached to it is called the **placenta**. What does its colour suggest to you? The placenta was embedded in the wall of the uterus. Food and oxygen pass from the mother's bloodstream through the placenta to the bloodstream of the embryo rat. Cut the wall of the sac enclosing the embryo. What is the function of the liquid you found inside the sac? How is the placenta attached to the embryo?

Fig. 6.17 shows human embryos at different stages in their development. Compare these embryos with the chick embryos and the rat embryos. How is each embryo fed and protected? Why is the egg of a hen larger than that of a human?

6.12 BIRTH OF A BABY

A human baby remains in the uterus of the mother for nine months. This is called the **gestation period**. At the end of this time the liquid surrounding the baby flows out of the body, and contractions of the wall of the uterus force the baby out of the vagina. The baby is usually born head first. The cord attaching the baby to the placenta, the umbilical cord, is cut and the baby becomes independent. The placenta comes away from the wall of the uterus and passes out of the body as the afterbirth.

6.13 GESTATION PERIODS OF OTHER ANIMALS

On page 104 is a table which shows the gestation periods of a number of animals.

Work out the gestation period of the mammals in your laboratory and make a table like the one shown.

Fig. 6.17 Stages in the development of a human embryo (a) 24 hours, (b) 4 weeks, (c) 8 weeks, (d) 10 weeks, (e) 20 weeks

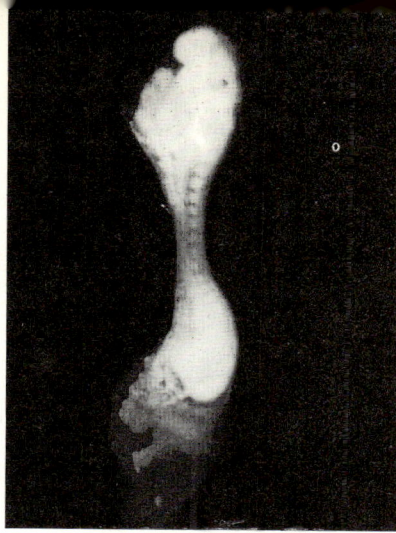

(a)

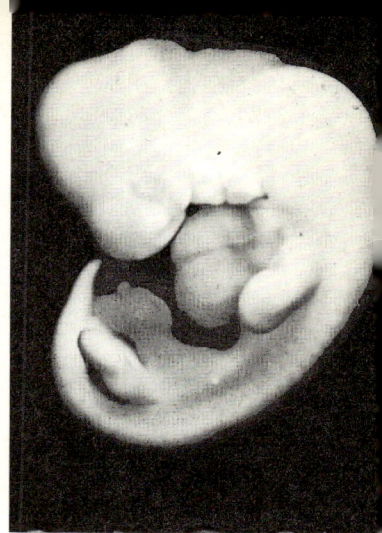

(b)

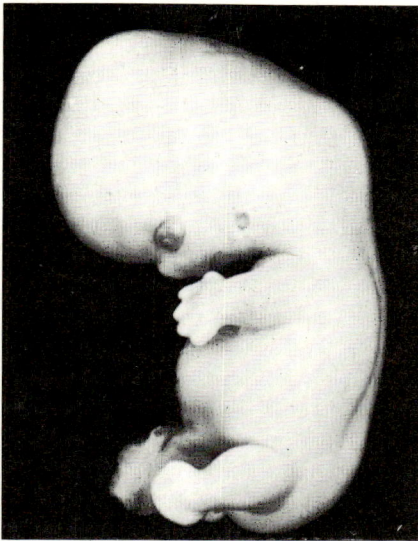

(c)

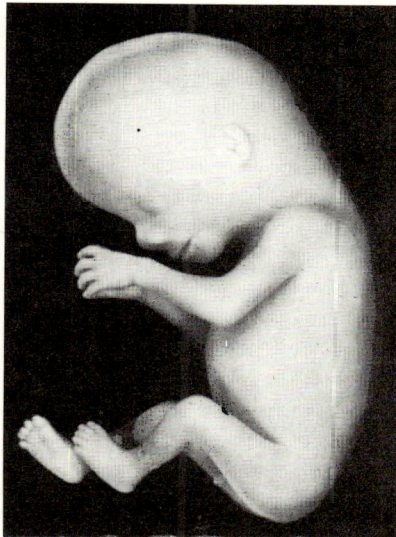

(d)

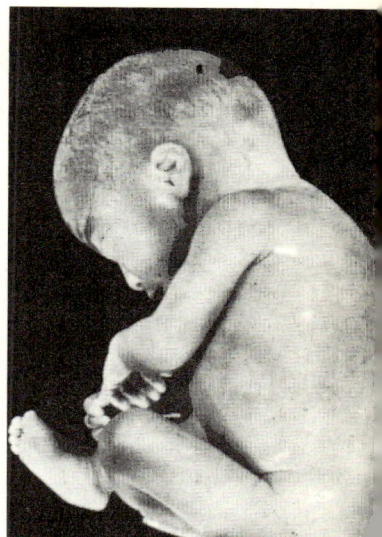

(e)

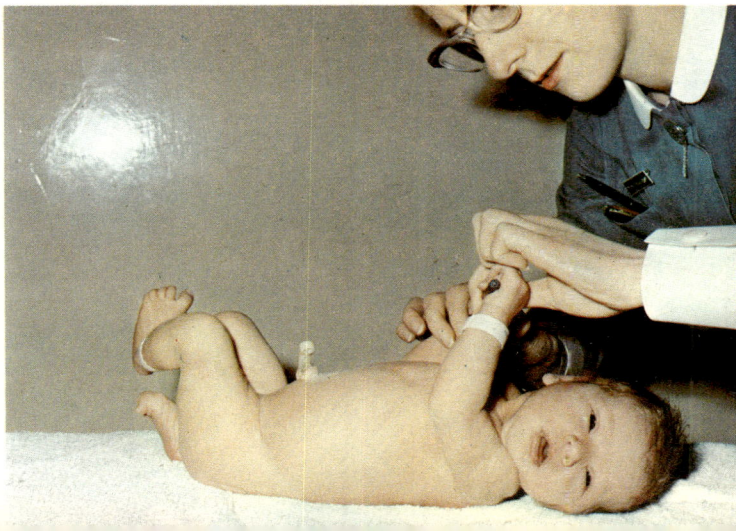

Fig. 6.18
A new born baby

Gestation periods of a few animals

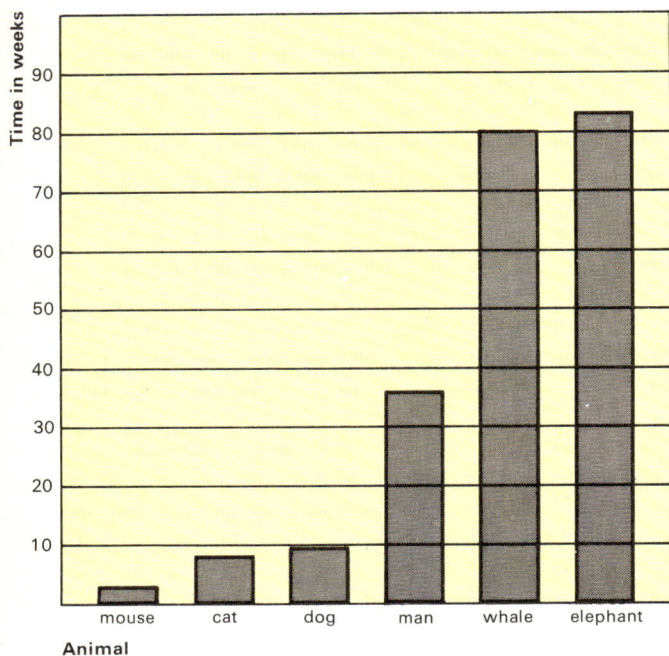

Animal: mouse, cat, dog, man, whale, elephant
Time in weeks (y-axis: 10, 20, 30, 40, 50, 60, 70, 80, 90)

6.14 YOUNG ANIMALS

How many kinds of young animals do you have in your laboratory? You may have the young of several of the following – mice, guinea pigs, locusts, trout, and frogs. How are these young animals fed? Young mammals are suckled: they drink milk made by special glands – the **mammary glands** – in their mother's body. Young locusts eat grass, just as their parents do.

Certain young animals are very similar in appearance to their parents; others look quite different. Look at Fig. 6.19, which shows a number of animals and their young.

Keep a record of the development of the young animals in your laboratory. If your class is divided into groups, each group can study a different animal. Pin a record sheet, like the one on the next page, beside the cage or aquarium of each animal so that others can see how your animal is developing.

Fig. 6.19 Animals and their young: (*top left*) blackbird and young, (*top right*) frog, (*bottom right*) tadpoles, (*bottom left*) baby mice, and (*bottom centre*) adult mouse.

Name of organism	. . . .	
Record sheet kept by	. . . .	
Class	. . . .	
Date	Length of organism	Additional features e.g. appearance of limbs or wings

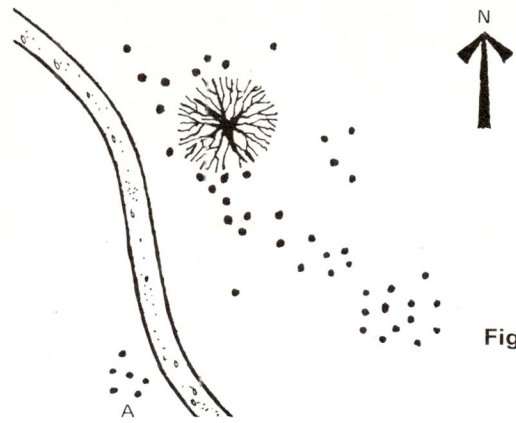

Fig. 6.21

Draw graphs to show the rate of growth of your animal. Compare your graph with those drawn by other groups. How does the growth curve of a locust differ from that of a chick or a mammal? What does the graph tell you about the growth of the locust? Look in the locust cage. Can you see any skins lying on the bottom? Mark on the graph when the skins are shed.

6.15 YOUNG PLANTS

Seeds develop in the ovaries of plants. If all the seeds dropped from the plant on to the ground below and grew, they would soon become over-crowded and die. The seeds must be carried away from the parent plant or **dispersed**. To aid the dispersal, the ovary wall or the receptacle in certain plants changes. Fig. 6.20 shows some of these changes.

Fig. 6.20 Fruits which are dispersed: (*top left*) dandelion, (*top centre*) acorns, (*top right*) apples, (*bottom left*) rosebay willow herb, (*bottom centre*) sycamore, (*bottom right*) lupin.

Suggest how these fruits are dispersed. A **fruit** is the name given to an ovary with a seed inside.

Some pupils should study a sycamore tree in a field. They should look for sycamore seedlings growing in the field and make a map showing the position of the tree and of the seedlings found.

With the help of the map, work out the prevailing wind. Can you suggest a reason why seedlings were found at region A in Fig. 6.21? Carry out a similar project using a tree near your school or home.

WHAT YOU HAVE LEARNT IN THIS UNIT

1. Living things are made up of cells. These cells are of different kinds according to the kind of organism they come from and the purpose they serve.

2. A group of similar cells doing the same job is called a **tissue**. An organ, such as the liver, the heart or the kidney, is made up of tissues. A **system** is made up of a number of organs which together have a certain job to do. Thus, in the human body we have a digestive system, composed of those organs which are concerned with the job of getting our food into our bloodstream; a nervous system, which is composed of organs which are concerned with transmitting messages from different parts of the body to the brain and taking back the responses; and so on.

3. Cells from plants are usually regular in shape – like bricks; but those from animals are not.

4. Cells contain a nucleus which controls the working of the cell.

5. Some plants and animals consist of only one cell; a complicated animal like man has millions of them, organized to do special jobs of work.

6. You have come across the following kinds of cell in this unit: cells from onion skin, cells from your cheek, male sex cells (sperm cells), female sex cells (ova or egg cells); but, of course, there are many other kinds.

7. One of the things that a living organism can do which non-living matter cannot is to reproduce itself, that is, make new organisms of the same kind as itself. This is accomplished through the sex cells. When the nucleus of a male sex cell unites with the nucleus of a female sex cell, we say that fertilization has taken place. The fertilized cell splits to form two cells; these two

split again to form four; and so on. This goes on until a new organism made of millions of cells is formed. This process takes place both in plants and animals.

8. To produce cells capable of uniting like this, plants and animals must be sufficiently mature.

9. Only one sperm cell can enter an egg cell, although thousands of sperm cells may try to do so.

10. Fertilization can be achieved either **externally** or **internally**. In external fertilization the male and female cells meet outside the female's body. In internal fertilization they meet inside the female's body.

11. In most animals that live in the sea fertilization is external. They use water to take the male cells to the female ones. As a lot of the sperm cells get washed away and never get near an egg cell to fertilize it, this method is very wasteful. Some fish (e.g. the trout) overcome the difficulty by the female laying her eggs in a safe place where they will not be washed away, and the male then secretes sperm over them.

Amphibians, such as the toad, pair off – one male to one female. Both get close together (with the frog the male sits on the female's back) so that when the female lays her eggs the male can shed sperm over them immediately.

12. Most land animals use internal fertilization. In this case the male deposits sperm cells close to the egg cells inside the female's body.

13. Plants achieve fertilization by pollen grains being dropped on to the stigma of another flower. Pollen grains contain male cells. The pollen grows a tube down the style, the column of which the stigma is the top. Each one penetrates an egg cell in the ovary, and the nucleus of a male cell then passes down the tube into the egg cell.

14. The developing animal or plant before it is 'born' is called an **embryo**.

15. When an embryo develops inside the mother's body, food and protection come from the mother. A hen's egg is therefore larger than the egg of an elephant or any other mammal.

16. The time during which the embryo develops inside the mother's body is called the **gestation period**. It varies from one animal to another. For humans it is nine months.

Unit Seven Electricity

In Unit 3 you have already carried out a number of experiments that had to do with electricity, and now we are going to learn more about the subject.

7.1 ELECTRICAL CHARGES

The ladies of ancient Greece were fond of wearing beads of amber. As they moved about the beads would rub against their clothes. They were often surprised that the beads sometimes sparked or attracted tiny pieces of fluff. We know now that these things happened because the amber beads had become 'charged' with electricity. Indeed the Greek word for 'amber' is *elektron* and it is from this word that we get the word *electricity* in English. Have you heard of 'electronics'? Later in the course you will understand more fully the meaning of this word.

Here are some experiments for you to do. Some you may do at school, while the remainder may easily be done at home. Remember that *you*

must never do any experiments with the mains supply of electricity unless you have had clear instructions what to do.

Experiment 7.1

Rub a blown-up balloon on a piece of woollen material — your jersey or blazer will do. Hold it near a pile of small pieces of paper. What happens? What does this tell you has happened to the balloon by rubbing it?

Now take two balloons which you have rubbed like this, hold one in each hand at arm's length, just touching, and let them go. Do they fall straight down or do they go apart sideways first?

They have both been rubbed with the same kind of material, and so presumably they both have the same kind of charge. Do they attract or repel each other?

Experiment 7.2

Here is another way of finding out about charges. You have four strips of plastic. Two are cellulose acetate (the clear ones), the others are polystyrene (the opaque ones — the ones you cannot see through). Rub one of these strips with a duster and then balance it on the watch glass. Now bring near it a rod of the same kind which you have rubbed with the same duster, and observe what happens as you bring the ends near each other. Do they attract or repel? Each strip has obviously been given the same charge because they were both treated in exactly the same way. What do like charges do to each other?

Fig. 7.1 Sticking a balloon on to the wall without glue! How is this done?

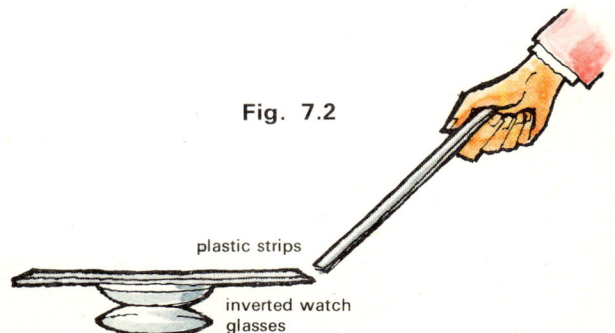

Fig. 7.2

plastic strips

inverted watch glasses

Now repeat the experiment using two strips of the other material. Do they attract or repel one another? Does this agree with what you found in the first part of the experiment?

Now rub a strip of one material and balance it on the watch glass, and bring up to it a strip of the other material which you have also rubbed. What happens this time? Can the charges be alike? If they are not they must be opposite or 'unlike'. What can we say that unlike charges do to each other?

No matter what different materials you might be able to charge by rubbing them, you would find that they either repel or attract the rod on the watch glass, and so we can say without any doubt that there are only two kinds of charge.

When rubbed with your duster the cellulose acetate strip usually becomes positively charged with electricity, while the polystyrene strip usually becomes oppositely charged, that is, negatively.

We have to say 'usually' in this statement because it depends on the material of which your duster is made.

Experiment 7.3

Fig. 7.3

Take a sheet of wrapping paper or a plastic bag and place it flat on a table. Now brush it vigorously with a clothes brush. Hold the sheet above the head of someone with fine hair who does not use hair oil or lacquer. What happens? What have you done to the sheet by rubbing it?

Experiment 7.4

Rub either a plastic fountain pen or a strip of material cut from an empty detergent bottle on a woollen cloth, and try to pick up some small pieces of wool or paper.

Experiment 7.5

Fig. 7.4

Take a sheet of glass and support it about 1 cm above a table top by letting it rest at the corners on pieces of plastic or plastic-covered books. On the table, under the glass, have some small pieces of paper. Now rub the glass with a cloth, preferably of silk. What happens to the paper underneath?

Some housewives dust glass mirrors with silk dusters. The dusters certainly rub dust off; but can you explain to these ladies why it is that very soon the mirrors are always much more thickly covered with dust a short time later?

Experiment 7.6

Some hearthrugs contain nylon. If you stand, wearing soft leather slippers, on a newly cleaned nylon rug and rub one foot on the rug, you can sometimes become charged with electricity yourself. When someone else touches you, you will hear a crackle as the charges jump from you to the other person. Even walking on nylon carpets can sometimes charge you up if the air is very dry.

Experiment 7.7

In school you will have a Van de Graaff generator, which is a machine for charging things up. When its motor is switched on, the dome of the machine becomes charged. It normally collects a positive charge. If your teacher points a finger at the dome, what happens? Some of you might be allowed to do this experiment for yourselves one at a time. The spark you see leaving your finger is due to charges being pulled out of your finger and then through the air with great force. Are these charges also positive charges? Obviously not, because like charges repel. We call these opposite charges 'negative'.

You will also see the effect of charges pulled through a neon bulb; it will glow when you hold it near the charged dome.

What happens when a wig is placed on the charged dome, as in Fig. 7.5? Can you explain why all the hair does not come together, but spreads out? This effect can be shown also with a pupil with fine hair. He should stand in a plastic basin and touch the dome lightly with one hand. If the boy now stretches out the other hand towards an unlit Bunsen with the gas on, what happens? The boy should always place one hand on the bench before he steps out of the basin. Can you suggest why it is best to do this?

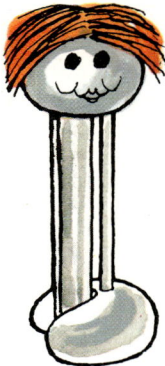

Fig. 7.5

Fig. 7.6 A modern MeV Van de Graaff generator (viewed from above) which is used to produce high-energy charged particles for nuclear research

Experiment 7.8

Here is a simple thing you can do at home. Try rubbing a balloon on your woollen clothes and then pushing the balloon against you. Does the balloon stick? Can you explain what has happened here? Your balloon will stick to other objects in the room such as upholstery or wallpaper, too, as in Fig. 7.1 on page 107.

7.2 ELECTRIC CHARGES IN NATURE

The air is always in motion and particles in the air can become charged. You will remember reading in Unit 5 about smoke particles being charged. Clouds can be very strongly charged, and aircraft flying near these clouds can themselves become charged and come down to land quite highly electrified. In the early days of flying, aircraft had a tail skid, and the charges escaped into the ground on landing. This did not happen when, later on, the skid was replaced by a rubber-tyred tail wheel.

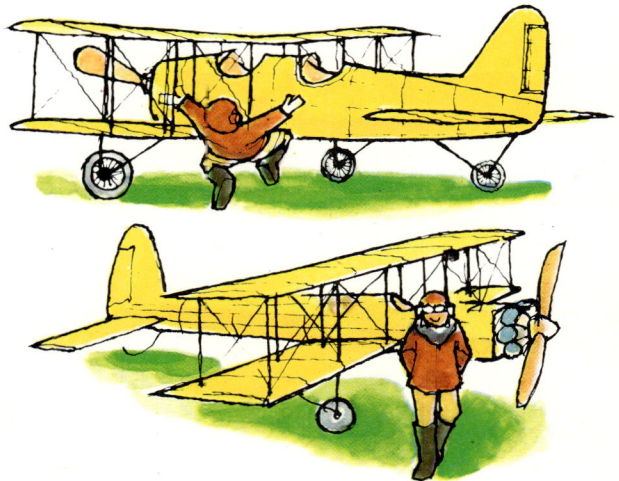

Fig. 7.7 (*Top*) A plane with a rubber-tyred tail wheel, (*bottom*) a plane with a tail skid

Airmen climbing out of these aircraft with rubber-tyred wheels got powerful electric shocks when they stepped on to the ground, and were sometimes flung some distance. Nowadays special tyres are used to allow the charges to get away from the aircraft before the passengers step out.

Perhaps you have had an electric shock when you have stepped off a bus while holding on to the bare metal hand-rail. Why do you think this happened? Why do road petrol tankers have metal chains dangling from them on to the road?

Some motorists have had the mistaken idea that electric charges which their cars might collect from the air can cause travel sickness, and they fit chains to let the charges leak away to the road. You must have seen the effect of charges jumping from cloud to cloud or from a cloud down to the ground. What name do we give to this? Why is it dangerous to stand under a tree or point an umbrella or a golf club up in the air when there is a thunderstorm?

7.3 ELECTRIC CHARGES ON CLOTHES

Many garments these days are made from plastic materials such as nylon. When we pull these garments over our heads so that they brush against our hair we hear crackling sounds. Why is this?

Not so long ago some surgeons in hospitals found that as they walked along their nylon coats became charged. Some anaesthetics are flammable and can explode if a spark is passed through the vapour. You can imagine that if a doctor whose coat was charged came near a patient on the operating table who had been given such an anaesthetic this could be very dangerous. One Scottish floor-covering firm devised special tiles for operating theatres which would carry away the charges from the surgeon's clothes so that accidents of this kind could not happen.

7.4 WHAT IS ELECTRICITY?

Experiment 7.9

When you connect up the battery, the bulb, and the meter as in Fig. 7.8, what happens to the pointer in the meter, and to the bulb? We say that what causes this is an electric current.

But what is an electric current? To find out we must go back to the Van de Graaff generator. It is a good idea to fit a pair of wooden leaves into a hole drilled in the dome. If you charge up the dome by switching on the motor, what do you notice happening to the wooden leaves? Why is this?

electrons

meter

gas tap

Fig. 7.9

Now find out what happens to the leaves if a boy points a finger towards the dome. What did we find in Experiment 7.7 about the type of charge being pulled out of his finger? If the leaves now collapse, what have the different kinds of charge done to each other?

Instead of pointing a finger towards the charged dome, a pupil may now bring up the free end of a long wire connected to a gas or water tap. Where do the sparks come from now – the wire or the finger? Cut the wire in two, bare the ends and connect them to the terminals of a very sensitive meter. Bring the free end of the wire up to the dome again. Watch both the wooden leaves and the needle of the meter. Do you see them both move together?

Negative charges are being attracted on to the positively charged dome, and there the charges are cancelling out. But as these negative charges move along the wire they make the needle of the meter move, and we know that this means that an electric current is passing through it. So we come to the conclusion that an electric current is a flow of charges.

Do you remember that in Unit 4 you came to the conclusion that matter was made up of atoms? You have found that when you rub a rubber balloon with your woollen clothes the balloon becomes charged, and so do your clothes. Where have these charges come from? They can only have come from the materials themselves, and hence from the atoms of which they are com-

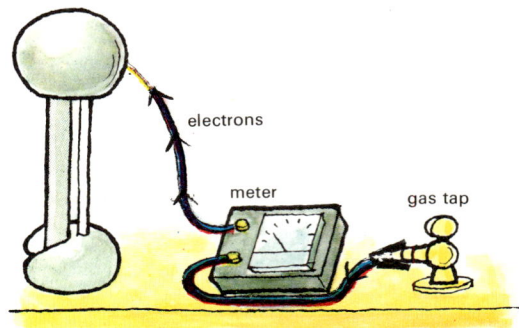

Fig. 7.8

posed. So we know something more about atoms. They must contain electricity. We call the negative charges in atoms **electrons**. As substances are not usually charged there must be in the atom somewhere or other just as many positive charges as it has negative ones, so that the whole atom is neutral. We think that the electrons in the atom are on the outside, and the positive charges, which we call **protons**, are deep inside it, in the nucleus of the atom. The word 'nucleus' here means the 'core', and is different from the nucleus of a cell.

7.5 ELECTRICITY IN MOTION

We can now visualize an electric current in a wire as a movement or flow of electrons hopping from the outside of one atom to the next. As each atom in the wire has both positive and negative charges in it, electricity is in the wire all the time. To get an electric current what we have to do is to make charges move. Can you name two things we have used so far to push or pull electrons from atom to atom? Of these the most handy for us to use is, of course, an electric **battery**, or a **cell**.

At this stage we must be quite clear about what we mean by a 'cell' and a 'battery'. A 'cell' is the unit of which a 'battery' is made. A battery consists of several cells connected together. To light a torch bulb you usually use a battery of two or three cells.

You are going to carry out quite a number of experiments on your own to find out about electric currents. The apparatus you will use is called a **circuit board**. Along with the board you will have a large number of pieces of equipment, or component parts. Underneath your circuit board you should have a diagram pasted telling you the names of these components and how many of them you should have. You must get into the habit of looking after these components carefully, and if any should be

missing you should let your teacher know before you start on the experiments. At the end of your work make sure that the complete set of components is handed back. On the list you will see some of the components are represented by symbols. Thus the symbol for one cell is ⊣⊢. The long stroke means the positive terminal of the cell, and the short one the negative. The electrons flow out along the wire connected to the negative terminal of the cell.

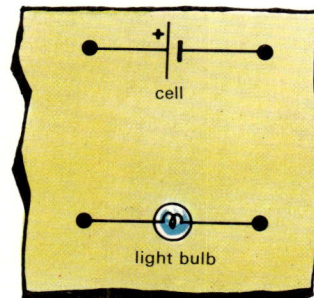

Fig. 7.11

Experiment 7.10
Making a circuit

Using your circuit board, connect up a cell and a bulb so that the bulb lights. Remember that you must be careful not to join the positive and negative ends of the cell together with connecting wires and switches because this would ruin the cell.

Now draw a diagram of the circuit you have made. What you have connected up is called a **complete circuit**. You should be able to see from your board and from your diagram that the electrons have a path to flow along from the negative terminal of the cell, through a lead to the bulb, and from the bulb through another lead back to the positive terminal of the cell. In other words the electrons are able to get back to where they started from.

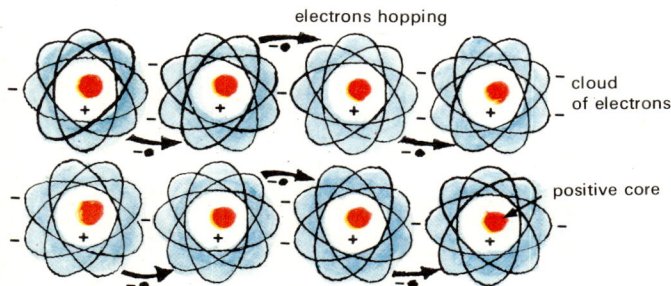

Fig. 7.10 Electrons in motion

Experiment 7.11
Conductors and insulators

If you take out one of your connector leads from your circuit, you can now find out what materials you could insert in its place and still get the bulb to light. You will have available strips of different materials to try. When the bulb lights, we say that you have 'completed the circuit', and the material you are using is a **conductor**. If the strip of material you have put in does not allow the lamp to light, the electrons are unable to flow through it and it is called an **insulator**.

Fig. 7.12 Is the material under test a conductor or an insulator?

In a table with two columns, one headed conductors, the other insulators, make a list of the conductors and insulators you have found. Is air a conductor or an insulator? Include it in your list.

How can we explain why some substances are conductors and others insulators? It is clear that in an insulator it is difficult to get the electrons to move from one atom to the next, whereas in a conductor it is easy. To what family of substances do most conductors belong? The electrons on the outside of atoms of metals must be more loosely held than those on the outside of insulators.

Experiment 7.12
Switches

When you have been replacing the connector lead with various conductors and so putting the bulb on and off, you have, as we say, been switching the current on and off. A switch is only something to make a gap in a circuit which

Fig. 7.13 A selection of switches

we can close or open at will. Open up as many types of switch as you can. Some are shown in Fig. 7.13. You will see that when the switch is off there is a gap between the metal contacts. What is there between the contacts when the switch is off? Is this a conductor or an insulator? We can close this gap by making a piece of metal swing into it. Then the switch is 'on'.

Something to do at home

Try to trace out the circuit in your torch, or the lighting system on your bicycle if you have a dynamo fitted. Often in a torch with a metal case the metal itself acts as one of the leads from the battery to the screw of the bulb. If the torch has a plastic case there must be some other way of doing it because the plastic is an insulator. Try to examine a torch with a plastic case and see how the circuit is completed or 'made' as we sometimes say. Have you spotted that the spring in a torch has two jobs to do? What does it do besides pushing the terminal of the cell against the bulb? Would a plastic spring do just as well?

Fig. 7.14 Trace the electrical circuit in the torch

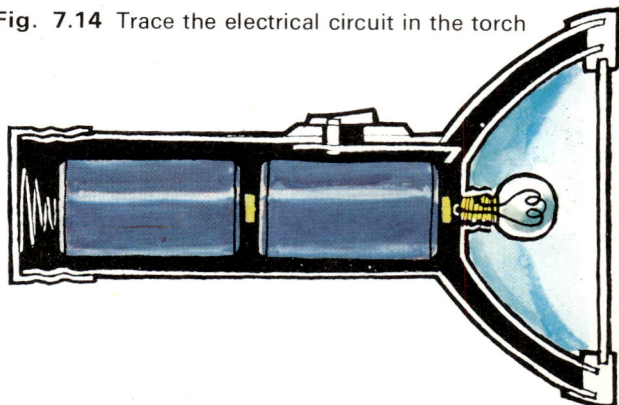

Experiment 7.13
A series circuit

Take two cells and three bulbs in their holders from the components that go with your circuit board and connect them up as you see in Fig. 7.15. The bulbs you are using have been chosen specially to be all the same, and so do not get them mixed up with anyone else's. Do you remember where the electrons start out in the circuit? Trace the path the electrons must be following in your circuit all the way round and back to the starting point. What do you notice about the brightness of the bulbs as you follow the circuit round? Does it seem as if the current gets any weaker as the electrons flow first through one bulb and then on to the other? In fact you should find that all the bulbs seem to be equally bright, and so the electric current, or the rate at which the electrons are flowing, must be the same all round the circuit. We call this a **series circuit**.

7.6 MEASURING CURRENT

We have been using the brightness of bulbs in this experiment as a guide to the size of the electric current passing. But it is not very easy to say for certain that one lamp is brighter than another, particularly if the difference in brightness is not very great. To find out more exactly whether the current is the same we have to use a meter. The instrument used to measure a current is called an **ammeter**, because the units in which we measure current are amperes (sometimes called 'amps' for short). Can you find out why the name ampere is used?

Experiment 7.14

Connect up the circuit with the three bulbs and the ammeter in place of one of the connecting links, as shown in Fig. 7.15. What does the pointer indicate? Connect the + on the meter to the + end of the cells. Now take the ammeter out and put it in place of one of the other connecting links. What does it read this time? Be careful to see that all your connections are tight.

Having done this with your own group's circuit board, try getting together with other groups and put ammeters into all the gaps in place of connectors. What do you notice about the readings on the meters? What happens to the readings and the bulbs as soon as the circuit is broken at any point?

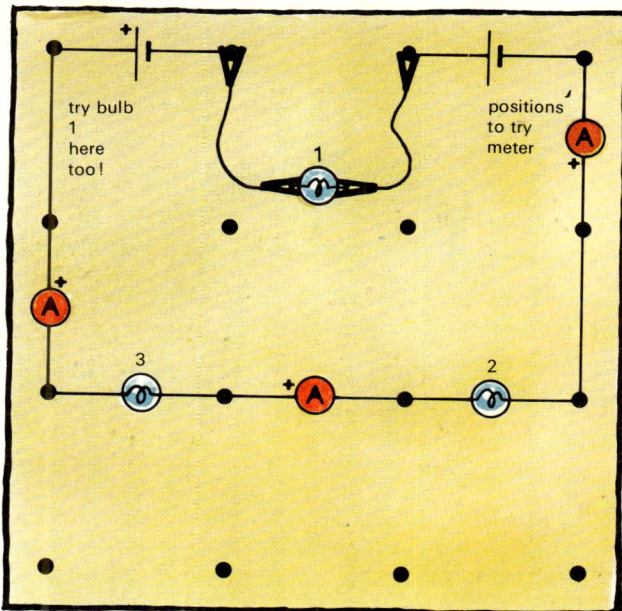

Fig. 7.15 (Note: Ordinary wire links should be used at all A's in Experiment 7.13)

Perhaps you have a set of lights at home with which you decorate your Christmas tree. How are they connected up? Can you remember what happens if one of the bulbs is loose in its holder, or broken? Do any of the bulbs light up then? Have you discovered how difficult it is to find which lamp is wrong when they do not light up? In what kind of circuit are these Christmas lights connected up?

Some boys and girls find it difficult to think of electrons flowing in a circuit because they cannot see them. Perhaps the following may help you. Think of water flowing along a pipe or a glass tube. To make water flow we might need a pump. What in your circuit makes the electrons flow and acts like a pump? We could say that water flows along at the rate of so many cubic centimetres per second. Each cubic centimetre of water is really many millions of particles flowing along the pipe each second. In an electric circuit the idea is just the same. When we have 1 ampere flowing this means that in each second 6 million million million (or 6×10^{18}) electrons are flowing through the circuit. What an ammeter really does then is to count the electrons which are flowing in one second through the circuit – a job we could not do ourselves.

Fig. 7.16 Counting trucks

When you come to think of it, the current in a series circuit must be the same throughout the circuit, because otherwise there would be a pile up of electrons somewhere. Suppose you were standing at the end of a tunnel watching a train pulling trucks going into the tunnel; and suppose you had a friend at the other end watching them come out. If you count say twenty trucks going into the tunnel in ten seconds, and your friend at the other end counted only fifteen coming out in ten seconds you would think there was something wrong, wouldn't you? There would have to be a pile up in the tunnel, or else some trucks must be falling through a hole in the line. You know that this is not the case. There must be the same number of trucks coming out as went in in the same time. So it is in a series circuit. There must be as many electrons going in one end as come out the other.

7.7 JOINING UP CELLS IN DIFFERENT WAYS

Experiment 7.15

In Experiment 7.10 you found out how to complete a circuit using one cell to light a single bulb. This time you are going to use two

Fig. 7.17 Will the lamp light?

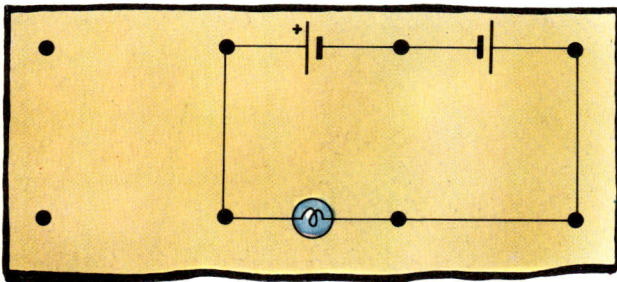

cells to light one bulb, and to find out if it lights brighter than it did with one cell. Put the two cells in the clips on the board any way round you like, and connect one bulb in series with them. Try turning one cell round the other way. What happens to the brightness of the lamp? You will find that, if you connect the + of one cell to the − of the next, the bulb will light much brighter than when you used one cell. If, however, you connect the + of one cell to the + of the other the lamp does not light at all. In the first case, + to −, the two cells obviously help each other; in the second they oppose each other and they give no electrons at all.

Your teacher will show you what happens when you use three cells in different arrangements. You will find that you always get the brightest result, and therefore most current, when the cells are all connected one way, the + of one to the − of the next. This is called connecting cells in series.

Try to examine an old car battery, and take to pieces an old PP9 or PP6 battery or a cycle lamp battery. You will see that the cells are all connected together either by bars or wires. To which terminal of a cell is the + of its neighbour connected? If your torch has a battery of two or more cells, notice how they have to be put in.

7.8 CURRENT IN PARALLEL BRANCHES

Experiment 7.16

On your circuit board fit up the circuit shown in Fig. 7.18, using connecting wires at A, B, and C. What do you notice about both bulbs? If you unscrew or disconnect one bulb does the other go out? Trace the path of the electrons and see that you understand why this happens.

Fig. 7.18

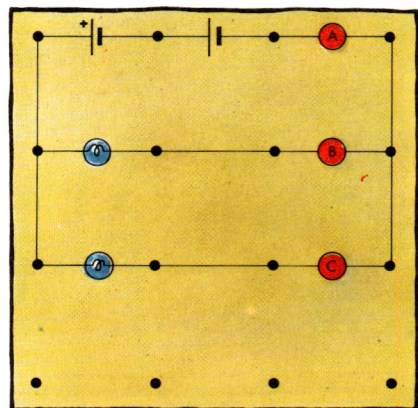

In this kind of circuit we say that the bulbs are connected in **parallel**. This method of connection has many advantages over connecting them in series. Can you think what they are? Do all the electric lights in your home or classroom have to be on at the same time? In which way must they have been connected – in series or in parallel?

Connect ammeters in the circuit in place of the links A, B, and C. Read carefully what each meter indicates. Add the readings of the meters at B and C together and compare the total with that shown by meter A. What do you find?

To help to understand this result think of a current of water passing point A and then finding a choice of path. Some of it flows along B and the remainder along path C, but quite obviously the total amount of water passing A must be the sum of the amounts passing B and C. This is rather like a flow of traffic too. Vehicles travelling along a busy road A come to a junction. Some branch off along road B, and the others along road C; but the total number of vehicles on roads B and C must be the same as the number that previously passed along road A.

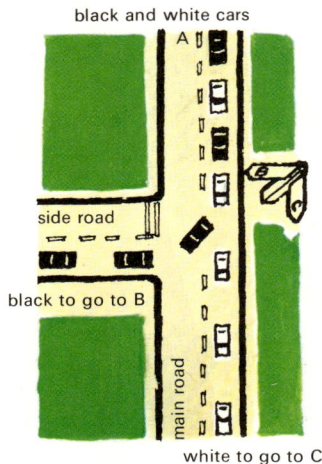

Fig. 7.20

been prepared for you. In some of these the wires are not broken. What should happen to the lamp in this case? What should happen if the wire is not complete? Sort the leads into different piles, one containing continuous wires, the other broken wires. An electrician might use this idea in his job.

If you were ever to try this experiment at home, remember that you must *never* interfere with appliances which are switched on, or even just plugged into the mains, even if they may not be working. You could, of course, quite safely test the lead to, say, an electric kettle *which you have unplugged from the mains* and from the kettle too. If you do this you should find three separate wires in the cable.

7.10 OPPOSING THE CURRENT

Experiment 7.18

Fit up the circuit shown in Fig. 7.21 on your circuit board. The wire XY is a piece of nichrome wire — the kind of wire used in heating

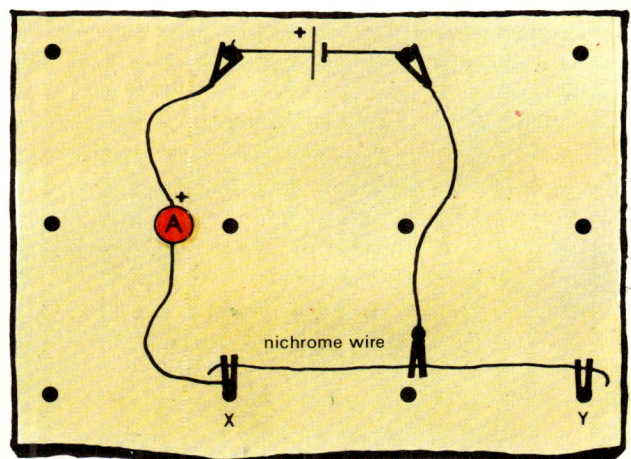

Fig. 7.19

7.9 A CIRCUIT TESTER

Experiment 7.17

A common fault with electrical appliances which have been in use at home for some time is that the wire inside the insulation breaks, and so the appliance does not work when it is switched on. Fit up a circuit like that in Fig. 7.20 and test a number of leads which have

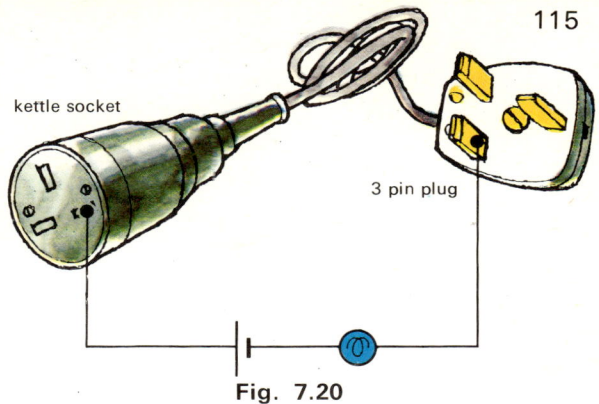

Fig. 7.21

appliances. Slide the clip from Y towards X along the wire. What happens to the bulb or the reading on the meter as you do this? As the clip moves nearer X, is more or less of the nichrome wire included in the circuit? As the length of nichrome wire is reduced, what happens to the size of the electric current flowing?

Do you think the current is managing to flow through this nichrome wire as easily as it does through your usual connecting links or copper leads? We say that the nichrome is opposing the flow of electrons through it, or that it is 'resisting' the current. So it is sometimes called 'resistance wire'. Which resists the current more, the shorter or the longer length of nichrome wire?

Now replace the length of wire XY with other pieces of nichrome wire of different thicknesses but the same length. The thickness of a wire is called its **gauge**; the smaller the number of the gauge of the wire the thicker the wire is. Thus 18 gauge wire is thicker than 24 gauge. Does the thickness of the wire have any effect on the size of the current? Why must we use equal lengths of wire in this experiment?

Now replace the nichrome wire with a variable resistor. Turn the knob both clockwise and anti-clockwise. Does this have any effect on the light from the bulb, or on the reading of the ammeter? Can you suggest what there is inside a volume control, and what turning the knob does? Now look at a volume control of which the inside is visible and see if you were right. Is yours similar to the type shown in Fig. 7.22.

As its name implies, this kind of variable resistance is used in radios and TV sets to change the volume of the output. Do you know of any other appliance where this idea is used? Some girls will have used electric sewing machines which have a foot pedal to control the speed of the machine. To get a big current to drive the machine fast what has to be done to the pedal? When it is pushed down what must happen to the length of resistance wire included in the circuit? Many boys will have model racing car sets or model trains. What do you do to the controls to speed up the cars or the trains? To make the cars go faster you need a bigger current. What must be happening to the length of resistance wire in the circuit as the cars are speeded up?

Perhaps your stage at school has some means of dimming the lights. Find out how this is done. Find out how a car fuel gauge works.

At fairgrounds the attendants can control the speed of the merry-go-rounds with large-scale versions of this type of control.

Variable resistances of this kind are called **rheostats**. A conductor which is used to cut down the flow of current is called a **resistor**.

You should have found that the longer the length of nichrome wire the greater is its resistance and the smaller the current through it. Using l for length, R for resistance, and I for current, we may represent this result in a diagram like this:

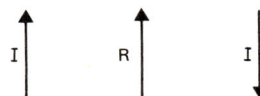

$$\uparrow l \qquad \uparrow R \qquad \downarrow I$$

Also you found that the thinner the wire the greater was its resistance. If t stands for thickness:

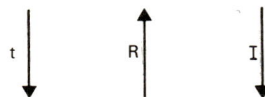

$$\downarrow t \qquad \uparrow R \qquad \downarrow I$$

Fig. 7.22 A variable resistor

These results make sense when we think of what happens when water flows through pipes or traffic flows along roads. The narrower the pipe or the narrower the road, the slower is the rate at which the water passes through the pipe or the traffic along the road.

It is interesting to try this experiment with other kinds of wire of the same gauge instead of nichrome to find out if they all have the same resistance. What else must be keep the same?

7.11 HEATING WITH THE ELECTRIC CURRENT

Experiment 7.19

As this experiment involves taking a very heavy current from an accumulator — in fact it is almost 'short circuited' — it is possible that your teacher will demonstrate this experiment. Fit up the circuit with an accumulator, a switch, and two lengths of copper wire of different thicknesses in series, as shown in Fig. 7.23. Watch

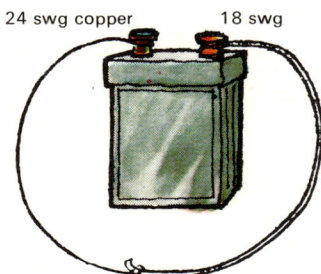

24 swg copper   18 swg

Fig. 7.23

what happens to the wires when the current is switched on. Touch the thick wire. Which wire is the hotter? What energy change has taken place? Which wire resisted the current more and used up more energy? What has happened to this energy?

Make a list of all the electrical appliances you can think of which produce heat energy like this. The resistance wires which are used in these appliances are often called 'heating elements'.

Experiment 7.20

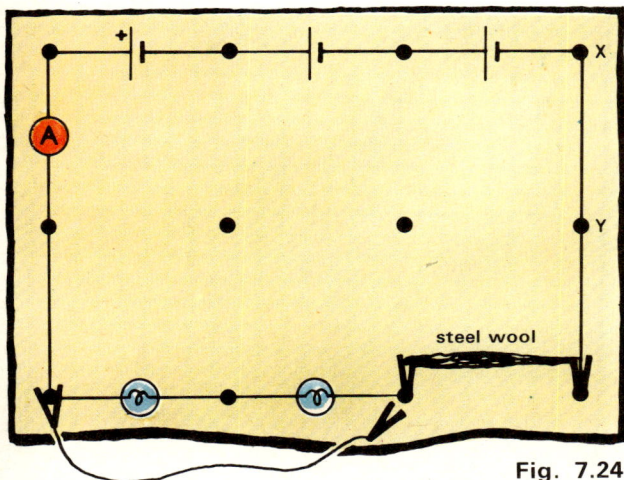

steel wool

Fig. 7.24

Here is another experiment which shows the heating effect of the current. Fit up the circuit on your circuit board as shown in Fig. 7.24. A 'wander' lead is connected across the bulbs, and can be made to touch some strands of steel wool connected to one of the posts. What happens to the steel wool, to the current shown on the ammeter, and to the bulbs?

Now alter the circuit to include a volume control instead of link XY and put in a piece of very thin fuse wire in place of the steel wool. Make sure your connecting leads are very tight. Slowly increase the current. What is the final result of this? For this experiment to be successful your cells must be new, or you can use accumulators recently charged instead.

7.12 FUSES

The soft thin wire you used in this experiment contained tin and lead, both of which have low melting points. Another word for melting is 'fusing' and so wire which will melt when a sufficiently high current is passed through it is called 'fuse wire'. In a house wiring system it is dangerous to allow the current to become too big. What could happen if the current became many times greater than was suitable for the cables?

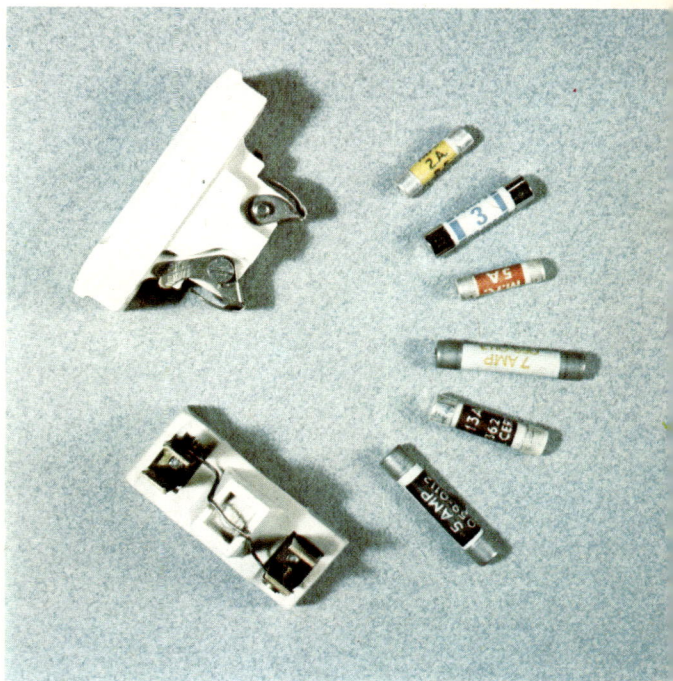

Fig. 7.25 A selection of fuses of various sizes. Find out what kinds of electrical appliances require fuses of each size shown in the picture

Usually the resistance of, say, the heating element in an electrical appliance prevents the current becoming more than the safe value. However, it may happen that something goes wrong with the wiring and the current may then become very big. Look at the diagram of the electric iron in Fig. 7.26. What do you notice

Fig. 7.26

about the wires and the insulation? Which way do you think the current will flow, the difficult way against the resistance of the heating element or the easy way from the one bare wire to the other where there is no resistance? We call this easy way a 'short circuit'.

What happens to the size of the current when there is a short circuit? Were this to happen in your house, what would prevent all the wiring from getting red hot and perhaps your house from being burned down?

Houses have sealed fuses where the cables enter the house, and there is also a fuse box after the main switch. You should know where this is in your own house. Nowadays, many plugs are fitted with cartridge fuses so that if the appliance connected to the plug takes too much current the fuse 'blows' and it is easy to replace. It is very important that the right size of fuse is used for the particular appliance.

Fig. 7.27 A plug fitted with its own fuse.

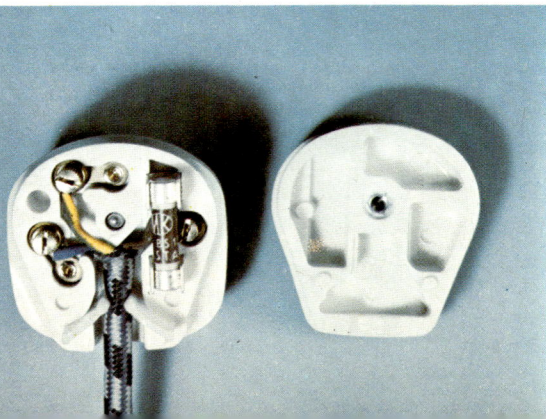

A mains operated radio set requires only about 0.2 A. (A is the abbreviation for ampere.) Keeping a 13 A fuse in the plug connected to the set could allow dangerously high currents to be supplied to the set without the fuse blowing. These high currents might cause excessive overheating of parts inside the radio, and the cost of replacing them would be much more than the cost of a fuse. In one word the main purpose of a fuse is SAFETY.

A piece of fuse wire is like an automatic switch, so that the circuit is broken when a dangerous level of current is reached, and the current is switched off. Try to find out the various sizes of fuse wire and cartridge fuses you can buy.

A fuse is the simplest kind of automatic switch. Some appliances, such as washing machines, often have another kind of 'circuit breaker' to stop the current if it gets too big. Some work by using the fact you already know, that when an electric current passes through a coil of wire it makes it act like a magnet. The greater the current, the more powerful is the magnet. When the current is big enough the magnet can pull an iron bar towards itself, and this breaks the circuit.

7.13 DRIVING THE CURRENT

Fig. 7.28 shows a coil of plastic tubing filled with water and connected to a pump. If we

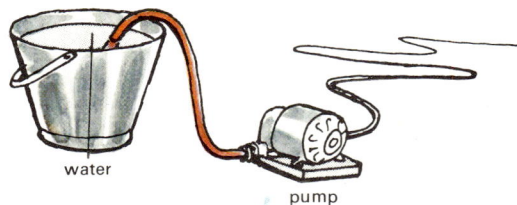

Fig. 7.28

wanted to make the water flow in the coil we should have to switch on the pump. It would not move otherwise.

In an electric circuit a cell is like a pump. It is able to make electrons flow through the circuit. We say that this is due to the 'voltage' of the cell.

Just as one pump might be able to push more water through a pipe than another, so one cell may be able to push more electricity through a circuit than another. We say that the second has a higher voltage than the first.

Current flows in a circuit because there are more negative charges (or electrons) at one point than at another. Voltage really indicates this difference in the number of electrons, and an electric cell is only one way of providing this difference of charges. A dynamo or a generator can do the same thing.

An instrument which is used to measure voltage is called a **voltmeter**.

Experiment 7.21

Connect up a series circuit of three U2 cells and three similar torch bulbs on your circuit board. Remembering that the terminal of the

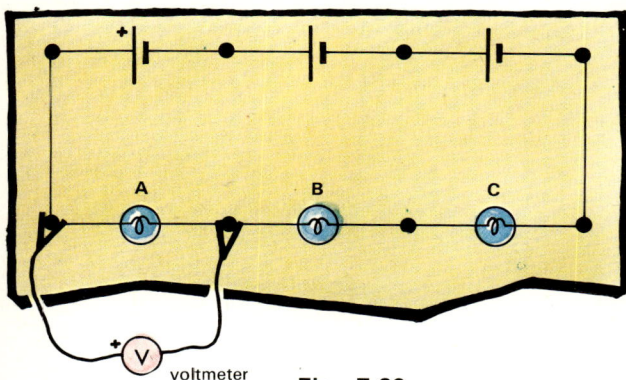

Fig. 7.29

voltmeter marked + must be connected to the + end of the circuit, connect the voltmeter across each bulb in turn, then across the pairs of bulbs A, B and B, C and last across the three bulbs A, B, and C. What is the connection between the voltage and the number of bulbs used? You should find that each bulb gets an equal share of the voltage, that two bulbs get twice the voltage of one, and that all three together get three times the voltage that one gets.

Now connect the voltmeter across one cell, then across two cells in series, and then across the three cells in series. How does the voltage of two cells in series and three cells in series compare with the voltage of one cell?

A PP9 battery gives 9 volts. How many single cells of a U2 type would be connected in series in this battery?

You will no doubt have spotted that by using a voltmeter it is possible to calculate the number of cells in a battery; in fact, one might look upon a voltmeter as a kind of cell counter.

7.14 VOLTAGE AND CURRENT

Experiment 7.22

Fit up a series circuit consisting of a bulb and an ammeter, using in turn one, two and three U2 cells in series. Make a table of results showing the current flowing in each case. (In this set of experiments do not keep the current flowing for more than the time taken to read the ammeter.)

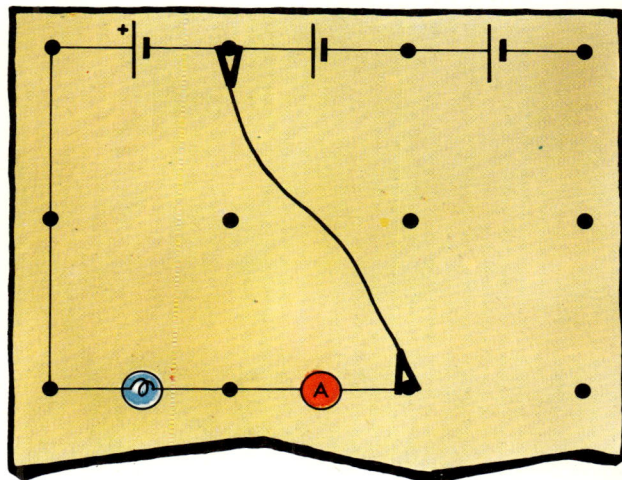

Fig. 7.30

What do you notice about the value of the current when you use more cells, and thus more voltage? Is there any simple connection between them?

We have already mentioned the voltage of a dry cell; it is 1.5 V. Find out the voltages of an accumulator cell, the power pack for a model train, a car battery, a NIFE cell, and your bicycle dynamo. If you look at one of the electric lamps you use at home you will see that it has on it perhaps 75 W 250 V. What do you think 250 V means? This voltage is very dangerous and could send a current through your body large enough to kill you. Find out the voltage stated on the warning plates on the pylons of the national grid system.

Experiment 7.23
Cells in parallel

Connect two U2 cells with the + of one to the + of the other and the − of one to the − of the other. Place a voltmeter across the combination. What does it read?

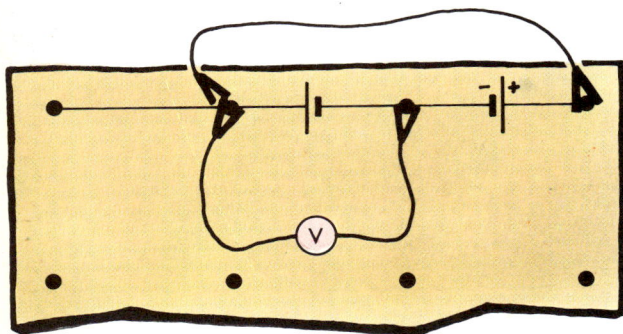

Fig. 7.31

The advantage of connecting cells in parallel like this is that sometimes bigger currents can be obtained; but the voltage of the two together is only that of one cell.

Some things to do

If you were given three bulbs, one of which was faulty, and a cell, draw a diagram of a circuit which includes all three bulbs and which would show up at once which was the faulty one.

Draw a circuit for the lighting system of a doll's house or a model railway layout.

Fig. 7.32

At home you may have a lamp on the stairs or in the hall which can be switched on or off by means of two switches, one at the bottom and one at the top of the stairs. Use your circuit board to devise a pair of switches which would do this, and show how they would be wired up.

7.15 ELECTRICITY AT HOME

At some time or other you will, no doubt, have to wire up a switch, a lamp-holder, or a plug; you do not want to have to call in an electrician every time there is a simple job like this to be done. So that you can practice doing this, try wiring up the components in the circuit shown in Fig. 7.33. Here are some hints about wiring up circuits like this.

1. Have about 1.5 cm at most of the wire bared of insulation at each end of your leads.
2. When tightening up a nut on a wire always make sure that the bare wire is bent into a hook pointing clockwise as you look at it.
3. Make sure that screws and nuts are tightened on to the bare wire and not on to the insulation. It is often a good idea to double back the bared end before tightening down the screw.
4. Most screws and threads in plugs, sockets, and switches are made of brass, which is a soft metal. Do not tighten screws too tightly or you may damage threads.
5. Make sure that inside plugs and sockets the wires are bent round the lugs which are meant to take the strain of a tug on the wire, so that the wire is not pulled out from under the screw.
6. Remember that bare wires inside plugs and sockets should not be long enough to touch one another and so cause a short circuit.
7. If you are dismantling a plug, etc. be careful where you put the screws, or you will not find them when you come to put the plug together again.

When you have completed your wiring exercise, and so that you will not be in any danger if by chance you should have made a mistake, connect the circuit first to a 12 V power pack (or a car battery) and a 12 V headlamp. See if the lamp can be switched on and off by the tumbler switch. If it passes this test it should be safe to connect it to the mains to light a 250 V lamp.

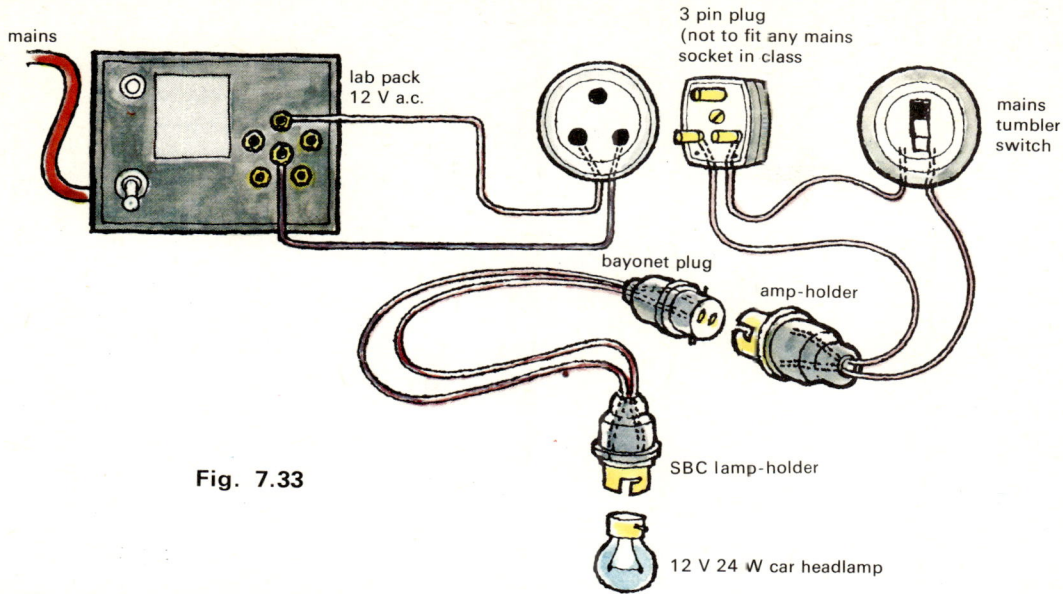

mains

lab pack
12 V a.c.

3 pin plug
(not to fit any mains
socket in class

mains
tumbler
switch

bayonet plug

amp-holder

Fig. 7.33

SBC lamp-holder

12 V 24 W car headlamp

WHAT YOU HAVE LEARNT IN THIS UNIT

1. When things made of plastic, rubber, glass, and such like materials are rubbed with wool, fur, silk, nylon and so on, they become charged with electricity.

2. There are two kinds of charge, positive and negative.

3. Bodies which have the same kind of charge repel each other; those with different charges attract each other.

4. When a piece of plastic is charged by rubbing it with wool, the wool becomes charged oppositely to the plastic, and the charge on the plastic is equal to the charge on the wool.

5. A possible way of explaining these observations is to suppose that atoms contain particles of electricity which can be 'rubbed off' from one body to another. The negative charges which atoms contain (if this theory is true) are called **electrons**. Like the atomic theory itself, this extension of it is only a guess, as no-one has ever seen an electron, but it seems very likely to be true, as it will explain all the observations that have been made about electricity. The theory has also predicted a lot of things which have been found to be true when tried out by experiment.

6. If the atom contains electrons it must also contain somewhere an equal number of positive charges, as atoms are not usually charged. These positive charges are believed to be deep inside the atom and form part of the nucleus of the atom.

7. When a Van de Graaff generator is discharged through a sensitive meter the pointer moves, showing that there is a flow of current. An electric current is therefore a flow of electrons.

8. Some substances allow electrons to flow easily through them; they are called **conductors**, and are usually metals. Others do not allow electrons to flow through them and are called **insulators**. They are non-metals.

9. If a current is to flow there must be a complete path for the electrons. We say that there must be a **complete circuit**.

10. Conductors, such as lamps, connected one after the other in a circuit are said to be connected in **series**.

11. Current is measured in amperes ('amps'). The meter used to measure a current is called an **ammeter**.

12. The current flowing in a series circuit is tne same at all points in the circuit.

13. In some circuits the currents may be divided between a number of branches. These branches are said to be in **parallel**.

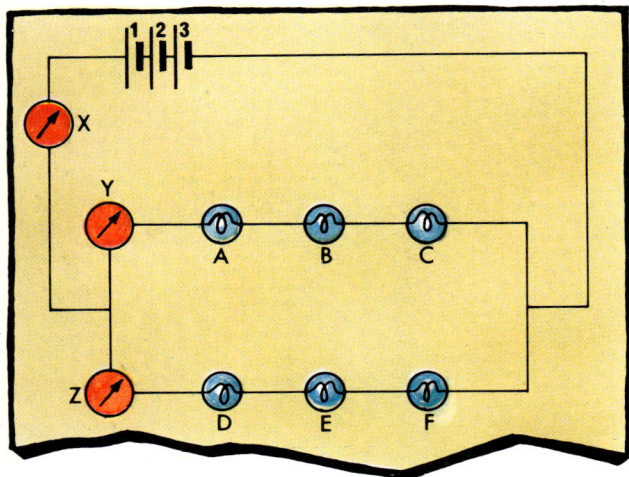

Fig. 7.34

In Fig. 7.34 the lamps A, B, and C are in series, as are the lamps D, E, and F. The circuit containing lamps A, B, and C is in parallel with that containing the lamps D, E, and F.

The cells 1, 2, and 3 are in series.

The current indicated by the ammeter X is the sum of the currents indicated by the ammeters Y and Z.

14. A battery is composed of a number of individual cells connected in series. Cells, batteries, and generators act like electron pumps. They drive electrons round the circuit.

15. Water can be driven through a pipe if the pressure is higher at one end than the other. Similarly an electric current can be driven through a wire if the **voltage** is higher at one end than the other. Voltage is measured by a **voltmeter**. A voltmeter is connected *across* the points at which we wish to know the voltage difference. An ammeter is connected **in series** in the circuit in which we wish to know the current flowing.

16. The greater the pressure of electrons (the voltage), the larger is the current flowing in the circuit. Do not confuse current and voltage. Although the current in a circuit depends on the voltage it is not the same thing.

17. Metals do not all conduct equally well. They all oppose the motion of electrons to some extent, but this opposition varies a lot from one metal to another. Some, like copper, offer hardly any opposition, and are very good conductors; others, like the alloy nichrome, oppose the current much more. This opposition to the flow of electrons is called **resistance**. Something inserted into a circuit for the special purpose of opposing the current is called a **resistor**. A resistor which can be varied is called a **rheostat**; this idea is used in the volume control on a radio set or TV, and in many other appliances.

18. The resistance (R) of two wires of the *same* material depends on the length (l) and their thickness (t). The longer the wire the higher is its resistance; the thicker the wire the lower is its resistance.

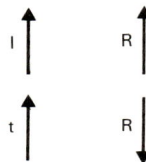

19. When the flow of electrons is resisted by a conductor, heat is generated. This fact is used in many appliances in the home, such as electric lamps, heaters, blankets, and irons.

20. A fuse wire is a wire made of a metal which is easily melted, so that if the current becomes too high and the wire becomes hot it melts and breaks the circuit. It is used to prevent overheating of cables and appliances.

21. The voltage of a single U2 cell is 1.5; that of an accumulator cell is 2.0; that of the *mains is usually* 250.

It is dangerous to experiment with the mains supply. The voltage is high enough to send a current through great enough to kill you. In carrying out repairs to electrical appliances working off the mains, *you must disconnect them from the mains* before you touch them.

Unit Eight
Some Common Gases

8.1 OXYGEN, NITROGEN, AND CARBON DIOXIDE

Gases are not so easy to study as solids or liquids. Often they are invisible. They are difficult to keep as they easily find their way out of tiny holes and cracks. Yet gases are very important indeed. The air around us, for instance, is necessary for our life, and that of all other animals.

First of all we are going to look at the properties of some common gases: oxygen, nitrogen, and carbon dioxide.

Your teacher will provide you with jars containing the gases nitrogen, oxygen, and carbon dioxide. Copy the following table into your note book and fill up each space.

From the results of your experiments can you say which would be the best test for (a) nitrogen, (b) oxygen, and (c) carbon dioxide?

Test	Nitrogen	Oxygen	Carbon dioxide
1. Hold a jar upside down in a basin of water. Remove the cover slip Gently rock jar.			
2. Hold a glowing splint in a jar of each gas.			
3. Hold a burning splint in a jar of each gas.			
4. Place a piece of moist pH paper in each gas.			
5. Add a little lime water to a jar of each gas and shake.			
6. Test a jar of each gas with a little bicarbonate indicator.			
7. Your teacher will show you the effect of burning magnesium in each gas.			

123

8.2 UNBREATHED AND BREATHED AIR

Is there any difference in the make up of the air we breathe in and that which we breathe out? We call the air we breathe in **inhaled air,** and the air we breathe out **exhaled air.**

Experiment 8.2
What gases are present in exhaled air?

First we must find out if exhaled air contains the same gases as inhaled air. How shall we collect our sample of exhaled air? Fig. 8.1 will help

Breathe out through a length of rubber tubing and then pinch the end firmly between thumb and finger.

Insert the end of the tubing into a boiling tube full of water as shown.

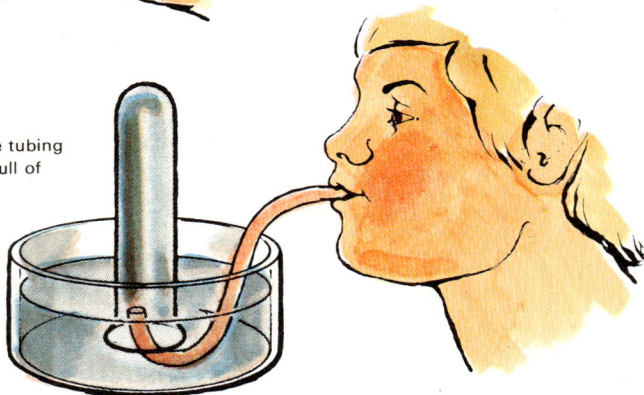

Continue breathing out gently until a sample of exhaled air has been collected.

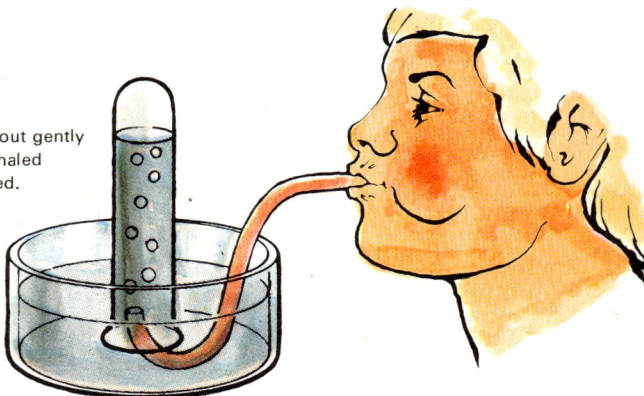

Fig. 8.1

you. We ought to take the same air into our lungs three or four times before we examine it, as there might not be much change if we breathe it in only once. (Do not, however, rebreathe the air too often.) A group of pupils thought out another way of collecting exhaled air. They attached a glass tube to a balloon and blew it up. Then they sucked the air into their lungs again, then once more blew up the balloon. They repeated this three or four times, then put the tube under water in a trough and let the air bubble out into a gas jar.

You have already found out some tests for distinguishing oxygen, nitrogen, and carbon dioxide. Try these tests on the exhaled air and the inhaled air, and put your results in a table like the one below.

Test	Exhaled air	Inhaled air

Before you did this experiment you might have thought that breathed-out air contained no oxygen; in other words, that we used up all the oxygen we breathed in. Is this correct?

If not, how much oxygen is left in it? To find this out we shall have to discover a way of analysing air. Let us see what happens when things burn in air.

8.3 COMPOSITION OF INHALED AND EXHALED AIR

Experiment 8.3
What happens to the air when a candle burns in it?

Take a piece of wood or cork and stick a small piece of candle on to it, as in Fig. 8.2. Float this on water in a trough. Light the candle and put a gas jar of ordinary air over it. What happens when the candle goes out?

Fig. 8.2

Does the candle use up all the air or only part of it? The part of the air that is used up is oxygen. The gases left obviously do not let things burn, and we know from the tests we carried out in Experiment 8.2 what these gases are.

How much of the air is oxygen? Can you find out *roughly* from the experiment you have just done? You will have to know two things – how much air you started with and how much was left.

Experiment 8.4
How much oxygen is there in exhaled air?

Now repeat the experiment you have just done with exhaled air instead of ordinary air. Is there any difference in the result?

There are much better ways of finding out the composition of air, but the above experiments, although not very accurate, will serve our purpose for the present.

You will probably have guessed that exhaled air contains less oxygen than inhaled air, and your experiment should have confirmed this. If it contains less oxygen, it must contain more of something else, and you will have found out what this is from the results of the tests in Experiment 8.1. Did you notice what happened to the lime water in the tests you did on inhaled and exhaled air?

You can now answer the question 'How does exhaled air differ from inhaled air?'

Both gases contain nitrogen. Why could you not detect it?

Here is a table showing an analysis of inhaled and exhaled air which sums up what you have found.

	Inhaled air	*Exhaled air*
Oxygen	21%	5%
Nitrogen	78.8%	85%
Carbon dioxide	0.2%	10%

Of course, the results for exhaled air depend a great deal on how many times the air has been taken into the lungs and breathed out again, but they do show that there has been a marked drop in the percentage of oxygen and a marked rise in the percentage of carbon dioxide.

Where does this carbon dioxide come from and what happens to the oxygen of the air when we breathe?

An experiment will help us to find out.

8.4 WHAT HAPPENS TO OUR FOOD?

Experiment 8.5
Burning food

We are going to burn some bread and some sugar in oxygen and see what is produced.

Your teacher will provide you with two jars of oxygen. Take a spoon with a long handle, which is specially made for burning things in gases — we shall call it a 'burning spoon', see Fig. 8.3. Put a piece of bread in it and heat it in a Bunsen flame until it starts to burn. Then quickly put it into one of the jars of oxygen. What happens?

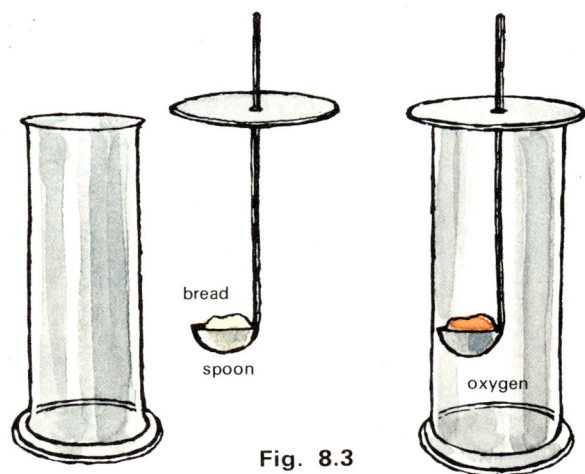

bread

spoon

oxygen

Fig. 8.3

Repeat with some sugar in a burning spoon, using the other jar of oxygen. What happens this time?

What is the gas now in the gas jars? We can look at our table of tests. It obviously will not let things burn in it because the sugar and the bread have ceased to burn; there cannot therefore be any gas left in which things will burn. Try the lime water test. What happens?

Does this experiment help you to find out first what you do with the oxygen you breathe in, and second why there is more carbon dioxide in the air we exhale than in that which we inhale?

A great deal of energy was given out when the bread and the sugar burnt in oxygen. There was a lot of flame and smoke. Why does this not happen when bread and sugar are 'burnt' in us?

Well, remember that for one thing you do not breathe in pure oxygen, but air, in which the oxygen is diluted (or weakened) by nitrogen. Look up your table of tests. Nitrogen does not let things burn. It 'damps down' the effect of the oxygen. You can see that this is so by comparing the way in which bread burns in air and the way it burns in oxygen. But even so, the bread does not burn up at this rate in your body. Nevertheless the bread *is* burned up, but it happens very slowly so that there is no flame at all.

You will remember burning magnesium in oxygen and noticing how fast and vigorous the reaction was. A white powder was produced. It is exactly the same as the white powder which is formed when magnesium is left out in the air. Look at the magnesium ribbon in the laboratory. It is not bright and shiny, but is covered with a thin layer of magnesium 'rust'. This is just the same stuff as you get when you burn magnesium in oxygen, but of course the reaction between the magnesium and the oxygen in the air has taken place very much more slowly. If, however, we were to measure the amount of energy given out when, say, 1 g of magnesium was burnt in oxygen and when 1 g of magnesium rusted away completely in air (it would take, of course, a very long time), the two quantities would be just the same.

We shall look at the question of what happens to food in our bodies again later in section 8.6.

8.5 ENERGY AGAIN!
(YOU CAN'T LIVE WITHOUT IT.)

Experiment 8.6
Body temperature

Fig. 8.4

Take your temperature with a clinical thermometer by putting the bulb of the thermometer under your tongue.

On another thermometer take the temperature of the room.

Here is something very odd! Your temperature is higher than the temperature of the room, and provided you are well it stays like that throughout the day (and night, too) – and it does not depend on what clothes you are wearing. Yet if you were to put some warm water in a beaker on the bench and leave it, it would cool down.

Why does the temperature of the warm water fall while your temperature does not?

What would you have to do to keep the water warm? Obviously you would have to put energy into it. If we are to keep warm we must have energy put into us too. We are not sitting on gas burners or radiators all day! Where does the energy come from?

Of course, it is not quite as simple as this. Our temperature remains very nearly *constant* – it does not fluctuate according to the amount of food we eat! So the body must have some regulating mechanism, which acts like the thermostat on a gas cooker, or on an immersion heater.

It would be interesting to find out if other animals take in oxygen. We can try an experiment with a woodlouse and see what happens with it.

Experiment 8.7
An experiment with a woodlouse

The apparatus shown in Fig. 8.5 will be set up by your teacher. In it a woodlouse is kept in a test-tube of air. What happens to the marker drop?

Another tube is set up with no woodlouse in it. What happens to the marker drop in this case? This is called a **control experiment**.

What does this experiment show us?

Why did we set up a control experiment? Ask yourself what would have happened to the marker drop if the temperature of the room changed. Would the effect have been the same in both tubes? This should help you to see the need for a control.

Can we prove from this experiment, and the fact that we know that *we* use up oxygen, that *all animals* use up oxygen? If not, why?

It seems probable from the experiments we have done that animals take in oxygen from the air, use it to burn up parts of their food – the carbohydrates such as bread and sugar – and in this process carbon dioxide is formed. This burning process is accompanied by the liberation of energy, which is used partly to enable us to move and to carry out all the things that living organisms do, and partly to keep our temperature at a constant level no matter what the outside temperature may be. Where does the carbohydrate itself get its energy – the energy which is liberated when it is burnt?

8.6 WHERE DOES THE ENERGY IN FOODS COME FROM?

All carbohydrates come from plants, and so we shall have to study how plants make carbohydrates, and where the energy comes from that is stored up in them.

In Unit 3 you learnt that plants need sunlight to grow, and that possibly the sun has something to do with the energy stored up in the food that plants make. We shall have to look at this more closely.

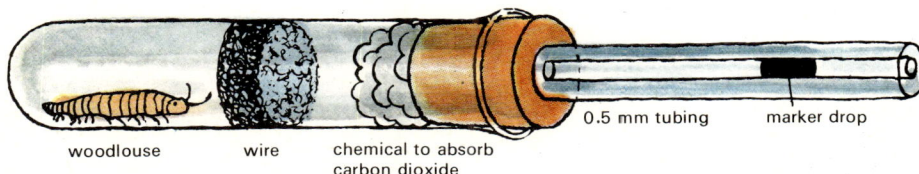

Fig. 8.5

woodlouse   wire   chemical to absorb carbon dioxide   0.5 mm tubing   marker drop

Obviously, from what you have learnt already carbon dioxide is a very important gas. It is a product of the burning up of food inside us to give us energy – a process that is called **respiration**. You have seen that carbon dioxide turns lime water milky, but in the experiments that we have to do now we shall need a more sensitive test than that. In the experiments with gases that you did at the beginning of this unit you tried the action of a bicarbonate indicator. This is a better test for carbon dioxide than the lime water test. We want to find out now how plants make carbohydrates, and for this purpose we shall have to see what part carbon dioxide plays in the process.

Experiment 8.8
The bicarbonate indicator

Take three test-tubes labelled A, B, and C. Put some bicarbonate indicator in each. Bubble air through tube A. Record the colour of the indicator. Blow through a straw into the indicator in the second tube B. You know that exhaled air contains more carbon dioxide than inhaled air. What colour does the indicator turn when you blow air containing more carbon dioxide through it? Using the third tube, C, set up the apparatus shown in Fig. 8.6. The potassium hydroxide removes carbon dioxide from air. If carbon dioxide is removed from the air, what gases will bubble through the indicator in the test-tube C? What colour does the

indicator turn when air minus carbon dioxide is bubbled through? Fill in your results in a table like the one below.

Test-tube	Gas	Colour of indicator
A	air	
B	carbon dioxide (exhaled air)	
C	air minus carbon dioxide	

If you were put in a glass case the composition of the air inside would change. The amount of oxygen would decrease, and the amount of carbon dioxide would increase. The same change would take place if you put any other living animal in the case, such as a dog, or a mouse, or an earthworm. What would happen if you put some plants in the glass case? Would the amount of oxygen go down and the amount of carbon dioxide increase? You can find this out for yourself.

Experiment 8.9

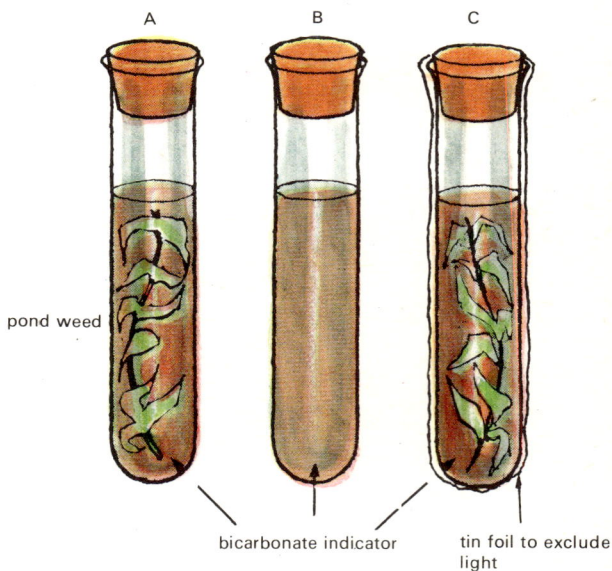

Fig. 8.7

Set up three test-tubes as in the diagram (Fig 8.7). Leave the tubes in bright light for about an hour. Note the colour of the indicator

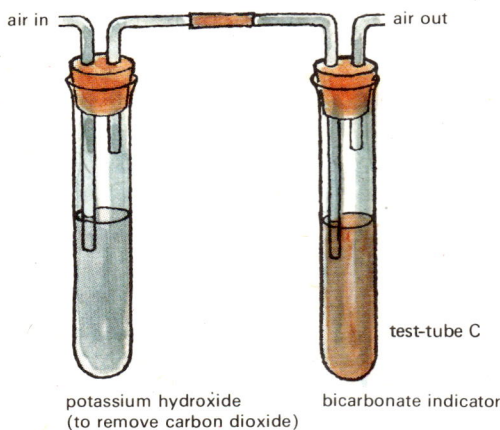

Fig. 8.6

in each tube, and enter your results in a table like the one below.

	Initial colour of indicator	Final colour of indicator
Tube A		
Tube B		
Tube C		

What colour did the indicator in tube A turn?
What gas caused this colour change?
What changes have taken place in tube A?
What *two* factors have brought about this change?

8.7 PLANTS AS FOOD BUILDERS

In the presence of light, plants *take up* carbon dioxide. This is strange, because we found that animals *give out* carbon dioxide. What does the plant do with this carbon dioxide? Is it taken up by the leaves, and does it then pass out again unchanged? Is it used to build up new substances in the plant? You can do an experiment which will help you to find an answer to this problem.

Experiment 8.10

Obtain two Iris leaves. Stand one leaf in water and set up the second leaf as shown in Fig. 8.8. Put both leaves in a bright place in the laboratory. After *two days* cut discs from leaf A. Grind up the discs with water and place the ground-up leaf in a boiling tube. Add about 5 cm³ of Benedict's solution and boil. For what food substance are you testing? If you cannot remember turn to page 88 (Experiment 5.39). What colour is produced in the tube? Is this food substance present in leaf A?

Test leaf B in a similar way. Record your results as shown in the table below.

	Colour of Benedict's solution	Glucose present or absent?
Tube A		
Tube B		

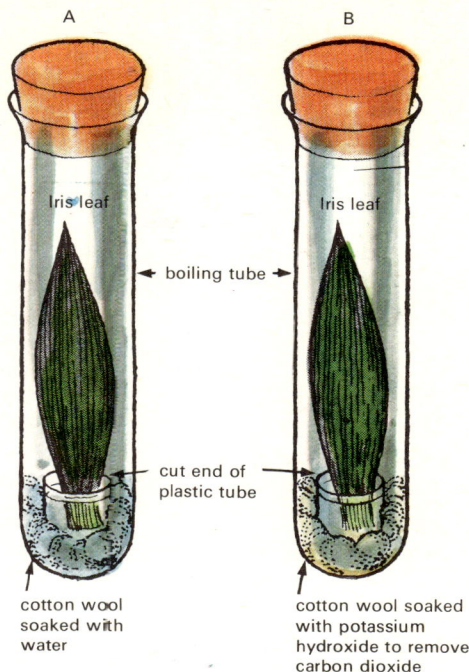

Fig. 8.8

You have found that Iris leaves which had carbon dioxide available to them contained glucose. Iris leaves which were in an atmosphere free from carbon dioxide contained no glucose. This result suggests that there is a connection between carbon dioxide and glucose. However, we have not proved that carbon dioxide taken in by plants is built into glucose. To do this we should have to be able to follow the carbon dioxide as it moved through the plant.

This is not easy, but it can be done if we use carbon dioxide containing radioactive carbon, or 'labelled' carbon as it is sometimes called. This labelled carbon can be detected by means of a special counter, called a Geiger counter, which can detect the presence of radioactive substances. Unfortunately radioactive material is dangerous to use, and you cannot do experiments with it in school. However, scientists have carried out experiments with this material. Green plants were surrounded by radioactive carbon dioxide. The plants were kept in bright light and then they were tested. It was found that the radioactive material had been built up into glucose in the leaves. Thus, using the results of experiments carried out by other people we can say that green plants take in carbon dioxide and build it up into sugars. In Experiment 8.9 you found that plants only absorb carbon dioxide when they are exposed to light. We can use the results of this experiment and of Experiment 8.10 to put forward the following hypothesis: 'Iris leaves make sugar only when they are exposed to light'.

Carry out an experiment to test this hypothesis.

Experiment 8.11
Do all leaves contain sugar?

Remove leaves from plants which have been in bright light in your laboratory. Grind up the leaves with a little sand and water and test the extracts with Benedict's solution.

Kind of leaf	Colour produced with Benedict's solution	Glucose present or absent
1)		
2)		
3)		

The results from this experiment may confuse you because you have found out that Iris leaves make sugar when they are exposed to light. The leaves tested above were all exposed to light but in some cases no glucose was found. Have these leaves been unable to make glucose? Has the glucose been removed? Have the leaves made some other kind of food? The last question is the easiest to investigate.

Experiment 8.12

1. Using a cork borer, cut discs from a geranium leaf which has been in light for several hours.
2. Drop these discs into a beaker of boiling water. Leave for two minutes to kill the cells.
3. Put out *all* Bunsen burners.
4. Remove the discs, and put them into a test-tube a quarter full of alcohol. Heat the test-tube in a water bath for three minutes.
   What colour is the alcohol?
   What colour are the discs?
   What has the alcohol done to the leaf discs?
5. Pour off the alcohol into the container

provided, and rinse the discs in water to soften them.
6. Place the discs on a white tile and cover with drops of iodine.

For which substance are you testing? (See Unit 5, page 88.)
What colour are the discs?
What does this show?

In Experiment 5.42 you found that starch could be broken down by enzymes into glucose. Can the reverse happen? Can glucose be built up into starch? You have found both glucose and starch in the leaves of plants. We can now put forward another hypothesis: 'Green leaves can change glucose into starch'. The following experiment will test this hypothesis.

Experiment 8.13

You are provided with a geranium plant which has been in the dark for a few days. Remove a leaf from this plant and test it for starch as in Experiment 8.12. Is starch present? When a plant is put into a dark cupboard, any starch in its leaves is removed and no further starch can be made. Such a plant is said to be de-starched.

Remove a second leaf and cut several discs. Label two Petri dishes A and B. Fill A with 5% glucose solution and B with water. Float half the discs on the glucose solution and the other half on the water. Make sure that the lower surface of each disc is in contact with the liquids. Leave the dishes in a dark cupboard for about three days. Test the discs in each dish for starch.

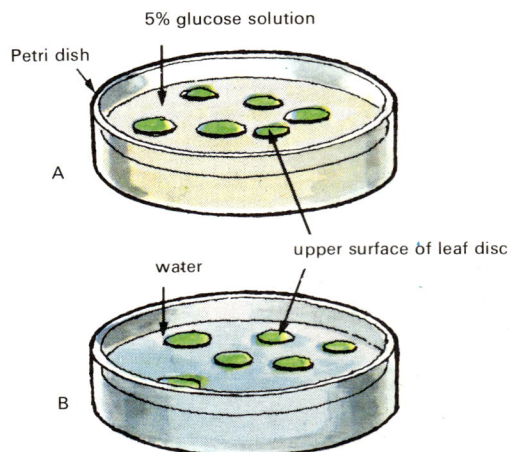

Fig. 8.9

Here are some questions for you to answer.

1. In which disc was starch found?
2. What liquid was in contact with these discs?
3. Why were the discs kept in a dark cupboard?
4. Why did you use a leaf from a de-starched plant?
5. What results would you expect if both dishes had been kept in the light?

8.8 THE MOST IMPORTANT REACTION IN THE WORLD – PHOTOSYNTHESIS

Your hypothesis has proved to be correct. We can trace the formation of starch in green leaves. In light, leaves take in carbon dioxide and build it up into glucose. As light is a form of energy and glucose is produced only in the presence of light, we can say that energy is required for the synthesis (building up) of this food. Enzymes in the leaves convert this glucose into starch for storage. You could not detect glucose in the leaves of geranium because it had been converted into starch. The process by which green plants build up food is called **photosynthesis**.

Both carbon dioxide and light are necessary for photosynthesis. If either of these factors is removed from the plant, would you expect starch to be produced?

Fig. 8.10 A variegated plant. Find out what it is called

Experiment 8.14

Devise apparatus in which plants or cuttings can be kept for several days under the following conditions. What must be done to the plants before setting up this experiment? Give a reason for your answer.
   These are the conditions:

1. in light with carbon dioxide in the air surrounding them;
2. in light with no carbon dioxide in the air surrounding them;
3. in the dark with carbon dioxide present.

Leave the plants for a few days then find out if starch is present in any of them.

Look at the leaves of the plants in your laboratory. You will see that some leaves are green all over while others have patterns of white on them. The patterned leaf is called a **variegated** leaf.

Experiment 8.15
Testing a variegated leaf for starch

Remove a variegated leaf from a plant which has been standing in bright light. Draw the leaf and label the green and white areas. Test the whole leaf for starch. Draw the pattern of starch areas. Do your two diagrams correspond in any way? The green colour in leaves is due to a substance called **chlorophyll**. What conclusions can you reach about the part played by chlorophyll in photosynthesis?

In Experiment 6.5 (page 94, Unit 6) you examined a leaf of a water plant and observed small green structures, the chloroplasts. Chloroplasts contain chlorophyll. What colour would you expect the chloroplasts to be if you mounted a leaf from the plant in iodine? Give a reason for your answer.

We now have additional information to add to our knowledge of photosynthesis. Energy, in the form of light, is absorbed by chlorophyll. This energy is used in the complex synthesis of glucose from carbon dioxide. Some of the energy is stored in the glucose molecules. In what form is this energy?

8.9 A BY-PRODUCT OF PHOTOSYNTHESIS

Experiment 8.16

Have you ever noticed bubbles of gas rising from plants in an aquarium? This gas is a by-product of photosynthesis. You can collect and test this gas by the following method.

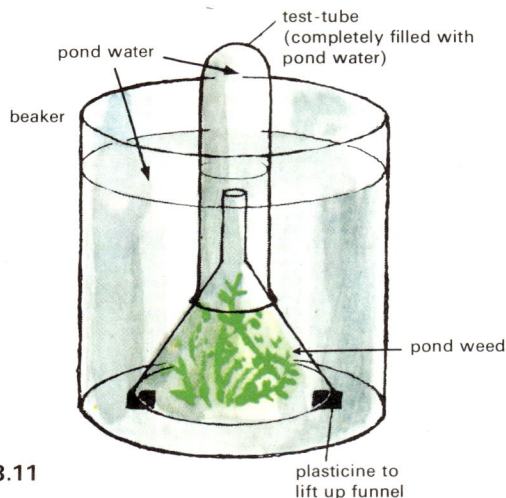

Fig. 8.11

Set up the apparatus as shown in Fig. 8.11.
Leave the plants in bright light. Remove the test-tube and quickly apply a glowing splinter to the gas in the tube. If the splinter glows more brightly or re-kindles, the gas in the test-tube is oxygen. Is the gas oxygen?

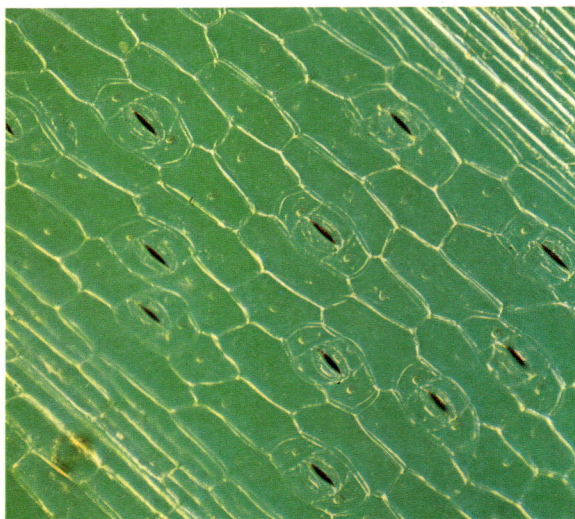

Fig. 8.12 A photomicrograph of the surface of a leaf showing the stomata

8.10 LEAF STRUCTURES AND PHOTOSYNTHESIS

The diagrams in Fig. 8.13 show the external and internal structure of a leaf. With the aid of these diagrams write down *four* ways in which the structure of the leaf is adapted to the process of photosynthesis.

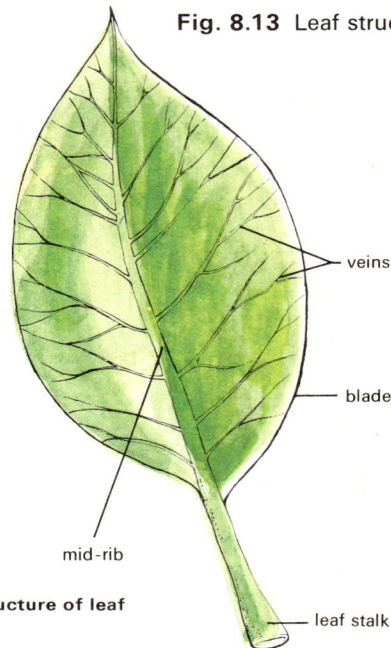

Fig. 8.13 Leaf structures

External structure of leaf

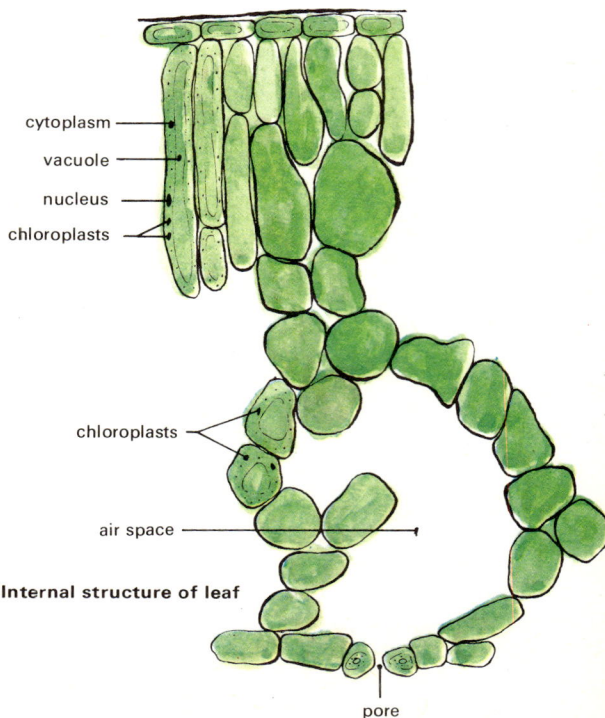

Internal structure of leaf

caterpillar

blackbird

green plant

hawk

rabbit

fox

Fig. 8.14 A food web

8.11 PHOTOSYNTHESIS AND ANIMALS

The process by which plants build up food is a very important one. Without it life, as we know it, could not exist. Animals depend on plants to provide them with food for growth and energy. You can argue that a large number of animals never eat plants. Make a list of animals which only eat flesh. One example you will probably have included in your list is the lion. Lions eat a variety of animals including antelopes. Antelopes eat plants. We can write the above relationship as follows:

plants are eaten by antelopes which are eaten by lions

or

grass ⟶ antelope ⟶ lion

This is known as a **food chain**. The grass uses energy from the Sun to produce food and so it is called a **producer**. When the plant is eaten the energy contained in it is passed on to the antelope. The antelope is called the **primary consumer**. Some of the energy in the consumer's food is used, but the rest is stored in the muscles of the body. The primary consumer is eaten by a **secondary consumer**, which is the lion in this case. By means of this food chain the lion can make use of energy which came originally from the Sun. The food chain above outlines a single energy pathway. Vegetation is however eaten by a large variety of animals (**herbivores**) and these animals are in turn eaten by a variety of flesh eating animals (**carnivores**).

The diagram shown in Fig. 8.14 illustrates a more complex series of energy pathways and is called a **food web**.

Here are some questions to answer.

1. What is the producer?
2. Name two primary consumers.
3. Name one carnivore.
4. What does the blackbird feed on?

Here is something to do on your own.

1.   Construct a food chain or a food web. You must begin with a producer and have at least *two* consumers.
2.   Select *four* items of food in your diet and trace them back to their original source.

8.12 ENERGY FROM CARBOHYDRATES – RESPIRATION

You have just investigated the process by which energy from the Sun is stored in sugar molecules in plants. This energy is transferred to animals when the plants are eaten. You are now going to find out how this energy is released in a variety of organisms.

Experiment 8.17
Detecting energy release

Cup your hands around the bulb of a thermometer. What happens to the mercury? Breathe on the bulb of the thermometer. What happens to the mercury? In Experiment 8.6 you found your temperature by putting a thermometer under your tongue. Try it again.

In all these cases the mercury rises, showing that energy has been released in the form of heat.

Experiment 8.18
Do other organisms release heat energy?

You cannot ask a hamster or some earthworms to breathe on to the bulb of a thermometer, and so you must investigate this problem in another way. In Experiment 4.18 you found that gases expand when they are heated. We are going to use this fact to help us to plan this experiment.

Set up the apparatus shown in the diagram in Fig. 8.15.

Open the clips. Look at the liquid in the U-tube. It should be at the same level in both limbs. Close the clips. Put your hand around

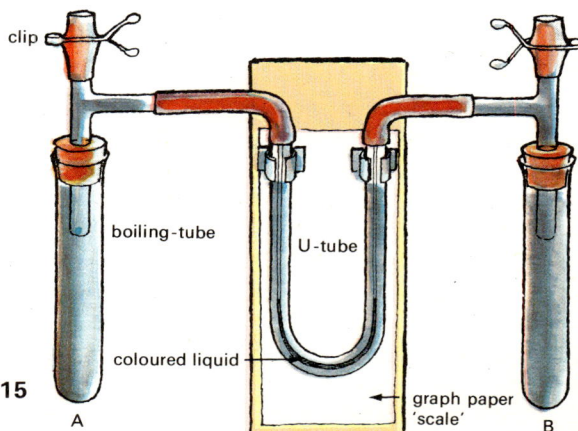

clip
boiling-tube
U-tube
coloured liquid
graph paper 'scale'
A
B

Fig. 8.15

tube A. What happens to the level of liquid in the limbs? How has this come about? Open the clips to bring the liquid back to the same level in each limb. Close the clips.

Place tube A in a beaker containing a chosen organism, e.g. a mouse, and tube B into an empty beaker, as in Fig. 8.16. (Your teacher will have wrapped cotton wool or felt around the beaker before the start of this experiment). Cover each beaker with a lid.

What happens to the liquid in the U-tube?
Is the mouse giving out heat energy?
Give a reason for your answer.

You can compare the rate at which energy is released in a variety of organisms, by finding the length of time taken to produce a result. You can

We know that living organisms obtain the energy they require from food. We must now ask two questions.

1. Where is this energy released in living organisms?
2. How is the energy released?

Experiment 8.5 will help us to answer the second question. You saw that when food was burned, energy was released. The burning of food in air or in oxygen and the breakdown of food in the body are similar in that they release energy, carbon dioxide, and water vapour. However, there are obvious differences between the two processes. Before we consider these differences, it is necessary to answer the first question.

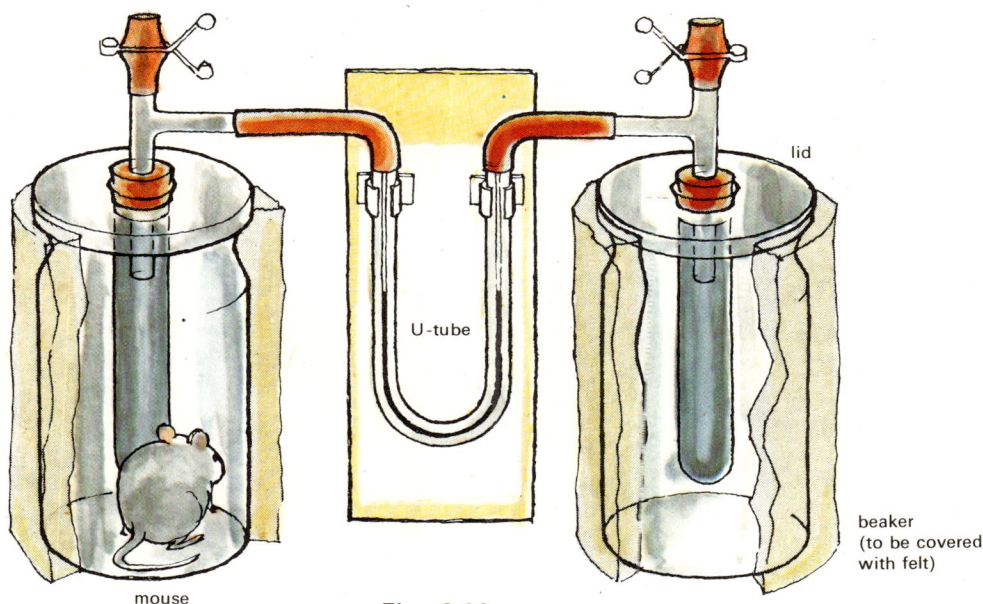

Fig. 8.16

use the following organisms – hamster, meal-worms, woodlice, earthworms, locust larvae, germinating peas, dried peas, flower buds etc. Put your results in the form of a table.
Here are some questions for you to answer.

1. Why were the beakers covered with cotton wool or felt?
2. Why was tube B put into an empty beaker?
3. How could you speed up the release of energy?
4. Do twelve locust larvae give out more heat energy than six locust larvae?
5. Where did the heat energy come from?

We know that our bodies are made up of cells; we also know that the food we eat is digested (that is, broken down into simpler substances), and that the digested food passes through the walls of the intestine into the bloodstream, and is then taken to the various cells of the body. It must be in these cells that the energy is released. Cells, as you know from your work in Unit 6, are filled with a watery substance. This is called **cytoplasm**. Here then, is the first difference. Food burned in a gas jar is surrounded by air; food broken down in the body is surrounded by a watery substance. The second difference concerns the rate at which energy is released. On page 126 we pointed out that when food is burned the energy is released in an uncontrolled manner; a great deal of energy is given out in one big burst. In the body the process takes place much more slowly, and is carefully controlled.

We have gone only part of the way towards answering the second question. The following experiment will provide us with further information.

Experiment 8.19

Half fill a vacuum flask with a solution of glucose which has been boiled and then cooled. Add about 2 g of dried yeast, and then pour a layer of oil on top. Set up the apparatus shown in Fig. 8.17 below, with the bulb of the thermometer below the surface of the oil, and the delivery tube leading into a test-tube containing bicarbonate indicator.

Set up control experiments with (a) only glucose solution in the flask and (b) only yeast solution in the flask.

Note the initial temperature of the liquid in each flask. Read the temperatures again after one hour.

In which flask has heat energy been released?

What does the colour of the indicator in the test-tube indicate?

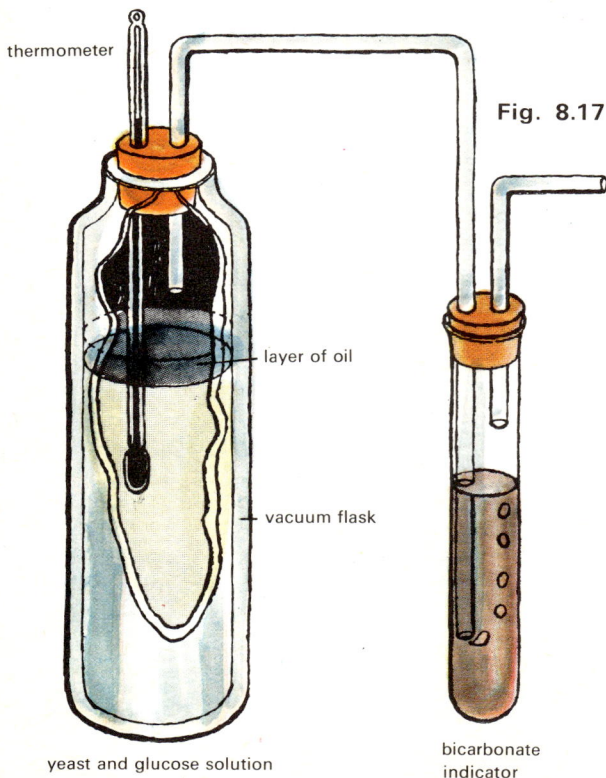

thermometer

Fig. 8.17

layer of oil

vacuum flask

yeast and glucose solution

bicarbonate indicator

In the absence of oxygen, glucose has been split by the yeast, or some substance in the yeast. What *two* steps were taken to ensure that no oxygen was available?

Yeast is a plant which contains enzymes. These enzymes started the breakdown of glucose.

We now have more information to help us to answer the question 'How is energy released?' Enzymes present in the cells of the body begin the breakdown of glucose. Some energy and carbon dioxide are released. Oxygen completes this breakdown. More energy and carbon dioxide are released. The complex process by which energy is released from food in the cells of the body is called **respiration**.

1. Write down *three* different ways in which you use the energy released in respiration.
2. In what form is energy released from (a) glow worms, (b) electric eels?

8.13 HOW DO WE TAKE IN OXYGEN?

We have noted that oxygen is required for the complete breakdown of glucose in the cells of the body. In very small organisms oxygen diffuses directly into the cells, but in large organisms special structures have developed to take in oxygen from the surroundings. In mammals these structures are called **lungs**. The oxygen passes through the lungs to the blood, which carries it to every cell of the body.

Experiment 8.20
Looking at lungs

Examine a sheep's lungs. Using the diagram in Fig. 8.18, find the following structures: (a) trachea, (b) bronchus, (c) lungs.

What colour are the lungs?

Are they moist or dry?

Prod a lung with your finger. Does it feel solid or spongy?

Place the lungs in a basin of water. Do they float or sink?

From your observations what *three* substances are present in the lungs? Run your finger down the trachea. What do you feel? What is the function of these structures?

Find where the bronchus goes into a lung. With a scalpel, cut the lung and find what

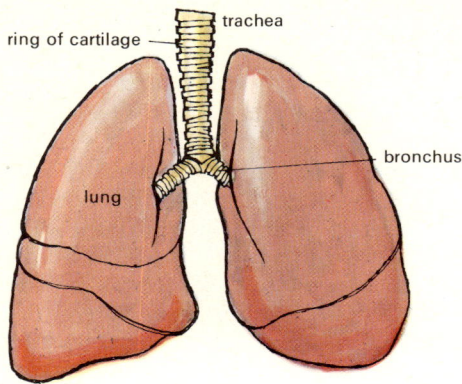

Fig. 8.18

happens to the bronchus. You will see that it divides into a number of thinner tubes. Follow one of these tubes: it also divides. This pattern is repeated so that a very large number of fine air tubes fill the lungs. Each tube ends in a small air sac.

Air passes from the nose or mouth, down the trachea and bronchi, through the fine air tubes to the air sacs.

The diagram in Fig. 8.19 shows the structure of an air sac.

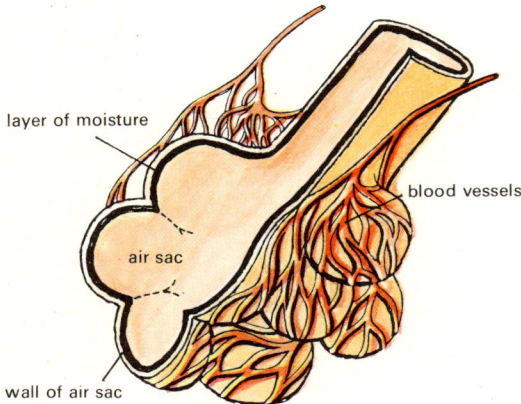

Fig. 8.19 The structure of an air sac

The oxygen has to move from the air sac into the bloodstream. Your knowledge about the movement of gases should help you to understand what takes place. If the concentration of oxygen in the air sac is greater than the concentration of oxygen in the blood, then oxygen will move from the air sac into the blood. However, there are no bubbles of oxygen in your bloodstream. The oxygen dissolves in the thin film of water lining each air sac and diffuses in solution through the walls of the air sacs into the blood.

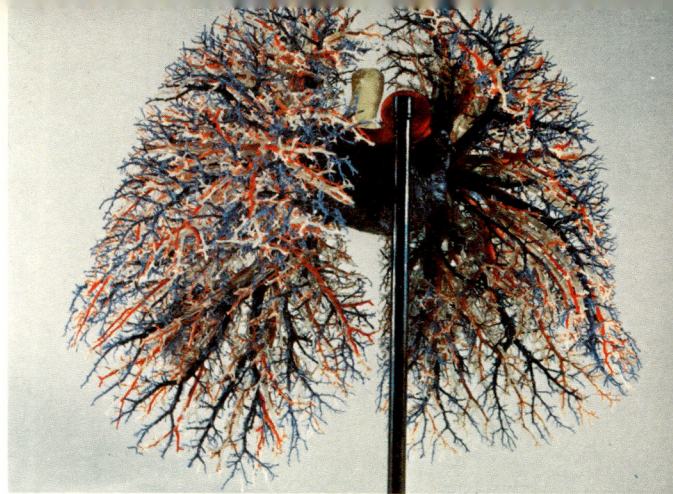

Fig. 8.20 A model of human lungs showing the fine structure of the blood vessels

8.14 HOW IS AIR TAKEN INTO THE LUNGS?

You have seen how oxygen moves from the air spaces in the lungs into the blood, but how does air get into the air sacs? Before we can answer this question we must look at the position of the lungs in the body.

The diagram in Fig. 8.21 shows the chest region of a dissected rat. Find the rib-cage and the diaphragm.

Both these structures are arranged close to the lungs, and they play an important part in the movement of air in to and out of the lungs.

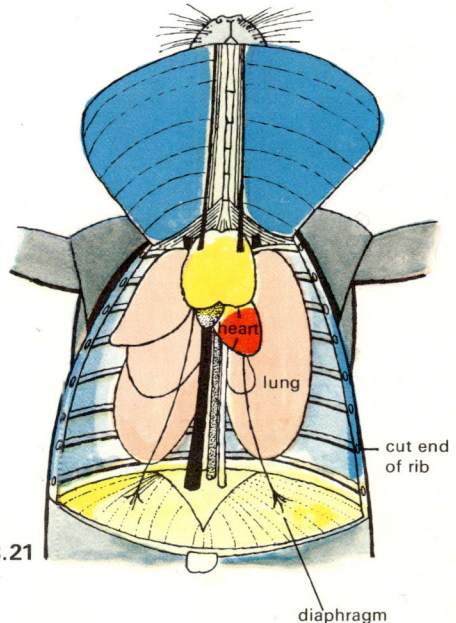

Fig. 8.21

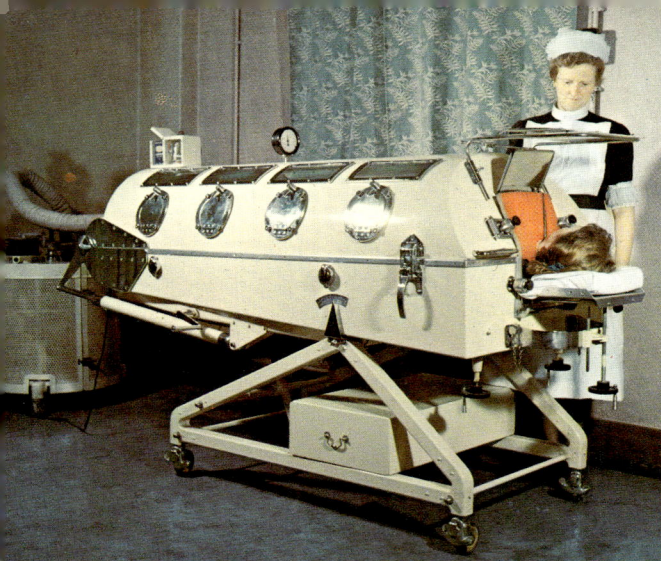

Fig. 8.22 A respirator being used to help a polio victim to breathe. Find out how these machines work

Action of the ribs

Place your hands on your ribs. Breathe in. What happens to your rib-cage? It moves out and up and the volume of the chest cavity increases. This movement is brought about by the action of muscles attached to the ribs.

When you breathe out the ribs move down and in. The volume of the chest cavity decreases.

Action of the diaphragm

The diaphragm is a sheet of muscle attached to the lower end of the ribs. Note that it is not flat, but forms a dome. When the diaphragm contracts, however, it becomes flat. As a result the volume of the chest cavity increases. When it returns to its domed position the volume of the chest cavity decreases.

Volume and pressure

As a result of the upwards and outwards movement of the rib-cage and the lowering of the diaphragm, the volume of the chest cavity increases. A change in the volume causes a change in the pressure. Because the volume increases, the pressure decreases. The pressure inside the lungs becomes less than the pressure of the air outside the body (atmospheric pressure). When the air pressure in one region is greater than the air pressure in another region then air will move from the region of high pressure to the region of low

pressure. In this case air moves from the surroundings into the lungs, which increase in size as a result. Intake of air is therefore caused by the movement of the rib-cage and the diaphragm.

The reverse happens when you breathe out. The rib-cage moves down and in, the diaphragm returns to its domed position. The volume of the chest cavity decreases and as a result the pressure increases. The chest cavity becomes the region of high pressure and air is forced out of the lungs. The following experiments illustrate the action of the diaphragm.

Experiment 8.21

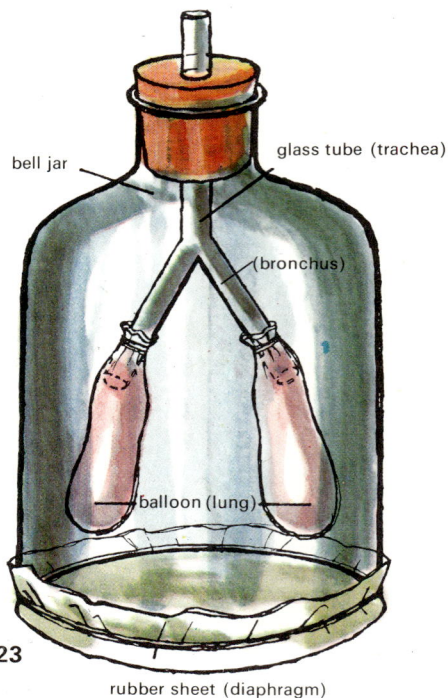

Fig. 8.23

Hold the neck of the bell jar in one hand and with the other hand pull the centre of the rubber sheet downwards.

What happens to the balloons?

Explain why this has happened. Your explanation should refer to changes in volume and pressure inside the bell jar.

Push the centre of the rubber sheet into the bell jar. What happens to the balloons?

In the diagram the bell jar represents the rib-cage. Does the bell jar make a good model? Give a reason for your answer.

8.15 THE AIR AND BURNING

We have been dealing with the importance of air to living organisms, and we have seen that in some ways the process of respiration by which all living things get their energy is very much like what happens when things burn. We now want to look at this process of burning – or **combustion** as it is called – rather more closely.

The first question to ask is whether air is necessary for things to burn. How could you devise an experiment to find out? Remember how we tackled things like this before. If a scientist wants to find out if a certain factor is the cause of anything, he cuts out this factor and sees if the experiment still works. We want to see if air is necessary for things to burn, so what would we do? Cut out the air, and see if things still burn. How could you do that?

Experiment 8.22
Will magnesium burn without air?

To heat magnesium in a vacuum is difficult, but it can be done. The metal would have to be heated electrically, and possibly your teacher may fit up an apparatus to do this.

There is, however, a much simpler way of preventing air from getting to the magnesium. All that is necessary is to put some pieces of magnesium ribbon in a crucible and cover it with something through which the air cannot pass. Which of the following would you select – a crucible lid, water, or sand?

Fig. 8.24

Heat the covered magnesium for a few minutes. Then allow to cool, and pour out the contents on to an asbestos sheet. What has happened to the magnesium?

Repeat the experiment without covering the magnesium. Is there any difference?

Can we conclude from this experiment that air is required for *all* substances to burn?

Experiment 8.23
What happens when magnesium burns?

You have already discovered that when magnesium burns a white ash is formed. Does this weigh more or less than the magnesium itself?

How can you account for the difference? There is only one possible answer.

8.16 IS ALL THE AIR USED UP WHEN A SUBSTANCE BURNS?

Experiment 8.24

To find out we shall have to burn something in a vessel which contains a certain amount of air, and no air must be able to get in while it is burning. An ingenious way of doing this is to use the apparatus shown in the diagram. The

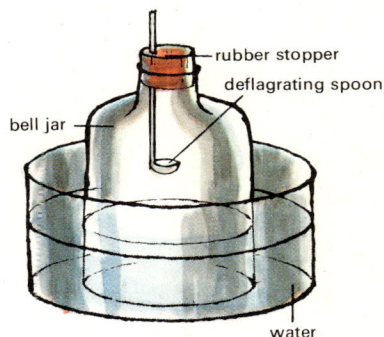

Fig. 8.25

magnesium in the spoon is lighted and quickly inserted into the bell jar and the stopper pushed home.

If all the air were used up, what would happen to the water level in the jar? What actually happens? What can you conclude from the experiment?

How could you find out the fraction of the air used up?

Will the gas left allow things to burn? You can easily find out if it is not obvious to you already. What is the gas left? Look at the list of tests you discovered at the beginning of this unit, and use them to find out what you can about the remaining gas.

Fig. 8.26 Plant for the separation from air of oxygen and nitrogen. These are stored in liquid form at very low temperatures

8.17 MAKING ARTIFICIAL AIR

Experiment 8.25

Take a gas jar. Find the total volume of gas it would contain.

Stick a small label on the jar to indicate where one-fifth of the total volume comes to. Fill the jar with water and invert it in water in a trough. Now put enough oxygen in the jar to displace water down to the level of the label. Fill up the rest with nitrogen.

Try experiments to see if this mixed gas behaves like air. Does it smell? Does it let things burn in the same way that air does?

8.18 USES OF OXYGEN, NITROGEN, AND CARBON DIOXIDE

Air is, of course, the cheapest raw material that any manufacturer could use. It is not always possible, however, to use the air as it is. It is often only the oxygen, or the nitrogen that is wanted, and it becomes necessary to separate them from the air. This is not a simple process, and it was some time before a cheap method was devised for doing it.

Air is, of course, a mixture of gases. If gases are cooled enough they become liquids. Compression helps this process. If you remember our theory about the nature of gases and liquids that we dealt with on page 58 you will know why. If air is cooled and compressed it turns into **liquid air** which is a mixture of liquid oxygen and liquid nitrogen. (The small amounts of carbon dioxide and water vapour in the air are removed before this is done, as otherwise they would become solid at the low temperatures used, and block up the apparatus.)

If we wish to obtain pure oxygen and pure nitrogen from liquid air we have to consider their boiling points. These are −183 °C and −196 °C respectively. Which of these gases boils at the lower temperature? Do not be misled by the *numerical* values without considering the sign. Remember how we separated a mixture of alcohol and water − two liquids which have different boiling points (page 77). The same method can be used here. If liquid air is allowed to warm up, the nitrogen boils off first, leaving liquid oxygen. When all the nitrogen has been boiled off, we have the pure liquid oxygen.

You have probably seen the large tanker lorries on the roads, with tanks which contain liquid oxygen. These are really huge 'thermos' flasks. Next time you see one look for the frost on the tap. To remain as a liquid, oxygen must be very cold.

What is oxygen used for? You can probably give some of the uses straight away. The most obvious one is in hospitals to help the breathing of patients with lung trouble. It is also used for getting very hot flames for welding and cutting metals − e.g. the oxy-hydrogen flame, and the oxy-acetylene flame. Look up some books in the library and see if you can find out any other uses for oxygen.

Fig. 8.27 An oxy-acetylene torch in use

cent of the air. It is interesting to know that the first of these gases to be discovered – helium – was found to be present on the Sun before it was found on the earth. That is where it gets its name – from the Greek word 'helios' meaning 'the Sun'. Are you wondering how we could find out that there was helium on the Sun when no-one could go there and collect some? This is a very interesting story and you should read about it in 'The Discovery of the Inert Gases' by Richardson and Hall (Nuffield Background Book, published by Longman and Penguin). The gases were found in the earth's atmosphere by Sir William Ramsay, a Scottish chemist. They were not found earlier because they were mistaken for nitrogen, which is also a comparatively inert (or lazy) gas. They

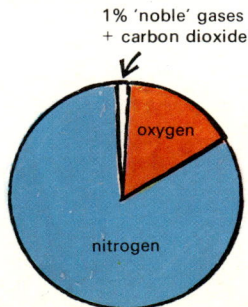

Fig. 8.29 The lazy ones!

Although nitrogen is rather inactive, it *can* be made to combine with other elements such as hydrogen and oxygen. With hydrogen it forms **ammonia**, one of the most valuable gases; this in turn can be made into **nitric acid**. Ammonia itself is used in the manufacture of substances from which nylon and other artificial fibres are made, as well as for making fertilizers for agriculture. Nitric acid is used in making dyes, explosives, fertilizers, and many other useful chemicals.

8.19 THE LAZY ONES

The air also contains some other gases which we have not yet mentioned. They are usually called the 'inert' gases or the 'noble' gases, and their names are helium, neon, argon, krypton, and xenon. Altogether they make up about one per

were first called the 'rare' gases because the percentages of them in the atmosphere is small; but when it is remembered that there is a tremendous amount of atmosphere, the total quantity of these gases present in the air is very large and they can hardly be called rare.

The inert gases do not react with most other elements, although a few compounds of xenon have recently been made. For this reason they are nowadays often called the 'noble' gases by analogy with the noble metals copper, silver, and gold. These were christened the noble metals by

1% 'noble' gases + carbon dioxide

oxygen

nitrogen

Fig. 8.28

Fig. 8.30 A xenon arc lamp is used to provide the light of this lighthouse

AIR

Oxygen (about 20%)	Nitrogen (about 79%)
used for medical purposes; hot flames	used for making ammonia (for fertilizers, artificial fibres etc.) and nitric acid (for explosives, dyes, fertilizers)
Carbon dioxide (less than 1%)	*Noble gases* (about 1%)
Carbon dioxide as a by-product from beer and spirit manufacture is used to make mineral waters, sodium bicarbonate etc.	helium, neon, argon, krypton, xenon. Helium is used for balloons. Argon is used in electric light bulbs. They can all be used for advertising signs.

the ancient alchemists. They are comparatively unreactive – that is why helium and its friends have been named 'noble' after them. One aim of the alchemists was to make the 'noble' metals out of common or 'base' metals like iron.

The inert (or noble) gases have their uses. Helium is used to fill balloons. It is a light gas, and, unlike hydrogen, is not flammable. (If it were, it would combine with oxygen – and helium is too lazy to combine with anything!) They are also used in gas discharge tubes for advertising signs. When a very high electrical voltage is applied to a tube containing a small quantity of any one of these gases it glows, each gas giving a different coloured light. Because it does not combine with anything, argon is used in making electric light bulbs.

We can sum up in this table our conclusions about the uses of air.

8.20 AIR DISSOLVES IN WATER

It is interesting that while solids usually dissolve more in hot water than in cold, with gases it is the other way round. Gases dissolve less in hot water than in cold. Does your theory of the nature of gases help you to explain why? You will have noticed that when water is warmed in a beaker bubbles appear on the side of the beaker long before the liquid boils. These are bubbles of air which were dissolved in the water. Obviously the hot water does not dissolve so much air as cold water.

Here is an experiment you can try at home

Leave a bottle of a fizzy drink uncapped in a refrigerator overnight and another uncapped bottle in the room. Next morning pour some of the liquid from the bottles into separate glasses. Which one fizzes the most?

The fact that air dissolves even slightly in water is very important for fish and other animals which live in water. All animals need oxygen to live. If air did not dissolve in water we should miss one of our most popular foods – we might have the chips, but no fish!

8.21 COMPOSITION OF AIR BOILED OUT OF WATER

It is not an easy matter to analyse the air boiled out of water, but when we consider the volumes of oxygen and nitrogen that will dissolve in a certain volume of water we could decide whether 'boiled-out' air contains a higher proportion of oxygen than ordinary air. Here are the approximate figures:

$35 cm^3$ of oxygen dissolve in 1 litre of water at room temperature;
$16 cm^3$ of nitrogen dissolve in 1 litre of water at room temperature.

What decision do you come to?
Can you see why this fact is important for animals and plants which live in water?

WHAT YOU HAVE LEARNT IN THIS UNIT

1. You have found out some of the properties of the gases nitrogen, oxygen, and carbon dioxide. Nitrogen is rather inactive. Oxygen, on the other hand, is a very active gas. Things burn better in it than they do in air. Carbon dioxide is rather more soluble in water than are oxygen or nitrogen. It turns lime water cloudy, and because it forms an acidic solution, it changes the colour of bicarbonate indicator.

2. Air breathed out (exhaled air) contains more carbon dioxide and less oxygen than air breathed in (inhaled air).

3. When sugar and bread are burned, carbon dioxide is formed and energy is released.

4. Essentially, food is burned in our bodies, and our energy is obtained in this way. However, the process takes place in a different and more controlled way than simply burning. Heat energy is produced, as is shown by the fact that we are warm-blooded. The process of obtaining energy from food is called **respiration**.

5. Green plants take in carbon dioxide and water vapour from the soil and convert them into glucose, and then into starch. This process takes place only in the light, and the green colouring matter of plants – **chlorophyll** – plays an essential part. The process is called **photosynthesis**, and it is the most important chemical reaction in the world.

A by-product of photosynthesis is oxygen. What happened on photosynthesis may be summarized as follows:

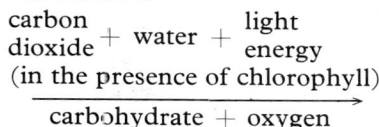

carbon dioxide + water + light energy (in the presence of chlorophyll) → carbohydrate + oxygen

6. The energy taken in from light in the formation of carbohydrates by photosynthesis is given out again when the carbohydrates are burnt, or in the process of respiration.

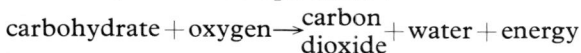

carbohydrate + oxygen → carbon dioxide + water + energy

This energy is used by animals for all the functions of living, and some of it is released as heat.

7. For respiration, animals and plants need oxygen. In very small organisms the oxygen is taken directly into the cells through the cell membranes but for larger organisms special structures have developed for the purpose. In mammals these are called lungs. You examined lungs and found how well they are suited for their special function.

8. Air is needed for things to burn, but not all the air is used up – only the oxygen. About one-fifth of the air is oxygen.

9. Air is a mixture, and a gas resembling air can be made by mixing oxygen and nitrogen in the proportions of 1 to 4.

10. Oxygen is made industrially from the air by cooling it until it liquefies, and then allowing the liquid air to warm up. Liquid air is very cold. Oxygen boils at -183 °C and nitrogen at -196 °C. As the liquid air warms, the nitrogen, having the lower boiling point, boils off first, leaving liquid oxygen.

11. The air contains, in addition to nitrogen, oxygen, carbon dioxide, and water vapour, small amounts of the 'noble' gases, helium, neon, argon, krypton, and xenon. They are very inactive.

12. Air dissolves slightly in water. Oxygen dissolves more than nitrogen, so air boiled out of water contains a higher proportion of oxygen than ordinary air does. This greater solubility of oxygen is vital to organisms that live in water.

Index